Tales
Out of
School

Tales Out of School

Implementing
Organizational
Change in the
Elementary
Grades

LEILA SUSSMANN

TEMPLE UNIVERSITY PRESS

 PHILADELPHIA

All names of persons, places, and schools in this book are fictitious, save those of authors quoted or paraphrased in the text, footnotes, or notes.

Temple University Press, Philadelphia 19122
© 1977 by Temple University. All rights reserved
Published 1977
Printed in the United States of America
International Standard Book Number: 0-87722-097-2
Library of Congress Catalog Card Number: 77-89413

For
Helen and Carl
and
Margaret and Joel

Contents

Acknowledgments ix

Introduction xi

Part I. The James Weldon Johnson: A Ghetto School

Chapter 1. A History of Innovativeness 1

Chapter 2. Johnson under a Militant Black Principal 11

Chapter 3. Innovation in 1972–1973 34

Chapter 4. Teaming for Individualized Instruction 62

Chapter 5. Goal-Defeating Behavior 85

Part II. Southside: A School in a Complex Environment

Chapter 6. The Institutional Setting 95

Chapter 7. The District's Innovation:
Individualized Reading 109

Chapter 8. Walton University's Innovation:
Open Classroom Teaming 115

Chapter 9. Open Classrooms:
Variability in Implementation 132

Chapter 10. Innovation in a Complex Environment 154

Part III. Coolidge: An Upper Middle-Class White Suburban School

Chapter 11. Professional Teachers, Powerful Parents,
and Misbehaving Pupils. 157

Chapter 12. Innovation at Coolidge: Open Classrooms . . .170

Chapter 13. The Conflict over Open Classrooms 193

Part IV. Conclusion

Chapter 14.   Implementing Organizational Innovations . . .211
Chapter 15.   The Social Organization of Innovative
versus Traditional Classrooms. 234

Appendix.   Research Methods 247
Notes 253
Index 263

Acknowledgments

A generous grant from the Spencer Foundation enabled me to spend a sabbatical year in 1972–1973 collecting the observations which are the basis of this study. An indispensable contribution was made by Professor Thomas F. Green of Syracuse University, then director of the Syracuse Education Policy Research Center, who offered me office space, the logistical support of the center, warm friendship, and immense intellectual stimulation. I am grateful to all the personnel at the center for their unwavering helpfulness.

During the field work phase of the study, I was assisted by Laura Schorr, then a graduate student in sociology at Syracuse University. Although this was Schorr's first field experience, she was a sensitive and competent observer.

I discussed the book with many colleagues and friends who contributed to the analysis of the material by asking the right questions. The graduate students in my seminar in the Sociology of Education in 1974—by writing papers from our field notes which came back to me ringing true—gave me confidence that the approximately 2,000 pages of typewritten field notes were complete enough to reconstruct a faithful image of the schools as Schorr and I saw them.

A special word of gratitude goes to the many subjects of the study, who tolerated my endless questions with grace, and encouraged me to "tell it like it is."

Introduction

The several waves of educational innovation which swept American schools from the mid-fifties to the mid-seventies included curricular reforms, technological inventions, and organizational changes. For the sociologist, the organizational changes were the most interesting. In 1970–1971, I had my first opportunity to observe these changes in elementary schools at close quarters. I did five case studies of the role of the teacher in innovative schools for the Organization for Economic Cooperation and Development (OECD).[1]

These studies whetted my appetite for more intensive analysis of educational innovation. Although it was my original intention to study more schools than are reported on here, I soon found that it would be impossible to do more than three, in any depth, in the course of one sabbatical year.

Because so many schools responded favorably to my request to study them,* I could exercise choice. I limited the locale to the Northeast, partly to eliminate regional variations and partly for convenience. I also limited myself to schools which had *organizational* innovations. One of them had a program of individualized instruction, and the other two had open classrooms. However, although these were the innovations which attracted me to the schools in the first place, when my research assistant and I arrived, we found other innovations in progress as well, and included them in our study of necessity. The simultaneous presence of more than one innovation in a school has important consequences which could not be ignored.

There was some planned variation in my selection of schools. They had very different pupil populations. The first was a ghetto school, 80 percent black, from the surrounding neighborhood, and 20 percent white; the white pupils were bused in voluntarily. The second was an urban school, which was ethnically integrated because its attendance district included white upper middle-class housing, as well as dwellings which housed low-income black and Hispanic families. The third was an upper middle-class white suburban school in a wealthy neighborhood.

*See Appendix: Research Methods.

xi

The reader should keep in mind that *no* three schools could be regarded as "representative" of their types: e.g. of urban, black ghetto schools. These three quite obviously are not. There cannot be many black ghetto elementary schools which have white pupils bused in voluntarily. Urban schools which are integrated without benefit of a court order, school board order, or local government order, but simply because of the social composition of their attendance district, are probably more common. However, minority group parents who search out affordable housing in the district of such a school—because it is widely reputed to be a "good" school—are probably unusually enterprising and competent people. Even the white suburban school was not quite like other all-white schools in wealthy suburbs, because the pupils were somewhat disproportionately Jewish.

In other words, I chose schools which varied socio-economically and ethnically because I wanted to see whether the same organizational innovation would fare differently among different pupil populations. There has been considerable disagreement on this point; for instance, as to whether open classrooms are as easy to implement with low-income minority children as with middle-class white children. Roland Barth has seemed to imply that they are not.[2] Charles Silberman has implied that they are.[3] I hoped to gain some insight into this controversial issue by varying the social composition of the schools I studied. But there should be no misapprehension that the three schools are a "sample" of any sort whatsoever.

It should also be emphasized that my focus of interest was not on the *adoption* of innovations. In all three cases the innovation had been adopted before I arrived on the scene. Nor was I concerned with changes in pupil achievement, creativity, self-esteem, and the like. Such outcomes can only be expected to appear after an innovation has been in effect for several years. What interested me was the process of *implementing* innovations. I wanted to see what this process was like, and what facilitated or hindered structural change in that special type of complex organization which is an elementary school.

Schorr and I went into the field with a set of questions, some of them formulated as hypotheses, generated by my OECD case studies. Those five case studies had been conducted through informal observation and interviews. My purpose in the present study was not to *test* any hypotheses; that would have required an explanatory survey with a large sample of schools, or else a field experiment. My goal was much more modest. I wanted to see whether deeper probing, using *participant-observation** would provide further grounding, or countervailing evidence, bearing on those original ideas. I was also prepared, as every participant-observer must be, to come upon completely unanticipated—and important—phenomena in the field.

The questions and hypotheses we took with us are best represented in the proposal I submitted to several foundations when I was in quest of funds. They are reproduced below. The reader who troubles to compare the contents of the book with these guidelines will find that: (1) for some of them, relevant evidence has been collected for all three schools; (2) some of them proved too complex for our method and our resources and we collected only scattered evidence or none at all bearing on them; and (3) there *were* unanticipated issues which we encountered in the field and which struck us as so important that we followed them up as carefully as possible.

Here are the guidelines, quoted from the foundation proposal:

1. In schools where the innovation is open classrooms and/or individualized instruction, pupils are given a good deal of autonomy in learning. They are provided with many choices concerning what activities they will pursue. The teacher is far less directive than in the traditional school. *In this situation, pupils spontaneously form into task-oriented peer groups which become crucially important in the classroom.*† Yet the literature on nongrading, open classrooms, and individualized instruction is written as though these informal peer groups did not exist. Teachers receive no guidance as to how to handle them.[4] My observations suggest that the peer groups fill the vacuum left by the partial withdrawal of the teacher's authority. Reaching academic decisions through an informal collective process relieves individual pupils of some of the anxiety attendant on choice.[5] The pupil peer groups of the innovative school deserve closer study. We need to

---

*Cf. Appendix for a description of how we used this method.

†This idea was first suggested to me by Maurice Gibbons' dissertation, cf. footnote 1.

know what their composition is,[6] how they function in the classroom, and how they are influenced by the teacher.

2. *If pupils are granted increased autonomy in learning, increased autonomy must be granted to teachers as well.* A teacher who is under authoritative constraint—for instance, to cover a pre-packaged curriculum in a semester's time—has no choice but to control the pace at which her pupils move. Conversely, the teacher who is expected to individualize instruction must be left free to make a host of professional decisions on her own. She must diagnose individual learning difficulties as they occur and prescribe remedial work. If remedial curriculum is not readily available, she must know how to create it herself. Innovative teachers write curriculum constantly.

3. *Is the increase in autonomy for teachers and pupils a chain reaction?* I suspect it is. That is, increased autonomy for teachers necessitates the same for principals, and so on up the line. In other words, these innovations entail a redistribution of authority throughout the school system, giving more of it to those who traditionally have had least. Thus far, I have observed only the effects on the teacher's role. The hypothesis that principals and others higher up are also affected should be investigated.

4. *The adoption of open classrooms and/or individualized instruction is nearly always accompanied by some form of teaming among teachers.* The self-enclosed classroom which insulates the teacher from observation by her colleagues as she performs her central tasks is abolished. That fact in itself needs explaining. Why do the new innovations seem to demand collaborative teaching? And what are the consequences of the fact that teachers at work become mutually visible? How are conflicts resolved in teaching teams? What happens to the traditional norm that all teachers are equal in status? Do new prestige rankings and authority patterns develop among teachers? What are the consequences of the formally organized teaching team for the informal society of teachers?

5. *Open and non-graded schools abdicate one of the major functions of the traditional school: that of competitive selection.* They do not give examinations or grades which evaluate students in comparison with each other. Instead, they write narrative reports assessing the pupils' progress toward academic and affective goals. The goals are not the same for every pupil.

6. *Under these circumstances, how do pupils form a self-concept?*[7] In the traditional school, self-concept is heavily dependent on the comparison of self with peers, aided by the

school's evaluations. Does this kind of self-assessment give way to some other process when competitive grading is abolished? How do the pupil peer groups influence self-assessment? There is some evidence that competitive evaluation dies hard.[8] One must also ask how innovative schools, which don't give the type of grades which make invidious comparisons among pupils, articulate with traditional schools when their pupils graduated or transfer. It appears that if pupils move on to a selective level of education, the burden of selection is put on the receiving schools.

7. *Under a regime of individualized instruction, academic achievement becomes much more widely dispersed than it is in the traditional classroom.*[9] The traditional teacher aims at the average achievement level in her class, thereby holding back the potentially faster students and pushing the slower to keep up. When pupils go more nearly at their own pace, a wide range of individual variability is released. One consequence is that achievement gets out of phase with age, so that the age-grading of academic work makes less and less sense.

These, then, were the ideas which some preliminary observation had already yielded and with which I began anew to work in the field. An example of systematic follow-up of an idea was our observation that all three schools in the present study had eliminated competitive grading, and were encouraging children to help each other with their academic work. In these classrooms the selection function had been much played down, although it didn't disappear entirely. Harried teachers could not literally individualize instruction and had to form their pupils into groups for whom the same assignments would be appropriate.

An example of scattered and unsystematic follow-up is the material on self-concept. The book contains some observations on self-concept but the question asked in the foundation proposal proved too complex for our resources and method.*

An instance of an unanticipated finding was that a school in a large urban system may be subject to orders from different layers of the educational bureaucracy, and pressure from the local community, to implement several innovations simultaneously; furthermore, the innovations may be based on mutually contradictory educational philosophies. The result is

*For a field experiment which compared self-esteem in open and traditional schools, see note 7.

terrible frustration for teachers and principals and a reduced probability that *any* change will be thorough-going. The extent to which a large educational bureaucracy can send out conflicting commands to its schools has to be seen to be believed. I hope these pages will help the reader to "see" it.

A brief guide to the organization of the book may be helpful. Parts I, II, and III are reports on the three schools. Each case study stands on its own feet. I have made no attempt to impose a common outline on them because the distinctive character of each school would be lost that way. However, I have assessed the degree of success each school had in implementing organizational change. My criterion of success was that the school should be moving toward a structure which resembled the one advocated in the official or influential literature of the innovation they had adopted. I have also tried to explain *why* the school was either relatively successful or relatively unsuccessful in putting the innovation into practice. The full flavor of the differences among these schools should come through to the reader in these parts of the book.

Part IV moves to a more conceptual level. In chapter 14, I compare my findings with those of other researchers who have done similar case studies of schools. My findings are for the most part in agreement with theirs. That is encouraging because it means that we are approaching a point where we will have enough well-grounded "middle range" theory[10] to warrant testing it with some rigor.

Chapter 15 compares the social organization of innovative classrooms of the kind studied here with Talcott Parsons' classic account of that of the traditional classroom—and finds them radically different.[11] It concludes that, so long as sectors of our social structure more central and powerful than the school system remain unchanged, innovations like open classrooms and individualized instruction at best produce little utopias which cannot thrive beyond the lower grade levels, where competitively measured achievement doesn't yet "matter." To flourish at higher grade levels in a society like the one we now have, these innovations would have to be badly bowdlerized. That is sad news for some, but not surprising for those who recall the fate of John Dewey's vision of progressive education.

PART I

The James Weldon Johnson: A Ghetto School

Chapter 1

A History of Innovativeness

The first of the three schools we studied, the James Weldon Johnson, is located in Centerville, a city of roughly 600,000 population in a mid-Atlantic state. The school is surrounded by a black ghetto neighborhood. Two low-income housing projects are in its district, and other low-rent apartments and houses accommodating large families are nearby. Between 60 and 70 percent of the nine hundred children in the school came from families living on welfare.

At the time we studied it, in 1972–1973, the whole school was involved in starting a new program of individualized instruction, and parts of it were engaged in other innovations as well. But it would be false to imagine that these innovative efforts were something new at Johnson. On the contrary, the school had engaged in a string of innovations, one after another, since the mid-1960's. Prior to that time, it had been a traditional school with a reputation for harsh discipline. In order to put the innovations we studied into perspective, we must give an account of the school's recent past.

Innovation as a Response to Protest

The Johnson School was not always named after a famous black man. Earlier, it was called the Pelham School. Pelham was a traditional elementary school with an all-white staff and a nearly

1

all-black pupil population. According to an ex-teacher there, it was not only traditional, but racist:

> It was the most dehumanizing experience that I have ever had. We had lovely white missionaries whose only job was to get through the day and earn brownie points for God. We had brutalization of kids going from verbal castration to physical beatings. I was told as a fairly young teacher that black kids couldn't really learn very well, but we were doing our job if we kept them off the streets. Young black boys would walk into school on a sub-zero day, and more than one teacher would immediately grab his hat off his head, whether it was strapped on or not, and say, "Gentlemen remove their hats."

Pelham became the James Weldon Johnson School in the midst of the civil rights agitation of the sixties. Centerville was often cited in the press as a city with *de facto* school segregation. The parents of Pelham's children staged a boycott to protest this segregation and also to protest the overcrowding of the school, which had 1,300 pupils at that time, as against 900 today. The school threatened to erupt in disorder. The Centerville Board of Education responded with three new policies. First, it inaugurated the Superior Educational Achievement Program (SEAP) as a way of attracting white children into the school on a voluntary basis. SEAP was a rather strange integration program. It included both white and black youngsters on a voluntary basis. They were chosen for their superior intellectual promise and were offered an excellent program, which was completely separated from the rest of the Pelham school. It was set apart in a new wing of the building. It had 80 percent white and 20 percent black children, while the rest of the school was nearly 100 percent black. It had a separate staff, chosen for their experience and high quality.

The second response of the Board of Education to parental protest against conditions in the school was to set up a compensatory program for low-achieving students. Located at Centerville University, it was called Pelham-on-Campus:

> The children were served for half a day at the school and for half a day at the University. There were six teachers up there and six at the school. We served third, fourth, fifth, and sixth graders; primarily black neighborhood kids, some white neighborhood kids as well.

The third response of the Board was the appointment of Dr. Henry Phillips, a white Professor of Education at Centerville University, as principal of the school. Dr. Phillips wanted to try out some of his innovative ideas in the inner city. He demanded special terms if he was to become principal. The school would have to be largely autonomous of the district. District supervisors might not set foot in the school without his permission. It would recruit its own teachers and have help in seeking federal funds.

These terms were agreed to. In 1966–1967, Dr. Phillips became principal of the renamed James Weldon Johnson School. He inherited the SEAP program, the Johnson-on-Campus program, and the regular school which catered to the large majority of neighborhood children.

Reform Under a Charismatic Principal

There is ample testimony from staff members who worked with him that Dr. Phillips was a charismatic leader:

> He was an evangelical guy, a tremendously powerful personality who enlisted an enormous commitment from teachers. During his years, teachers were in the school morning, noon and night, seven days a week. He was there himself, from six in the morning until midnight. Some teachers left after the first few years from sheer physical exhaustion. The commitment was so tremendous those first few years that, literally, there were teachers who separated from their husbands because of their commitment to the school. On the other hand, a lot of people couldn't take what was going on and left. In many cases, these were people we *wanted* to have leave because they could not adapt to what we were trying to do.

Another teacher, recalling the beginning days of the Johnson School, said:

> That man rallied two camps. There was no middle camp. For me and many others it was like a shot in the arm. I don't know what pure heroin is like, but I think that that is the feeling. It was the most "up" time that I can remember. It was like, "Stand up! Let's go do that job!" From that time on, it was just a very solid kind of feeling. Either solid against Henry Phillips or "Let's do it all together." Most of the people who stuck with Henry would never

say, "I work for Henry Phillips." They would say, "I work *with* Henry Phillips." You know—a kind of "We are working together" thing. The norm at the school was changing. The new norm came in, and the philosophy of Johnson was that every child can learn.

Continual Innovation

With this kind of devotion from his staff, Dr. Phillips began to introduce into the Johnson School a train of innovations which followed one another in constant succession until he left. Almost at once he put an end to the traditional pattern of grading academic work. Instead of the usual letter grades which rank-order children's performances and distribute them on a normal curve, Dr. Phillips introduced a report card which listed age- and grade-appropriate skills and informed the parents which skills the child had mastered and which he had not yet attained:

> The parents asked, "Why don't you give them grades?" and we tried to explain. The first year we had training sessions for the parents. Now we still have some savvy parents who want a report that says, "Mary is able to recognize such and such letters of the alphabet; she can do such and such specific things." But there are still many parents who want a grade of A, B, C, or D.

Also during the first year, Dr. Phillips took a number of steps to bring the school and the community closer together. He created a body of parents and teachers, with a majority of teachers, called the Johnson Cabinet. It was elected by the Parent-Teachers Association and was supposed to be the governing body of the school. Its most important power was the recruitment of teachers. The Cabinet screened new teachers carefully for their racial attitudes. They hired a number of people who did not have conventional teaching credentials but had talents—for instance, in the performing arts—which they thought would be useful. They instituted a rule that every teacher must visit the home of each pupil no later than the second month of the semester. That particular requirement caused a number of "traditional" teachers to leave the school— to the satisfaction of the Phillips devotees.

Dr. Phillips announced that the prime goal of the school was to raise the children's self-esteem. To that end, he obtained a Title III ESEA grant* to develop a self-esteem curriculum for inner-city children. The curriculum included projects to help children acquire an identity. They wrote about such things as: "What makes me different"; "What my family is like"; and "What my neighborhood is like." The idea was to work outward from things which were familiar and to help the child develop a feeling of self-worth. The curriculum was used for a short time and then dropped.

In the second year of the Phillips regime, it was decided that the segregation of the SEAP program within the school was absurd, and SEAP youngsters were moved into the classrooms of the regular school. That meant that the school became 80 percent black and 20 percent white, with the white youngsters bused in on a voluntary basis. Also in the second year, a large variety of unconventional courses were introduced:

> We found out everybody's special talents and hobbies; that is, among the staff. We had 127 different courses, including everything from philosophy to Japanese, to folk myths, to guitar lessons. We changed the curriculum every ten weeks. Toward the end, we began to feel a little guilty about neglecting the children's reading and mathematical skills.

After reading and math scores dropped, the staff reverted to the more conventional curriculum.

During the third year, a number of the teachers went to Toronto to observe open education schools and returned to begin introducing a version of open education into Johnson. An example of this was a project which "incorporated the reality of life around the school into the curriculum." A murder was committed on one of the streets bounding the school, within view of a large number of students, and that murder became the curriculum of the school for weeks afterward. The students examined who was there, who knew the victim, how they felt about it, what the reasons for the murder were, what the political aspects of the situation were, and what the legal aspects were. They examined the murder from every conceivable point of view. However, the exposure of the staff to open education had been brief and superficial, and its effects on Johnson quickly faded.

*Title III of the Elementary and Secondary Education Act of 1965 financed educational innovations.

Another innovation of the third year was "political training" of the pupils. The staff tried to teach the children to do things like write a letter to the mayor which would elicit a reply. They felt that a child of a certain age should be able to talk to his teacher about a problem he was having and to get a response from her. He should be able to negotiate with his parents about the hour at which he was required to come home. They were trying to "teach the children to deal with the environment in everyday sorts of ways so that they could assert themselves and get the things they were entitled to, not by being belligerent, but by having factual information and good communication skills." This particular training in demanding their rights made Johnson pupils disliked at the junior high schools to which they were graduated. The behavior they were taught at Johnson got them into trouble at junior high:

> When one of our youngsters arrived in junior high school wearing pants, she was led to the principal's office and told she was suspended from school. She told him, "I have a right to wear pants. There is no dress code." He said, "No such thing." And she replied, "I think if you call the district headquarters, you'll find out that I'm right." When the girl returned to school with her mother as directed, the principal had discovered that she was right and she was not suspended. But the staff was so angry, and she got so much backlash, that her parents had to take her out of the school.

In year four, Johnson began an experiment in team teaching. The teams were large and departmentalized, with fourteen to twenty teachers on each. Every teacher taught one subject for the whole day. At first, teams were appointed, but later in the year there was an attempt to introduce some choice as to who would work with whom. This was the first of a series of experiments with different types of team teaching involving small and large, departmentalized and non-departmentalized teams.

Also in year four, Dr. Phillips made the momentous decision to "throw the textbooks away," since "they are not teaching the kids," and to "write our own curriculum" instead. Johnson was free of district supervision; so it received no district curriculum guides. Now, in abandoning the textbooks, the school was left completely without a course of study in any subject. The curriculum goals had to be specified anew, and the curriculum material for reaching the goals had to be created *ab initio*. The decision produced an almost inconceivable burden for the teachers: "That meant that teachers were in school until evening every day creating their own curriculum material." One of Dr. Phillips' greatest admirers felt that this policy had been his biggest mistake:

> Phillips did a terible thing when he said, "Get rid of textbooks. They are not teaching kids." What he didn't clarify was, "Get rid of textbooks as soon as you know how to develop all the skills and not handicap a kid by a single approach." But many people felt it meant "Burn the books." So while they were floundering—rediscovering the wheel—the kids, you know, weren't learning. They just were not learning. The teachers couldn't create a whole curriculum no matter how hard they worked.

Another serious problem which resulted was the absence of continuity in a child's work as he moved from one team to another. The teachers were free to write their own material, but there was no mechanism for co-ordinating or sequencing its parts. Teachers receiving children from other teams at the beginning of a school year had no idea what the child had been taught the previous year. This lack of articulation gave rise to a saying among the staff: "We have seven teams but no school."

Predictably, the staff soon reverted to ordering books and other kinds of curriculum material, but since each teacher made curriculum choices independently of all the others, the chaotic situation was reflected in the materials bought:

> That was part of the negative thing that occurred. We spent a lot of federal money. We got a lot back for the money. But in terms of the materials that were purchased, there was almost no continuity. There was no sequencing. There was no evaluation. There was nothing. We didn't even make an inventory of what we got. So we've got books and materials in this building that have never been used. By now, no one knows what we have, or if they do, they don't know where it is stashed away.

The Destructive Effects of Premature Publicity

One early experience which Johnson shared with many other innovative schools was involvement in a large amount of public relations activity. No sooner does a school begin to innovate, it seems, than it is inundated with visitors who want to see the not-yet-developed innovation; with invitations to instruct others in accomplishments not yet achieved; and with requirements to make interim reports to funding authorities on outcomes not yet realized. Few innovative schools seem able to resist the temptations of widespread publicity. Johnson was no exception. Nearly all its impact on education was in distant parts of the state and at the national level, rather than in Centerville:

> The teachers at Johnson did a lot of educational work outside the school. For example, they went to a meeting of the National Elementary English Teachers Association and talked about what they were doing in English. They gave an in-service on differentiated staffing to a board of education in another city. Many of the teachers trained by Dr. Phillips at Johnson went on to key positions in education in other parts of the state, where they introduced the things they had learned. Places where they went sent visitors to the school.

The relative lack of impact on Centerville's school personnel was due to the fact that Johnson had deliberately isolated itself from the rest of the district:

> We refused, for instance, to go to city-wide meetings of school people. We didn't go because we were afraid of some kind of negative reaction to what we were doing. But we got it anyway because people didn't know what we were doing and inferred it was bad.

However, in presenting itself to the Centerville public, Johnson emphasized its success and glossed over its problems. For instance, Dr. Phillips made large claims concerning improvements in academic achievement scores:

> Phillips bragged all over the city—on the news and everything— about how well we were doing; how we were really dealing with the kids and building up this incredible school. He used to always walk around with all these statistics—you know, about how the grade scores were going up and all that stuff about the achievement tests.

What Phillips failed to mention publicly was that Johnson's improved test scores were due to the high-achieving bused-in students rather than to any change in the scores of neighborhood children.* Yet any meaningful evaluation of the effects of Phillips' innovations would have had to concern itself primarily with their benefits for neighborhood children. The trouble was that Phillips had enemies in the district—other principals who would gladly have seen the privileged position of Johnson School withdrawn. It was only by producing continuing "evidence" of success that the Johnson School could fend off its envious rivals and maintain its freedom to experiment with unorthodox educational practices. Needless to say, these were not conditions under which the effects of innovation on educational achievement could be objectively studied or constructively discussed in a public forum. Instead of meaningful evaluation, there was a public relations facade. This has been a continuing legacy of the Phillips regime.

The Residue of the Phillips Regime

After four years as principal, Dr. Phillips resigned to take a new university post. One innovation which survived his departure was the abolition of conventional, competitive marks. The basic pattern of reporting each child's mastery of specific skills, and of eliminating all comparison of children with each other, has remained in Johnson to the present. Many of the other innovations that Phillips introduced vanished without a trace.

Nonetheless, important change was accomplished, though not as a result of any specific innovation. It was, rather, the spirit of the innovators which counted. They revolutionized the moral climate of the school. First, Johnson was largely purged of racism. The hostile authoritarianism of the white staff of Pelham toward their black pupils disappeared. So did the use of the school as a dumping ground for incompetent teachers. New teachers were recruited by the parents and staff of the school, not the district, and they were carefully screened for their racial attitudes.

---

*The reader will recall that the bused-in children had been selected for SEAP in the first place because of their academic superiority. They were all middle-class and most of them were white. The neighborhood children were lower-class and nearly all of them were black.

Second, pupils were treated warmly and respectfully. The strict discipline of the traditional school was abandoned by Johnson and replaced by a loose, somewhat "progressive" discipline style. Children, for instance, sat around tables with friends who had mutually chosen each other. They were permitted considerable freedom of movement in the classroom. The traditional rule of silence except during recreation periods was relaxed; children had a lot of leeway to interact spontaneously. Johnson's pupils were fairly noisy and very active, but the school was not chaotic or undisciplined. It was rare for a class to get out of control.

There can be no doubt that the pupils of Johnson lived in a more humane environment and were happier at school than the pupils who had attended Pelham. But this happened without any improvement in academic achievement among pupils whose achievement badly needed improving.

The point is a significant one because the literature on urban schools is filled with documentation of how black pupils are victimized by teachers' assumptions that they cannot learn, by corporal punishment, by the hypocritical promise of upward mobility for the diligent while the school is actually preparing the pupils for "getting nowhere."[1]

It is certainly true that all these things happen in black urban schools and that they are more typical than what happened under Phillips at Johnson. But this literature contains an implicit assumption that if the conditions referred to disappeared, achievement would rise. The Johnson School casts doubt on that assumption. Humaneness, high expectations, the assumption of responsibility for children's learning, a positive attitude toward the parents and the neighborhood, black teachers as role models—all these were not sufficient to raise achievement. Nor did any of the succession of innovations help.

Thus we entered a school which had achieved political independence of its district, which had a humane climate, and a history of continual innovation. Yet this school had failed, over a four-year period, to raise the low achievement levels of its black pupils. It seemed possible that the fault lay in the innovative implementation process. Fortunately, during the year we observed at Johnson, several innovations were initiated. That gave us the opportunity to get a close look at the process of innovation. In the chapters to come, we shall discuss it in detail.

Chapter 2

Johnson under a Militant Black Principal

Phillips, who was a white integrationist, was succeeded in 1970 by his assistant principal, John Wilder, who was black, militant, and temperamentally very different from Phillips. Wilder put his own stamp on the school. Although he lacked Phillips' charisma, his style as principal had a strong effect on how others in the school played their roles. In this chapter, we shall discuss how each of the major roles was played under Wilder's leadership. In the chapters to follow, we shall describe how innovation took place in the context of this role structure.

The Principal

Wilder's politics placed him in a delicate position, since he adhered to a highly personal variety of black separatism while being the principal of an integrated school in a district which had a policy of voluntary integration. On some occasions, he carefully differentiated his personal views from his actions in his role as principal; on other occasions, he did not. During a formal interview, he did make the distinction:

> Now I'll tell you what I feel personally—me as a man—OK? I personally feel that blacks in America must come together to develop their own nation. I feel that we must begin to look to ourselves as resources. I feel that we must teach our young, mold their minds in a way that is beneficial to them and for us as a people first. We're really African-Americans. We didn't come here to be under the banner of the red, white, and blue. We're under the red, black, and green. We didn't come here by choice; we're prisoners of war. We are black. Therefore, our history is African. When I say a separate nation, I do not mean a separate land, body, that kind of thing that people are hung up with. I'm talking about a nation in the mind. I'm talking about a nation in the heart.

11

As for the school, I feel that my role as principal in this building, the fact that I accept a check from the Board of Education, means that there are a wide number of people with a wide number of beliefs. Therefore, I do not have the right to totally impose my personal beliefs on them or on this school and its programs.

Later in the same interview, Wilder noted:

We're in the business of indoctrinating children whether we like to call it that or not. And if I have some power, then I'm going to indoctrinate the kids into blackness—teachers, too. It would be better for our kids if this were a black school with a black staff, because then you wouldn't have to deal with the problems of white people relating to blackness. All you'd have to deal with is black people relating to it, which is problem enough. We could say things to each other that differ from what you can say in a mixed group of staff or kids. That would be good. Unfortunately, we're in the stage of development now where we as blacks must separate and develop our own, or else we'll still be swayed by other people. We don't have a culture that's strong enough yet not to be swayed. We haven't had a chance to come together and pull it together.

Further on, he described his view of the school as an agency of political socialization:

Along with the basic survival skills go: What do you do when you run into a racist son-of-a-bitch? How do you deal with it? How do you deal with grievance procedures? How do you challenge the system effectively without getting killed in the process? How do you begin to move together collectively? This applies to children, staff, custodians, aides, teachers, administrators, and parents. The school should be developing all of them. The student is not the only product in this kind of school. The community is the product; the custodians, the teachers—everybody who touches the school becomes part of that product. This is a revolution. These are the goals that eventually will begin influencing the bigger circles.

Wilder rejected the innovations of the Phillips regime, just as he rejected Phillips' integrationist views. He felt that Dr. Phillips' innovations were appropriate for white middle-class children but not for the majority of low-income blacks in Johnson:

During that period [when Phillips was principal], we didn't have the basic skills we need with our kids. Our kids were not learning—our neighborhood kids. I would say that four or five years ago we were closer to an open setting, and we found this to be unsuccessful with the greater numbers of black kids. And I've got the figures to show it. Our kids were not responding to that setting. People made assumptions that once you give the kids all these materials and you provide an open setting, all of them will respond similarly. But that was not happening. They were making some assumptions from the white perspective that were wrong for black kids, and black kids were losing out on it.

The point is, we did magnificently with some white kids who came in here that were bright, but failing in other schools, because the system was just killing them in terms of motivation. It's easy to motivate those kids. You just stay out of their way and you're doing the best thing in the world for them, because the average teacher isn't that bright anyway. Now, you stay out of the way of a black kid who is struggling with a language barrier, who's struggling with a lot of social ills, and you're not helping him— particularly not if you're dealing in white middle-class values. That's what makes me sick about the white man, anyway. They come up with something they think is innovative, and it works for them in a certain setting, and they say it will work for everybody. That's bullshit.[1]

Mr. Wilder's political preoccupations kept him out of the school a good part of the time. Johnson gained some benefits from his political know-how. For instance, it got $25,000 of Model City money, which paid for the supervisor of student-teachers. But the school also paid a price for his frequent absence. Teachers were alienated by what they felt was a lack of leadership from him:

Everybody was sort of angry last year. We had a lot of teachers who set up their own programs. They had ideas on what they wanted to do, and they sort of decided they were going to direct themselves. Our principal we have looked at as being an absentee landlord, because he is so busy doing things in the district and not really doing things within the school. We noticed the absence of administrators in there, to sort of do a little bit of guiding and see that things are carried through. You need someone who isn't in the bustle of kids to kind of help you keep your head straight and help you pick up the pieces and put you on the track again when you're down. It got so bad that teachers just couldn't take it anymore. And only when you threatened to quit—then the administrators listened.

Six of the seven team leaders, and most of the teachers interviewed, were more or less critical of the principal:

> There isn't too much leadership from the administration in terms of the curriculum and in terms of instruction. There isn't too much attention paid to reading and math skills. I thought they could have exhibited a little more leadership in that area.
>
> And there was the general unstructured approach to time. It boils down to the fact that meetings didn't get started on time, didn't end on time. If I was going to do the job, I would be much more organized and more clear and precise about what I wanted from people and what I expected them to do. And a lot more stuff would be done in written communication. John tends to rely on the personal things: "We're friends. We'll talk about this problem. We'll resolve it somehow." To me, the job is just too immense. The building is too big to let that kind of thing go down.

> I don't think we've got as much support from the administration as we could have. I'm talking about a leader as such—somebody who is pushing the program because it is so good; somebody who is as excited about it as I am.

> I generally look for more leadership from him. I don't need somebody to tell me what to do to discipline my children or handle team problems, but I do need someone who is a leader in curriculum and an example himself for the total staff. I don't particularly feel he sets a good example for the staff as far as stupid little things like being on time, following through on a job, taking initiative in all areas. And I don't mean to be an expert; I just mean to know what's happening. I don't feel that he does. I also think he should be a little more willing to play the heavy, when it comes to someone not doing their job. I don't mind taking responsibility for things on the team, but I would expect an administrator to take as much responsibility as I do. I don't always feel that's the way it is.

One or two teachers were aggrieved because they felt the principal took credit for their work:

> For instance, two teachers had written a proposal to get $500 from the campus fraternity, for a project on self-awareness of black children in their team. They decided it would be a good idea just to go to the principal and let him know what they were

doing. Wilder insisted on calling the district superintendent in charge of grants to find out where they should send the proposal, although they already had that information. They felt he was making political capital out of their work: "He's playing his little game again." He wanted the district to know that the school was sending in a proposal, but he didn't mention the teachers who had done it.

The principal's relationship to the pupils was informal, just like his relationships with the staff. For the most part, he interacted warmly with the children, despite the fact that he was the administrator of corporal punishment in the school. The corporal punishment was not severe; not nearly so severe as it was in the homes. And there was a code as to who could use corporal punishment on whom. The principal only punished boys in this way. If he thought a girl needed such punishment, he called in her mother and explained the offense, leaving it up to the mother to decide what penalty was due. He also punished only *black* boys, since he knew that the white upper middle-class parents would be angered by corporal punishment given to their children.

In general, the Johnson code was: No male teacher could corporally punish a girl; no black teacher could corporally punish a white; no white teacher could corporally punish a black—for fear of charges of racism. Black teachers in the primary teams occasionally spanked a black child. However, the teachers were personally acquainted, through home visits, with the parents of their pupils, and the threat of a telephone call or visit to the parents was very potent—since it usually meant that the parent would beat the child. The principal described corporal punishment as part of the neighborhood culture:

> Most of our parents use corporal punishment. In telling the parent the child was doing something wrong around the school, that can often result in a severe beating; not necessarily a negative one either. Corporal punishment is not very productive, but I wouldn't dismiss it either. Again, getting back to blackness, you'd make a mistake in a black school to dismiss corporal punishment, unless you had the full support of the community to abolish it. This stuff about not having corporal punishment comes from two areas. One is the lily-livered liberals, who don't beat their kids and don't want anybody else to touch them, and pretty much

let the kids make their own decisions; and two, black people who have gone to white schools where whites think the only way to control them is to put their hands on them. Here, I think, a white teacher who uses corporal punishment on black kids is going to find himself in trouble—both from me and from the neighborhood parents. But on the other hand, the parents will tell me to beat them more often than I do. In a school where I could, I'd totally dismiss corporal punishment. But to do it here would be denying the neighborhood its own personality.

The neighborhood's attitude toward the black principal was ambivalent. Most of the local blacks were in favor of integration. The previous year, when Wilder had proposed setting up a Black Board of Education, the parents had opposed the proposal strongly. Many were resentful of him as an outsider, not a Centerville native, telling them they were "backward" because they were not sufficiently militant. On the other hand, if he or the school were attacked by outsiders, they rallied to his support. The Director of Elementary Education in the district recalled such an occasion:

> A couple of years ago, there was an attack made. I can't remember the problem, but it ended up that there was a lot of letter-writing in the newspaper in support of Mr. Wilder and the school. There was a tremendous outpouring from the people in the neighborhood and also the parents who had children bused in. I think we've never had an example of any stronger support than at that time.

And a black junior high school guidance counselor, who was himself very critical of Johnson, said:

> Johnson is supported by more parents than it would seem. Black parents have never been very active in school activities. Most of them work. Most of them are one-parent homes. Most of them feel they have very little competence in education. Various factors like this would make for a small black turnout at school affairs. But, in this case, I don't think there's any alienation there, because the black parents I've talked to all seem to be satisfied with Johnson. I think if they really knew the standards of education there, they would be alienated, but they don't know. They're snowed. So, basically, those parents would have gripes not with Johnson, but with the school where the kids go after Johnson: "Well, my kid did so well in Johnson, why isn't he doing well here? Something must be wrong with this place."

Wilder, in sum, was a highly political principal. He gave his staff no instructional leadership, no guidance on curriculum, and little administrative support—and they resented these lacks. Rather, he was concerned with ways to use the school as an instrument for raising the level of black militancy in the pupils and in the community. He had to move with great care because he had an integrated school with many parents and teachers who were integrationists. He had more trouble on this score from the Centerville blacks in Johnson than from the whites. The black parents and teachers felt they knew how to deal with the white power structure of Centerville better than Wilder, who was not a native of the city. But, on the whole—and especially if attacked by whites outside the school—Wilder could count on the parents' support.

The Parents

In theory, the Johnson School was governed by a Cabinet made up of parents and teachers, who were elected by members of the larger Parent-Teachers Association. Dr. Phillips and a collaborator at the university had devised it as a "participative policy-making body." In a sense, the Cabinet was a charade, since, under the laws of the state, it could not have ultimate authority over the school. At one meeting, Mr. Wilder said that the Board of Education did not like the Cabinet's statement of its power. He said he had promised to obey the laws of the state, and he passed the whole matter off as a joke.

In 1972, Mr. Wilder decided to underline his position that Johnson was a "community school." He wanted especially to break the pattern of greater white than black parent participation in school affairs:

> White people have a tendency to come out to meetings better than black people. The reason is that a lot of black people have never found anything positive in school. We're trying to break that pattern. In other words, the only time they had to go to school was when the kids were in trouble. They themselves are not successful products of school and therefore do not view going there as something rewarding. When they do go to meetings, they are talked to in terms they don't understand and are made to feel put down if they ask maybe stupid questions. That wasn't done by the staff so much as by white parents who were very

bright and very verbal. These busy little mothers, who didn't have jobs but did have college degrees, came in here to show their expertise. The whole matter was run on a very intellectual basis, my dear, and left no room for the neighborhood people to get in. Those mothers just ran off at the mouth from the time they got here until the time they left. The pattern isn't broken yet. We've got really poor people here. We've got people who have gone through maybe sixth or seventh grade."

Mr. Wilder's idea was to shift the composition of the Cabinet so that parents would outnumber teachers, thereby making the school "community controlled." Under the new rules, there were to be seven elected parents and four elected teachers, with the principal and assistant principal serving *ex officio*. Participation in the voting was very low. One white teacher and one white mother were elected. The remainder of the elected candidates were black. The Cabinet chose a black mother as its president. She conducted meetings with Mr. Wilder at her elbow, guiding her closely. It was Wilder who actually ran Cabinet meetings. As he said in his interview: "For the time being, I hold the reins. Someday, when the parents have had enough political training, they will be able to take it over."

Two important policy questions came before the Cabinet during 1972–1973. The first had to do with deciding whether to press for an Afro-American studies curriculum for Johnson, involving collaboration with Centerville University. The Cabinet voted to approve this innovation.

The second was a statement of the school's position with respect to integration. The principal persuaded the Cabinet to take an anti-integration position. Its final form was a cryptically brief statement, sent home to parents, which said, "We favor busing children into our school for its superior programs, but we oppose busing for integration. We also oppose forced busing of black children out of this community."

The statement was contrary to district policy, which was to promote voluntary busing for integration. There was no forced busing in Centerville. About 400 children in the district were bused out to white schools on a voluntary basis.

Wilder originally intended to confront the Board of Education with this statement and to try to force some kind of showdown on integration policy. However, he thought better of it and dropped the matter after the flyers went out to the parents. So far as we could tell, the statement never came to the attention of any district official or Board member.

Some parents were puzzled by it, however, and some white parents concluded that their children were no longer wanted in Johnson. That contained a grain of truth, since Wilder would have preferred an all-black school. However, enrollment was falling, and the school was threatened with a loss of staff positions. The only way to avoid that loss was to recruit, not fewer, but some 100 *more* white pupils. The position Wilder finally took in the Cabinet was that white pupils should be recruited informally, but that he wanted only recruits who were coming for the superior programs of the school, not recruits who were coming "for integration."

Although white parents continued to turn out to meetings in disproportionate numbers during our stay at Johnson, the black community was involved in the school through the paraprofessional aides, all of whom were black mothers from the neighborhood. These aides assisted teachers, sometimes with clerical work, sometimes with minor teaching duties. Since they often knew the children's families, they did not hesitate to discipline pupils. They were also a bridge between the school and the neighborhood. The aides had a lounge of their own where they gathered to exchange gossip about the teachers with whom they worked. This gossip got back to the homes. Similarly, a great deal of information about children and their backgrounds was communicated to teachers by the aides who knew the children. At least one black member of the staff, who came from the South, said she thought the aides "understood" the children better than anyone else in the school. These aides were "boundary spanners," or what Litwak and Meyer have called "common messengers."[2] They were in a good position both to represent the community to the school and the school to the community. However, at Johnson they made little political use of their opportunities. Most of them simply looked on their positions as lucrative jobs.

Teachers and Teaching

Teachers at Johnson had an unusually strong input into the school's policies by virtue of their representation on the Cabinet and also through the IGC (Instructional Guidance Committee), a committee of team leaders, which met weekly with the administration and acted as a liaison between the administration and the teams.

The teaching staff valued their influence and autonomy:

> It was a total about-face in teaching so far as I was concerned; nothing like the school where I did student teaching. The kids here are very open. I like the relationship of the faculty to the principal and to each other. I always perceived the principal as someone you wouldn't approach with a problem. But John Wilder welcomes people, and he has a total commitment to the faculty, and you can go to him with any problem anytime at all. The atmosphere is easy. You feel free. Your ideas aren't disregarded here. They are taken seriously and they are given a try.

> I'm pretty happy with the school. You have enough freedom to do practically anything you want to do. If you are willing to do the work, there is an opportunity for you to design your own type of situation. It treats people with respect and gives them the opportunity to solve problems; whether it's the problems of the community, parent relations, or problems of instruction or classroom management or anything like that. You are allowed to do whatever you can do. That's what makes me happy.

Teachers were encouraged by the administration to think of themselves as a potent force in the pupils' lives. Both Phillips and Wilder disavowed the validity of any social research, such as the Coleman report[3] or Jencks' *Inequality,*[4] which implied that schools are ineffective:

> Dr. Phillips always said anybody who believes that because you only have the kids six hours a day, and the home and the community have them the rest of the time, that the school can't possibly overcome the effect of the home had better get out of teaching. Because if you lose hope, you can't be an effective teacher. You have to recognize that if you find out what the kids' problems are the rest of the day, and if you start helping the kids to deal with the problems, out of that eventually you get around to teaching him reading. Then, what you do in those six hours may be more important than what happens during the rest of the day.

The other side of potency was accountability. It was a Johnson motto that "every child can learn." If he did not learn, the fault was not his, nor the home's; it was the fault of the school. And the school had to search until it found an effective way to teach that child:

> I like the school because the teachers are always trying different things, and they try very hard to make it possible for the children to learn. If I lose a child's attention, it's because I haven't made the lesson compact enough. It's my fault if I can't keep the child's attention. It's not the child's fault.

Teachers carried the pattern of democratic governance, which they themselves experienced, into the classrooms. Pupils had occasions on which they might choose among several alternative activities—for instance, in their post-lunch recreation period or on Resources Day. Among older children, problems were discussed collectively and decisions were made by consensus or vote. There was a clear understanding that pupils had a right to reasonable treatment from teachers:

> At 9:22 Mrs. Waters called a class meeting and the kids drew their chairs in a circle. She said, "Does anyone want to say something about anything that happened during the three days that I was absent?" A girl in the class complained about the behavior of the substitute teacher. Her complaint was that he was sarcastic with her. She said he sneered at the class and that he yelled at them. Mrs. Waters said, "He'll have to modify his behavior some, because it's not satisfactory to you, but we have to remember that we have to hear his side of the story." Then she said, "I want you to remember that there are going to be teachers that won't be able to tolerate you, and you won't like all your teachers either." Another child complained that a teacher on the team had pushed him out of the room when he tried to come in, and several other kids confirmed this. Mrs. Waters asked some questions, and then she pointed out to this child that he had had no pass to leave the room. The teacher shouldn't have pushed him, but he was also wrong in not having a pass.
>
> Then she said, "Let's problem-solve a little about passes." There was a long discussion of this topic. The kids mentioned that children pick up passes on the ground and steal them. They write their own passes and forge the teacher's signature. Mrs. Waters pointed out that the reason for the passes was so that people couldn't just go off and wander around this big school with nobody knowing where they were. The kids acknowledged that their behavior was a problem for the staff.

The teachers did not always agree about the standards of behavior to be required from children. In the following field notes on a meeting of the IGC, all the team leaders insisting on strict behavior standards were middle-class blacks. The dissenters were middle-class whites:

> The meeting got on to the topic of standards of behavior teachers imposed on black and white pupils. Carla Young (black) said, "If you don't treat pupils as your own children regarding expectations, you shouldn't be here. I don't want my own child calling me a motherfucker and I'll be damned if I'll let somebody else's do it." She said that if you just teach a child skills and no other development of the whole child, you're doing that child a great disservice. Alice Nelson (white) disagreed to some extent, saying that you could be a good teacher anyway. The principal concurred with Carla. He said that he knew teachers who could teach skills very well, but they had racist attitudes which totally discounted their effectiveness. Carla was saying that we must have high expectations for the behavior of the children. We can't let them curse, run around the halls, and wear their coats in classrooms. Mrs. Washington (black) nodded emphatically. The director of pupil services, Ellen Smith Goldberg (black), said that many times she passed kids in the hall who should not have been there, and she made sure they went where they were supposed to. However, she has seen other teachers pass them by and do nothing. Ellen said that she had visited another school in Centerville where there was a very high standard of behavior for the white children, but the black children were allowed to run wild up and down the halls. She called this a "plantation school." Cliff Wallace (white) said his class had made a rule that a child could curse if he were angry. He said it was more important to find out what made the child angry than to stop him from cursing. Ellen disagreed. She said that when these kids got to junior high school, they would be expelled for the kinds of cursing they do. "If it's not stopped now," she said, "you will have black children in the street once again."

Thus, at this meeting we see that it was the black middle-class teachers who were inclined to be somewhat authoritarian with the black lower-class children and the white middle-class teachers who were inclined to be more permissive. Their permissiveness was interpreted by the principal as a kind of racist condescension. This matches the experience of Roland Barth and his colleagues with black administrators and parents when they tried to introduce open education into a black school.[5]

Johnson was afflicted by a high teacher turnover, because it attracted many young women whose husbands were doing graduate work at the local university. As a result, there were a number of inexperienced teachers with a lot to learn. But there were also old hands who were poor teachers. Some of them planned lessons with an obvious lack of understanding of the pupils' capacities:

> The film on the life of Martin Luther King contained all sorts of words which the children didn't understand. Words like "boycott," "segregation," and "civil rights" meant nothing to them.
>
> After the film, they were given a worksheet and dictionaries so that they could fill in blanks in sentences. However, many of the most important words on the worksheet, like "NAACP"* and "doctorate," were not in the dictionary. So it was largely an exercise in futility, very frustrating to the children.
>
> I asked a girl, "Who was Martin Luther King?" "A civil-rights leader." "What is a civil-rights leader?" She shrugged and walked away. The teacher commented, "They have no sense of history," but she should have known that this film was way over the children's heads.

Another teacher planned an art lesson ineptly:

> She asked them to draw a bottle of Elmer's Glue—a very small bottle about six inches high—which she put on a large table in the center of the room. Many of the children were several yards away from this little bottle and couldn't see it very well. She told them to draw it and not to touch it, but they came up to the table to look at it. They handled it. The kids who crowded around the table made it impossible for the others to see. They seemed to feel that in order to draw the bottle they had to copy literally every word on the label. Some of them wanted to trace the bottle. The kids went around to each other saying, "How do you spell 'Elmer's Glue'?" They seemed to have very little experience with art. Their sole concern was to give a literal rendition of the bottle, and this was impossible to do from the distance they were at.

Some teachers were satisfied with rote learning by the

*National Association for the Advancement of Colored People.

pupils and made no attempt to help them understand concepts. This was especially true in arithmetic:

> Mrs. Washington pointed out to me a girl who had done perfectly on the test in counting by twos, by fives, and by tens. The child started counting by twos for me, but she got stuck at eight and asked me what came next. I said, "What's two more than eight?" and she looked at me blankly. I said, "What's one more than eight?" and got another blank look. I discovered that this counting by twos and so on, for her, is just a memorized chant, which she sometimes forgets. She doesn't have any idea that it has some connection with adding or that the concept "one more than" has something to do with the counting. The teacher's only concern is that the children memorize their "number facts."

A problem which plagued many classrooms was poor planning of time by the teachers. Often the students were given activities which didn't fill the time allotted to them. They were given nothing to do with the unexpended time but were expected to wait quietly until everyone else was finished. It was during such periods that discipline most often deteriorated:

> Mr. Jenkin was supervising a project which involved attaching name tags of the team's members on a large fishnet and then hanging it in the corridor. Once the pupils were given certain instructions—for example, "You take this section and attach these five tags to it"—they were quiet and hard working. Unfortunately, some of the tags were attached in a very short time, which left those pupils bored and restless. I saw Lenore standing in a corner looking unhappy. A boy from another class came over and teased her, and suddenly this usually sweet-dispositioned girl hurled a cup of hot coffee at him. Things deteriorated rapidly, and I suggested to Mr. Jenkin that we put off hanging the net in the corridor until a more calm moment, since the group at this point was on the verge of chaos, with everyone running around and fighting.

Poor logistical planning by teachers and failure to provide enough work to keep the class busy meant a lot of wasted time:

> One day I counted up the division of time in one intermediate team classroom. They arrived in school at 8:40 A.M., but nothing really got started until 9:20 A.M. They did their handwriting and some homeroom language arts until 11:00 A.M. This morning they watched the film *David Copperfield* for forty minutes. From

11:00 A.M. to 12:00 P.M. they went to their math group. From 12:00 P.M. to 12:30 P.M. they ate lunch. From 12:30 P.M. to 1:00 P.M. they had recreation. When they returned from that, it took until 1:20 P.M. to settle them down and redistribute them to their reading groups. By 2:45 P.M. they returned to their homerooms. The period from 2:45 P.M. to 3:20 P.M. was simply wasted. In some rooms, the children used it to finish their morning handwriting or to do homework. In Marsha and Jack's room, they just marked time, playing tic-tac-toe, or Hangman, or cards, until dismissal time. In short, in Marsha and Jack's room, the kids were in school for six and a half hours, and they worked only three hours of that time

Teachers at Johnson felt they had a strong influence on school policy. They could always make their views known to the principal by way of their team leaders on the IGC, by way of their representatives on the Cabinet, or by going to him directly. They felt they were listened to seriously and given considerable freedom to do what they thought best. In their turn, the teachers gave their pupils a respectful hearing, and a say in making the rules which governed their behavior.

Unfortunately, while there were almost no harsh teachers in Johnson, there were not a few unskilled ones, both new and old. There were teachers who seemed unable to plan for the efficient use of time, teachers who used materials inappropriate for the pupils' abilities, and teachers who encouraged rote learning without understanding. We have already pointed out that the staff got no guidance with respect to instruction from the principal, who never even bothered to observe them. And we shall see below that they got very little help from anyone else. So Johnson was a school with many teachers in need of on-the-job training, who were not getting it.

Pupils

The black pupils at Johnson came from low-income and frequently one-parent homes. The school social worker estimated that 60 to 70 percent of their families were receiving welfare. Many of the parents had less than an eighth-grade education. Since these pupils were 80 percent of the pupil population at Johnson, it was their subculture which was dominant in the school. The most salient fact about this subculture was that it involved a great deal of fighting, both physical and verbal. But not all of the fighting was serious:

> I observed at this time that the standard means of communication between the sexes among the pupils was a pushing, shoving, or punching, and insulting which was really meant to be friendly, though it didn't seem that way to me at first.

In a sense, the white students were left out of the fighting because they didn't know how to "play the game": that is, they didn't retaliate. That did not, however, protect them from a certain amount of physical attack:

> Debbie, a black girl in the classroom, was punching a white girl, Sally, sitting next to her, and Sally tried to ignore her. Debbie kept saying, "I'm going to beat her butt." There is also a white girl, Pamela, who sits right in front of a black girl, Joanna, and Joanna is constantly taking her books and throwing them on the floor and hitting her. Pamela does the same thing as Sally, she just tries to ignore Joanna. At the same time a black boy, Harry, was slapping Tom, a white boy, on the back of the head, continually, with no provocation. Tom tried to ignore it just like the girls, but he got very frustrated and sat in the corner of the room sulking. None of these three white students made any attempt to defend himself.

While a lot of the fighting arose out of the usual quarrels among children, some of it was a structured pattern of ritual challenge and response which established the order of dominance in the classroom:

> Vera and Marcie were out there from Mr. Jenkin's class, and I heard them discussing the fact that Marcie had beaten up a girl, and they were discussing whom Marcie had to beat up next.

Here is a quote from a junior high school counselor about a child she knew personally:

> "When Monica transferred to Johnson, I saw her wind up within five or six weeks as a kid who was more interested in social combat than in just relaxed friendships."
> Question: "What do you mean by social combat?"
> Answer: "Well, it was all about who was going to war with whom the next day and who certain kids had to go after next, whether verbally or physically."

Cliff Wallace, a white teacher, explained that not every challenge resulted in a fight. A kid could lose a challenge by backing off from fights; that would be the same as fighting and losing. Kids who were natural leaders were not often challenged:

> Kids don't always have to fight. They have to be ready to fight. Lots of kids go along, you know, and they don't get bothered much, and some kids get picked on all the time. I don't think this is much different from any other school in that the kids that get picked on are the kind of kids that want to be a leader, but they don't have it in them to be a leader. They get beat up all the time. But most of the kids, since it is a tough place, they have to fight once in a while but not very often.

The fights among the black children were not exclusively physical. They played their own version of "the dozens," a game of ritual insult in which the insults are usually obscene aspersions on the other person's close relatives. The audience decides the winner on the basis of superior wit. The children did not play the game quite correctly, however, and it often ended in a fight:

> A little girl was crying. I asked the teacher why, and she said the girl had walked up to a boy and said, "I'm your sister," and he punched her. The statement was meant to imply that, though they had different mothers, they had the same father.
>
> Often "the dozens" was so ritualized that it was enough to walk up to someone and say "Your momma" for the exchange of insults to begin. Again the white children were left out because they didn't know the rules of the game. One day David (black) walked up to Peter (white) and said, "Your momma." Peter replied "I'm not going to be a momma; I'm going to be a poppa." David walked away with a look on his face that seemed to say, "What can you do with someone like that?"

Most of the teachers tried hard to get the children to channel their aggression into verbal negotiations, in middle-class fashion. However, Mrs. Waters said she was loath to forbid the children to fight since their parents encouraged them to defend themselves physically whenever attacked. To do any less was to lose prestige in the peer group:

> Well, we have tried very hard to deal with it. We have a Johnson Students' Bill of Rights: "Every child has a right to learn. You

can't interfere with what other people want to do." And one key thing is "no fighting." Well, you can't really say "no fighting" because that's what's taught in many black homes. If you're hit, hit back. The teacher can't say, "We must never fight." You can say, "Maybe your parents taught you to fight back, but I also, as your teacher, can't permit you constantly to hit someone else. I'm here to help you deal with it another way." Let's face it: fighting is the only way to survive many times. Otherwise you're going to get hell knocked out of you. So you would tell some of the white children that sometimes you are going to have to begin to learn to deal with that kid that is poking you all the time. One day you're going to turn around and sock the hell out of him, and you're going to set him back on his heels because he's going to keep going like that until you've had enough, and you're going to give him a little bit of it, and he might leave you alone. A lot of times, I'll just say to the children, "Do it at home; do it at 3:30; do it any place but here."

Relations between the black neighborhood pupils at Johnson, who are lower-class, and the bused-in white pupils, who are upper middle-class, seem to be neither very good nor very bad. Since the children in each room seated themselves as they wished, the seating was to some extent an indicator of relationships. In general, the races segregated themselves, although the self-segregation of blacks and whites was not nearly so complete as the self-segregation of boys and girls. Instances of interracial friendships could easily be found, though they were not very numerous. Nearly every staff member interviewed thought there were some benefits for children of both races from the integration:

It's not all "black and white together and into the sunset," you know. But there is an awful lot of interaction among white and black kids. A lot of stuff I don't even think they would be able to verbalize. But the kids have really gotten to accept each other, sharing and meeting each other as individuals. Since the white kids are in a numerical minority and their cultural upbringing isn't as aggressive and forceful as it is in the ghetto, those kids do tend to be intimidated somewhat. But those instances are really diminishing, and the general tone now is working together, without any big blowup of the fact either.

I've had white kids in my classes that I thought it's been an almost joyous experience for them to be at Johnson. It was hard at first. Then they stayed here, and now their relationships with black kids are healthy kinds of things.

Black teachers objected strenuously to white parents who "sacrificed their children" on the altar of integration under the illusion that they were "doing good" for blacks:

> My first year here, the most horrible experience I had was a whole family of white kids that had been bused in, and I had the daughter in my room. She ran out of the room everyday. She used to come to school with clothes with holes in them on purpose, telling me that if she didn't, the kids would steal her things; just paranoid about things happening. At first, I kept going after her. Finally, I said, "I've got twenty-four other kids in the room, and I cannot run after this girl everyday." I called her mother in to talk to her. She said, "Well, why are our kids here, if it's not to bring up the values of the black kids?" And she was complaining, "My kids come home with filthy language." And her kids had the filthiest mouths I've ever heard in my life. I said, "I don't like it any more than you do, but when a kid comes in like Lenore does and flaunts everything she has, it's going to get taken. I don't care where she is." And finally the mother just took them out of the school.

We saw one white boy in first grade who was evidently terrified of his black classmates. He kept his arms around his books like a fortress and kept saying, "Don't touch my things, don't touch me, don't even look at me, don't look at my things." Another white first grader, a girl, had hysterics after a brief scuffle with a black girl on the playground. No one could understand her disproportionate reaction until a black teacher came along and said to her, "Don't worry, honey, the color won't rub off on you," and she calmed down.

The effect of integration on the black children was problematic. We came across many expressions of self-hatred stemming from blackness among the pupils. But we could not tell whether such feelings were intensified by the presence of whites. The recent literature on black self-hatred suggests that blacks do not experience this feeling so long as they are insulated from whites. However, they do begin to experience a loss of self-esteem when they come into contact with higher-achieving whites.[6] Here are some instances of black self-hatred that we observed at Johnson:

> A black girl came over to me and said, "Do you see that girl next to you?" I looked up in surprise and said, "Yes, of course." Then she said, "I don't know how you can see her because she's so black." I said, "Black is beautiful, isn't it?" And she said, "Well, yeah, but she's ugly, she's so black." Then she sat down and said, "I'm ugly. I know I'm not pretty, but it doesn't matter, because my mother's satisfied with me anyway."

In an intermediate classroom one day, we helped pupils who were working on a "self-esteem" project to make silhouettes of each other's profiles:

> Then we did Robert's silhouette. And when it was done, Robert said, "No, no! I don't want to have that put up." We did Dennis' silhouette, and he snatched it and looked at it and tore it up. Jeff, a white boy whose silhouette was done by a black boy, had his profile done to make him look like a black. I said, "That doesn't look anything like Jeff." And the artist said, "Yes it do." Later, the girls did their silhouettes, and they liked them—in stark contrast to the boys. Not only that, but they did the silhouette of a white girl who was a member of their peer group. They lovingly arranged her hair and traced her profile exactly along the lines of shadow on the screen. It's true that Jeff was not a member of the clique which made him look like a black, but that does not explain why the girls were so much more accepting of their appearance than the boys. I have no clues as to what the answer to that might be.

An important difficulty that many black children faced at Johnson was that they spoke some form of black English. This meant they had to learn to speak, as well as to read, standard English. So far as the observers could tell, the problem was never explicitly dealt with by the teachers and there was no official policy for dealing with it. One administrator said that in Phillips' day the children were coached as to when they might and might not speak black English. Mr. Wilder said he would want every teacher in the school to learn black English, so that he could be sure they didn't view it as an inferior means of communication. But then he would be just as happy to have them drop it and teach standard English, since that was what the children needed to survive in school.

All of the teachers, black and white, spoke standard English to the children. The paraprofessionals from the neighborhood spoke black English about as often as they spoke standard English. We ourselves got into occasional difficulty with the issue while trying to help the children. For instance, a child asked the observer how to spell "axed." When she gave the complete sentence, it turned out that the word she needed was "asked." Another child asked how to spell "steer." The word he wanted was "stair." A third child, a good reader, read out of a book which said, "She comes down the stairs." He read it as, "She come down the stairs." In these instances, we did what we saw the teachers do. We repeated the child's word in standard English and then spelled it out. Or, we pointed to the "s" at the end of "comes" and had the child reread the sentence, pronouncing the final "s." At no time was black English labeled "incorrect." It was more nearly ignored. However, the children faced the same difficult problem that British working-class children face who must acquire an entirely new accent to be upwardly mobile, or that second-generation American children faced who learned a foreign-accented English at home and had to learn American-accented English if they wanted to be upwardly mobile.

Another difficulty pupils faced, which was common throughout the school, had to do with what we, at first, classified as inadequate spatial perception. Our field notes contained observation after observation of children who got into trouble with their classroom work because of this handicap:

> I noticed another child who was copying from the blackboard as instructed and who showed the characteristic spatial perception problems we have seen in this school at every grade level. The blackboard had, on the upper left-hand side, the word "name" which meant that the child was supposed to write his name. On the upper right-hand side, it had the date to be copied, "February 5, 1973." This little girl wrote "Ellen" on the upper left-hand side, and she wrote "February" opposite, on the right. Then she copied the first sentence, "We have it," and right next to that, on the right, the remainder of the date, "5, 1973."

> The teacher was showing them what he called "renaming" numbers. For instance, 8,615 was translated into "five ones, one ten, six one-hundreds," and so on. Then he gave out a dittoed sheet

with numbers to rename. I found a boy who was having great trouble with it, and I tried to work it out with him. However, he had a difficulty I have often seen at Johnson. Each problem was on a different line of the sheet. The child would frequently lose the line he was on and start reading off how many ones and how many tens from another line. He also had trouble calculating how much space he had in the parentheses to put in, say, "two times 100," or "two 100's." He would make the numbers too big and go outside the parentheses and then find he didn't have enough room to finish the problem on one line. As Johnson children often do when something like this happens, he said to me, "I messed up," in disgust with himself.

The children were copying a sentence, "Rats like to come out at night," from the blackboard. Again, I noticed their poor use of space. For instance, one girl put the word "Rats" on one line of her paper, left the remaining three-quarters of that line blank, and finished the sentence on the next line.

The teacher gave the children an assignment to make up a full day's menu for each day of the week. She laid out the page for them on the blackboard. Leaving room on the left-hand side as a margin, she wrote the names of the days of the week, starting with Sunday, across the top of the page. Then, below in the left-hand margin, she put "Breakfast, Lunch, Dinner," one under the other. About a third of the class, in copying this layout, didn't leave the margin when they put in the days of the week. They put "Breakfast, Lunch, Dinner" directly under "Sunday." Then they experienced puzzlement and frustration because they didn't have room for Saturday's menu. They were genuinely unable to "see" what they had done wrong.

Observations of the spatial perception problem* were piling up rapidly in our notes, but there was no indication that anyone in the school was aware of it, much less thinking about how to deal with it. One day, in conversation with a new teacher, we discovered that her team had discussed the problem at a weekly team meeting and had decided to test the children

---

*There is no certainty that all the examples we have given, and the many more we saw, were all the same problem, and there is controversy among experts as to the source of such difficulties. Some would suspect "minimal perceptual impairment" a physiological problem, while others would feel that the child had simply failed to learn an essential skill. Of course, there could have been some of both these causes underlying what we saw.

for their perceptual-motor abilities. Out of this testing came an innovation which is discussed in the next chapter.

As the semester wore on, we noted that Johnson's pupils, who were seated in their classrooms around tables in places of their own choice, were becoming melded into small collectivities. For instance, in one primary classroom, each table-group had a name and was treated by the teacher as a unit so far as behavior was concerned:

> There are five tables in the room. They are the Jets, the Supremes, the Dallas Cowboys, the Supers, and the Angels. The children selected their own seats, so these are self-chosen peer groups. The names of the groups are on the blackboard, and the groups get merit and demerit points for behavior as the day goes on.

Gradually, the children at the same table started to work as a collectivity, too, rather than as individuals. They began spontaneously to help each other and seemed to become dependent on their groups to get their work done. Here is an example of the effect of isolation from the group on a pupil's work:

> As a punishment, Mr. Jenkin removed Carole from her table and put her by herself in the back of the room for the whole week. Her personality really changed over the week. Before, she was a participant in a group. She was quiet, but she was always included in the group. She became withdrawn and couldn't do any of her work because of her isolation. I also noticed this with Bud. When a child must sit by himself, he can't do anything. But once he joins his group, his work gets done. I would say, in summary, that work was an individual function at the beginning of the term, but now it is totally a group activity. The only people who want help from me any more are the ones who are sitting individually.

This, then, was the context in which we observed the innovations of 1972–1973 in Johnson: a black militant principal who had to adapt as best he could to the rules of a district with voluntary integration; a somewhat apathetic majority of black parents combined with an active and articulate minority of white parents; a staff which needed instructional guidance and was not getting it; and pupils whose lower-class subculture and perceptual difficulties placed obstacles in the way of academic achievement.

Chapter 3
Innovation in 1972–1973

In the year during which we observed at Johnson, we saw four innovations which originated at three different levels of the Centerville school district. Two were introduced by the teachers, one by the principal, and one by district headquarters. We know that neither of the latter two had raised pupils' achievement scores by the end of the year, since the district collected that information. The first of the teachers' innovations raised achievement scores startlingly, but neither the principal nor the district officials believed that the scores rose as much or as rapidly as the teachers claimed. When the whole school was tested simultaneously, the achievement gains of the relatively few classes exposed to the innovation were not visible in the overall scores. Evidently the district didn't think it worth the bother to separate this subgroup of children to see if perhaps the teachers were right. But a study of the outcomes of innovation is logically preceded by a study of how the innovations are implemented. Adoption of an innovation does not guarantee that it will be effectively carried out. That has been convincingly demonstrated in previous studies.[1] In this chapter and the next, we shall examine how the four innovations were implemented at Johnson.

The Teachers' Innovations

There is reason to believe that a good deal of unheralded innovation takes place in the nation's classrooms, initiated by teachers and sometimes emulated by their immediate colleagues.[2] But time constraints and structural barriers to communication among teachers in different schools, not to speak of different districts and cities, prevents these innovations from spreading very far. The teacher's work leaves little time for such activities as professional communication with colleagues. And the occupation has not organized itself so as to provide a broad audience of colleagues for teachers who have ideas to disseminate.

The teachers in Johnson were notably innovative. Their first innovation was the adoption of DISTAR (Direct Instructional System for Training for Arithmetic and Reading) as the program of instruction for many of their pupils. And the second was their attempts to diagnose and provide remediation for perceptual-motor deficits in their pupils. In both these efforts to improve instruction, they were quietly but firmly opposed by their superiors in the school and the district.

DISTAR

The main teacher-initiated innovation was the use of DISTAR, the Bereiter-Engelmann reading and math curriculum in a programed form put out by Science Research Associates.[3] DISTAR had been introduced into Johnson by informal diffusion in 1970. The child of an office worker went to a nursery school where it was used. This three-year-old girl was often in her mother's office reading. There was a teacher at Johnson who became fascinated with the fact that the preschool child could read and went to visit the nursery school, where she saw the DISTAR program in action. She was so excited about it that she brought other Johnson teachers to see it. One or two teachers adopted DISTAR in the primary grades, and by 1972–1973, many of the primary teachers were using it. According to Lucy Roberts, the supervisor of student teachers, the program is highly structured. "You can't deviate from it," she said, "It is done with small groups and a great deal of repetition." She said that it worked very well; it was lots of fun and the kids enjoyed it. Some teachers tired of it rather quickly, but the kids didn't tire of it. "When it's taught with animation by the teacher, it works marvelously. It can go dead if the teacher goes dead." One primary teacher made quite a claim for DISTAR:

> I was talking with Mrs. Wise about DISTAR, which she swears by. She said, "We couldn't get it from downtown, because they said it was too expensive, so we bought it ourselves." She told me that in previous years she had had some kids jump twenty points in IQ* after one year of working with DISTAR reading and math. She told me that she had kids in "Special Ed" (slow learners) who were the younger siblings of kids she had had in "Special Ed"

*She may have meant "achievement," but she said "IQ."

before them, and sure enough, by the end of the year, the younger kids could all read better than their older siblings. She said that DISTAR simply worked, and they scrounged everywhere looking for money for it. It's expensive, because the workbooks can't be reused. They have to be bought new every year.

Cliff Wallace was another devotee of DISTAR. He said he hated it for himself because it bored him, but it worked for the kids, so he used it:

> The main thing about DISTAR is the analysis they've done. You've got the controlled introduction of words, and you've got the phonics approach. Then you have the behavioristic way of teaching. You're supposed to reward correct responses and ignore inappropriate responses and not to criticize the kids. And the program is built so that the kid would have to be an absolute moron not to know the right answer 95 percent of the time. I've heard some teachers say, "Well, they're not being challenged." But it gives the kids a hell of a lot of confidence. They've taken apart the phonics. They say the kids need to learn that the sounds in a word are in progression; that the letters are there for a reason, even though the language is not phonetically regular. So "was" doesn't come out "friend" or "have" or something like that. See—it comes out something like "was." They have all kinds of good tricks. They collected a number of excellent teaching techniques and put them into a program made up so that any idiot can follow it. It would take me years to work out all this technique myself.
>
> There are a couple of problems with the program. For awhile, especially the first six months, the kid doesn't learn words really. I mean, he's learning a bunch of skills that, when he begins to apply them, will be much more powerful, but the other kids are into little primers. They know maybe fifty or sixty or 100 words. They can go down to the library and read little books just made for them, so the DISTAR kids might get discouraged for awhile.

Some of the DISTAR advocates thought that all of the children in the school should start with it in kindergarten, not just those who fell behind grade level in the primary teams:

> We took kids who had been in school for three or four years and were still reading at the primer level. We figured that they had

had enough failure experience, and we put them on to DISTAR. I personally think that if it works for a kid after he has failed for three years, why not start right away and have them succeeding right away, rather than waiting until they have had a bad experience with something else? I would like to see it started in kindergarten for everybody.

These were the proselytizers. Other teachers had some reservations:

I think DISTAR is very good programed learning material. I don't think it's the answer to every child's needs. There are other programs that can do just as much.

Even the school's most enthusiastic DISTAR teacher made other arrangements for the few children who were too advanced for DISTAR. They had come to school already reading or in such a state of "reading readiness" that the program moved too slowly for them.

One obstacle to the further diffusion of DISTAR in Johnson was the district's refusal to pay the higher price that the program cost. Even more important was the low-keyed, but firm, opposition of the principal. He said nothing against DISTAR to the teachers who were using it. However, he could have persuaded the district to pay for it, but this he did not do. He told the observers he disapproved of DISTAR, but did not say why. Since it was a program meant for children lagging below grade level, widespread adoption of DISTAR in Johnson would have amounted to a public admission that achievement levels were generally low. And Wilder was as much concerned as Phillips had been to maintain a public image of Johnson as a school with "superior programs" and constantly rising achievement levels.

So the teachers' first innovation was one which they claimed raised academic achievement. It diffused somewhat within the school, but was prevented from getting very far, even inside Johnson, by the district's refusal to pay for it and the principal's failure to apply pressure on the district to reverse this policy. The principal was opposed to it because its adoption throughout Johnson would have damaged the public relations image of a high-achieving school.

When we asked a district official in charge of reading programs why *he* didn't investigate the teachers' claims for DISTAR, he said the claims couldn't be true. If they were true, everyone in the country would know about it, because everyone was looking for a reading program which would do for children of relatively uneducated parents just what DISTAR teachers said DISTAR did.

Ironically, three years later, the Johnson teachers' DISTAR results appear to have been replicated on a large scale in Chicago:

> After students were exposed to a concentrated reading program called DISTAR, performance on achievement tests rose dramatically.
>
> The DISTAR program is used most extensively in Chicago's District 10, which covers Lawndale, one of the most deteriorated sections of the city.
>
> In all second-grade classes in District 10, with a total of 1,470 children exposed to DISTAR, mean reading scores were 2.6 in 1974, higher than the city-wide mean of 2.5 and 30 percent higher than the inner-city mean.[4]

In Centerville, the low status of teachers in the school system hierarchy, and their powerlessness in educational matters—to which they were closer, and about which they knew more than the decision-makers knew—was tragic for the children. In many organizations, it is the direct-service personnel, who are encountering day-to-day problems, who can most effectively judge the merits and demerits of an innovation but who are least likely to be consulted about it. This is often the situation of teachers in the United States. It never occurred to the Johnson DISTAR teachers to put their test data together and make an organized attempt to convince the district officials that they were right. Elementary school teachers in this country are not accustomed to communicating with an audience wider than their colleagues in the same building, and they are too accustomed to accepting, passively, their relatively low professional status. So the Johnson teachers, instead of mustering the data to prove they were right, and challenging the decision of their superiors in the educational bureaucracy, paid the excess cost of DISTAR for their own pupils out of their own pockets and allowed the issue to die. Under the circumstances, it seemed unlikely that DISTAR would last long.

Perceptual-Motor Remediation

The second teacher-initiated innovation during 1972–1973 was not widely publicized, even within the school. The only teachers who knew about it were those on the team which was doing it. The staff of this primary team had noticed the perceptual problems which we had recorded repeatedly in our field notes. They discussed the problems at a team meeting and decided to test their pupils systematically for perceptual-motor deficits.

They began by assigning one teacher to give the Kephart Perceptual-Motor Tests to the Special Education children on the team. These were children who had been in school three or four years, but hadn't learned to read. The teacher said that every one of them turned out to have either fine motor problems or gross motor problems. She showed us a test paper on which a child had copied geometric figures incorrectly. He was ten years old, and he had a three-year-old capacity to copy shapes. Many of the children could not track a moving point with their eyes, a great obstacle to learning to read. There were also defects in terms of large muscle control. They couldn't do "jumping jack"; that is, they couldn't make their arms and their feet move together. The teacher told us that she found the same problems widespread among pupils on her team who were *not* in Special Education. She said the team's idea was that, once they discovered what a child's problem was, they could work out some remediation program for the child. Kids who could not follow a moving point with their eyes, for example, would get special training in that; kids who had gross motor problems would be trained by having them practice jumping rope, for example. Another thing they would try to do would be to teach kids in terms of their strengths; that is, if the kid had ocular problems, he might be taught the shapes of letters by tactile methods, only gradually approaching the use of the eyes, in the hope that some connection would be made from the tactile to the visual.

All of this innovative behavior at the team level seemed very much in line with the spirit of the school. However, when we asked for the principal's opinion of the Kephart tests, his response was striking: "If we started diagnosing all the children for this type of problem and trying to do remedial work," he said, "the problem would be absolutely massive, and the school wouldn't be able to do anything else. So we have to act as if they were normal perceptually and try teaching them to read with conventional methods."

In short, the principal seemed quite aware of the nature and scope of the problem being uncovered, but was not prepared to have the school tackle it. He defined the problem as so huge that he preferred to ignore it. Perhaps there was some justification for this stand. It is true that problems of this nature are so frequent among children of low socio-economic background that remediation is an enormously expensive strategy. Prevention—as practiced by the health program of Head Start—is cheaper and more effective.[5]

However, Mr. Wilder also had other reasons for not wanting the school's energies to be spent on perceptual remediation. First, widespread use of this type of program, like widespread use of DISTAR, would have been an admission that achievement levels were low. Second, he had a project afoot much more to his political taste.

So the innovations made by teachers and teams didn't spread much beyond their originators. They had no organizational support. When the district was asked by the teachers for help, it refused to give it. The principal was covertly opposed to both of the teachers' innovations. This opposition from above proved decisive.

The Principal's Innovation

Just before the beginning of the school year in 1972–1973, Johnson-on-Campus was closed by the Board of Education, because, they alleged, tests showed that the children there were not profiting by contact with the university. Their achievement scores were low and were not improving. The black community itself had been critical of the school and its director, Richard Harris. However, when the Board ended the project, at least part of the community was outraged. Harris set up a small African Free School, but the majority of the children returned to their neighborhood schools.

Meanwhile, the building which had housed Johnson-on-Campus stood empty. It was a small structure with movable room dividers intended for an open-space school. In early

October, Johnson's principal made it known to the parents that he and the head of the AAI (Afro-American Institute) at the university had made a proposal to the Board of Education and the university. Their staffs would work together to develop an Afro-American elementary school curriculum and to introduce it into Johnson. The empty building on campus would be used to send Johnson teams, one at a time, to spend five weeks working with the university's African specialists on the curriculum, while at the same time continuing with their regular program.

Mr. Wilder and Dr. Brown, head of the AAI, wrote the proposal. Wilder handled the delicate political job of getting approval for it from Centerville University and the Board of Education. He had a still more delicate problem of avoiding dissension among the black leadership in Centerville. Some of Richard Harris' supporters felt that returning to the building after Johnson-on-Campus had been "kicked out" would look like a capitulation to the Board of Education. The subject was thoroughly aired at a few Johnson Cabinet meetings. Finally, Harris took the position that he would not oppose the proposal, and he released his backers from any obligation to oppose it. However, he forecast gloomily that the "racist" Board of Education would never allow Johnson and the University's African staff the freedom to develop the kind of curriculum they wanted.

The next item on Mr. Wilder's agenda was to get the approval of the Johnson staff for the proposal. Their support was vital, since it was they who would have to supply the expertise as to what kind of curriculum material was appropriate at the elementary level. Mr. Wilder suggested that each team discuss the proposal and that 80 percent of the team in favor should be considered a vote of "Yes." Wilder wanted Karen Waters' team to be the first to use the new facility, since it was the only team in the school with a majority black staff. This was the team called "Soul." Karen Waters, the black team leader, was an old hand at Johnson. As it happened, however, this was the only one of the seven teams in the school which voted "No." Here is a condensed account of the meeting which arrived at the negative decision:

> Joanne Patterson [a black Teacher Corps member who was on the team] started off the discussion by saying, "I'm feeling very ambivalent about the whole thing. The more I think about it

and talk with Marley, [another black Teacher Corps member of the team], the more difficult it becomes for me to make a decision; because I have some feelings like Paul's feelings, [Paul Harris, a black teacher and brother of Richard Harris] about that building and what it means politically. Then there is another whole set of feelings about the dangers and hazards of walking the kids up to that building in a month like February, when we have snow and ice. We would lose a lot of time. On the other hand, it also seems that whatever personal feelings we have about the building, perhaps we ought to set them aside if this curriculum is going to do the kids some good."

Jack Bellini [a white Teacher Corps member of the team] agreed about the safety considerations, but he definitely wanted to be involved in the program. He referred to what Mr. Wilder had said in an earlier staff meeting to the effect that Johnson had been talking about a curriculum like this for years, but hadn't done anything about it. There had never been any large-scale opposition to it, yet it never got off the ground. Here was a chance to do it with some outside stimulation. But he was not sure, Wilder said, that the staff really wanted to do it, and that was what he needed to find out. If the staff really didn't want to do it, he indicated he was going to go somewhere else and do it. This threat had made the team leader angry.

Paul, in a way, replied to Jack's remarks. He said he felt as his brother, Richard Harris, did. "I couldn't set foot inside of that building because of what happened to my brother there. Also, the fact that the kids have to walk up there. They wouldn't do that to white kids. They'd provide some kind of transportation for them. What does that say to people about what this program means? I don't care what they say—you haven't really got control over this program." Joanne thought the same. Marley put in, "Why is the Board of Education doing this to us? Why does it have to be in that building? Why can't we have it in this school?" Sandy Ferris a black special-education teacher added, "You know, it's like feeling you've messed up, and they're making you stick your head in it again."

At this point, the black team leader indicated that because of the feelings that people were expressing around the table, "Maybe those people up there can't give us any more than we can give ourselves in terms of developing an Afro-American curriculum." Paul agreed: "We can get other consultants. And another thing: we ought to find how the parents feel about this before we come to any decisions at all."

Then Joanne suggested that, instead of voting, they write a

position paper. They decided to let her be the secretary for this. As the discussion went on, negative arguments were repeated over and over. Joanne said that no team could be ready to go to the Afro-American Institute before March. Karen said she didn't see why it was necessary for every member of the team to go early. Marley suggested that the institute should be used as a resource center, instead of them moving themselves up there bodily. Eventually, Karen said, "I think we are talking ourselves out of it." And somebody added, "It sounds like that." Joanne read off what she had written:

"1. The place was mandated, and we want it to be stated that the funds should be used in this building if the team wishes it.

"2. There are problems of transportation, safety, and time.

"3. We should consult parents before deciding about the use of the campus building.

"4. No team should go before March.

"5. It is not necessary for every member of the team to go.

"6. The Afro-American Institute (AAI) should be used as a resource center, rather than as a school.

"7. We are committed to an Afro-American curriculum.

"8. The Afro-American curriculum should be in the Johnson School."

Then they talked about what they should do with this statement. Were these conditions to be met before they would vote? Finally, they decided to vote "No" and to give this as their list of reasons. Karen ran around getting everyone's signature on the statement.

When the principal received this statement the following morning, he was quite disturbed. He explained to Karen that the campus building had to be the center of the program, because he wanted the curriculum to spread eventually throughout the school district. If it started in one school, the other schools in the district would be envious and would resist. However, he was ready to make many concessions to get the Soul team's support. They need not begin before March. He would make further efforts to secure bus transportation. They could use the AAI as a resource center, if that was what they preferred. In fact, he said, it was because Soul was such a thoughtful team that he wanted them to be the first in the program.

Karen went back to the team with these concessions, and discussing them with each member individually, rather than as a group, she got a 100 percent vote of "Yes."

The next near disaster which befell the principal's innovation was an in-service conducted by the AAI staff for Johnson
teachers. It was held at the campus building. Dr. Brown had
explained to the teachers that the Africanists would work sometimes with them and sometimes directly with the pupils. This
in-service was supposedly a demonstration of how they would
work with teachers:

> The staff was divided into four groups, and I joined one
> which consisted of an intermediate team and a sixth-grade team.
> There was a presentation made by each of four members of Dr.
> Brown's staff. These people circulated to all four groups.
> The first presentation we had was made by an American
> black in his early 20's. He talked about various theories of racial
> prejudice. He discussed how children learn about color and ac-
> quire race consciousness, and here he used some research which
> went back to the 1950's and was quite outdated. At one point, he
> asserted, "In grade school, white children won't have anything to
> do with blacks. In junior high school, they become more diplo-
> matic." This could not have sat very well with the Johnson
> teachers, who had white and black pupils who interacted a great
> deal. The young man was showing a total ignorance of the
> Johnson School and what went on there. I looked around at the
> audience. It appeared to me that most of the faces were either
> bored or reserved.
> The next person to come into the room was an African folk-
> lorist. He talked about the folk tales of Africa and the Caribbean.
> He said, "The folk tales transmit inherited beliefs of the civiliza-
> tion. They contain moral lessons, like the lessons of generosity,
> patience, truthfulness. In Africa, the grandmothers are the ones
> who sit around and tell stories to the children. They tell them in a
> very indirect way, and stop and ask a lot of questions, and the
> children are expected to answer the questions and ask questions
> of their own."
> The third presentation was given by a young woman who
> taught at a nearby junior high school. She distributed a printed
> curriculum which she emphasized was meant for teachers' use,
> not for children. We barely had time to leaf through it. It in-
> cluded a time-line on black history in America, which began with
> Crispus Attucks and ended in the recent period. It mentioned
> Eldridge Cleaver, H. Rap Brown, Bobby Seale, Martin Luther
> King, and Thurgood Marshall. It did not mention Roy Wilkins or
> the NAACP, nor did it include Whitney Young and the Urban
> League. One part of the curriculum was called "The Black

Family" and consisted of an attack on the Moynihan report.[6] Another was called "Birth Control or Extermination?" and was devoted to the idea that advocates of birth control for poor blacks were trying to exterminate the black race; they were committing genocide.

The final presentation was made by a sociologist from what was formerly French Africa. He launched an attack on American sociology. He said, "American sociologists, both black and white, have espoused an equilibrium theory of society. The ideology implicit in their work can be harmful to the objective of black self-esteem that we are working toward, and so I am hoping that we will be able to analyze these ideologies so that we will be aware of the ideologies behind the social science. Our kids have to be made aware that there isn't just one kind of family structure in the United States; there are two or three kinds of family structure. And if the father is absent, that should not be interpreted as pathological."

When the presentations were over, both presenters and audience gathered in a large room for a question period. Karen Waters came storming in with a woman whom I didn't know. She was saying, "Didn't that infuriate you? It infuriated me. They can take it and they can shove it." Then she turned around and walked out. Someone asked her companion why Karen was so angry, and she said, "We got nothing out of this afternoon that we can use. It was all terribly academic and straight out of books. It had nothing to do with our kids or us."

Dr. Brown then called for questions. There was a long silence. Finally, Marley Winston raised her hand. "I have a question, or what I have to make is really more of a statement. All of the things you did this afternoon didn't deal with kids. It wasn't relevant to anything we can do with our kids. I want to know whether your staff is going to come down to the school, to the Johnson School, and get into our classrooms and get to know our kids and get to know us and find out where we are really at before we come up here somewhere around March 1 and start using this facility." Dr. Brown responded that the AAI's staff wanted to negotiate that separately with each team. "Yes, we will come down if that's what your team wants us to do. Some teams might feel that we were trying to take over if we came down. Other teams might feel we are trying to back off if we don't come down. So we want to know from each team what you want us to do."

There were other questions. But the team leaders kept coming back to the question of how the university personnel would relate to elementary school teachers and grade school pupils. Carla Young, who headed the youngest primary team at Johnson, made the point that there was a need for a very special relationship with the primary grades, that everything presented that day was on far too high a level for use in any form with primary grades. Janet Carruthers, who headed an intermediate team, said, "I hope you people really do plan on spending time in Johnson with children in the classrooms."

On the way out of the meeting, I asked Mrs. Washington, a black primary team leader, what she thought of the in-service. She said that she didn't believe in the idea of the Afro-American curriculum at all. "They are going to teach these children to hate, but not to read." Someone asked Cliff Wallace if he would like to go off somewhere for a baloney sandwich, and he said, "I'm not hungry for any more baloney this afternoon." Since Karen Waters, Carla Young, Janet Carruthers, Cliff Wallace, and Mrs. Washington were all team leaders, that was five out of seven team leaders heard from. The other two also gave negative reactions to the in-service in their interviews.

So far, there had been three major objections to the Brown-Wilder Afro-American curriculum proposal. The first was the use of the building where the Johnson-on-Campus school had been located. Many people felt that to use that building would constitute a symbolic defeat for the black community. The second objection had to do with walking the children to the campus up a steep hill in mid-winter. That idea was thoroughly impractical, and when he realized that the whole project might founder on that rock, Mr. Wilder did obtain busing for the children. The third objection grew out of the in-service. The teachers had been exposed to four sessions which were like university classes in style and content. To translate what they had been given that afternoon into a curriculum usable by their pupils was impossible, they felt, and yet no one had made any concrete suggestions as to how they and the African specialists could collaborate on the new curriculum.

In fact, the situation was even more difficult than the teachers realized. They had been given the impression that the Afro-American Institute staff would spend a good deal of time working with them. They were not told that, except for Dr. Brown and his administrative assistant, the staff all had full-time university commitments and that any time they gave to the project would have to be "extra," voluntary, and unpaid.

In the end, there was almost no collaboration between the university African specialists and Johnson teachers. Nor was any work done on an Afro-American curriculum at the campus center. The two major goals of the innovation were unmet. Yet Karen Waters' team, Soul, which was the first to go to AAI, felt their experience there was an exciting one for reasons that no one had considered before the program began. The positive effects were produced by the campus building itself, and the new organization of space which it forced on the team. We learned this from an interview with Karen Waters in the late spring, after the Soul team had returned to Johnson. On the subject of the AAI staff, Mrs. Waters said:

> We had an awful lot of trouble with the AAI staff relating to the children. We actually got a commitment from only one staff member there, who was going to work with them on photography. They had committed themselves to Dr. Brown about time, but then when they would start with the children, they either petered out or didn't show up. We had to keep constantly pulling them back in to discuss and talk about their commitment to the program. It was very touchy. There was even hostility between the two staffs, and we had to discuss that quite a bit.

As the Johnson teachers had anticipated, the AAI staff did not know how to deal with children:

> Drama was a very sad experience, because we had a young woman who'd never worked with children before and didn't know how to get children to open up. She was very critical, the way you would be if you were working with an adult, trying to produce a professional product. She gave the kids no positive encouragement when they did something. She just said, "No, that's not the way you do it." And she got a lot of overreacting to that, not just from the kids, but from the teachers, too.

One of the biggest disagreements between the Soul team and the university African staff had to do with classroom discipline. The Africans expected a very traditional kind of authority-centered discipline in the classroom. Their attempts to impose this discipline did not succeed and elicited hostility from both the teachers and the pupils:

> Most of the African staff were just hung up on discipline, because our children didn't sit at attention and just hang on their every

word. I think that was what discouraged participation on their part. And the way they dealt with discipline was something we had a lot of confrontations with them about.

Another disappointment was that the AAI had no materials on Africa that the Johnson staff could use. As a result, there was no African curriculum. Instead, the team dug up and worked with the old "self-esteem" curriculum which had been developed in the 1960's under Dr. Phillips.

Since the Afro-American staff had not lived up to the expectations the Johnson teachers had of them, it was a bit difficult to understand the positive aspects of the Soul team experience on campus. Mrs. Waters tried to explain it to us:

> I think what it did for the team was it developed the feeling that we could handle problems. We could always come up with a solution that maybe not everybody liked, but everybody could live with. I don't know whether it was the size of the place or the fact that we were on our own. It wasn't easy to turn to anybody else but the team. It did away with this sort of sitting in the teachers' room and a sort of gossip kind of thing about what your team isn't doing for you.

Dr. Brown and his administrative assistant were also important factors in the situation. They acted as "observers" who, as soon as they saw an interpersonal problem of any kind developing, dealt with it, or helped those involved to deal with it:

> Then, of course, Harry Brown did his job. When something was going wrong between two people, he would see it immediately because of the small size of the building, and he could deal with it. Like people can come together and he can say, "I think for five minutes we need some conversation among us." Harry wasn't around as much as Bob Allen, who was assistant director. Bob was an observer of the whole situation, and as soon as he noticed something going wrong between children, or teachers and children, or teachers and teachers, he would bring it to my attention. And I would bring it to Harry's attention. And then we'd come together and solve it. It was nice. I had somebody to work with, not just myself. John Wilder at Johnson is just not available to you anytime you want him, but up there I could grab Bob or Harry anytime at all and say, "Hey, we need to discuss a problem that's occurring."

This passage suggests that the visibility of everyone on the team to everyone else, in the specially designed open space of this building, made it possible for an observer to nip problems in the bud. In another passage, Karen Waters suggested that the mutual visibility of team members increased their interaction and consequently their cohesion:

> When you're up there, that's when you're forced to deal with every kid on the team, because you come across them. You're in and out of everybody's room all the time. You see something happen. There's nowhere you can go to get away from it all. It's something about the way the space is organized. You're not off in a self-enclosed classroom. You can do that if you want to, but it's very, very difficult to do. I don't believe anybody taught with their doors closed. Theater and Dance had their doors closed for obvious reasons, but a lot of activity was taking place in the hall. Marley used the hall for her reading, and my kids had their classes in the hall, and kids would constantly flow in and out. The bathrooms were in the center of the building, so kids just had to come from everywhere. There was no place for kids to hide, no place for teachers to hide. Everyone was always looking for a place to work, so if you went into one of those little quiet rooms, you weren't there alone for very long. There was just no place to go to be completely isolated. Teachers became friends who were only acquaintances before. Teachers found out new things about kids whom they had labeled, for instance, as nonachievers. There was a lot of touching going on, too, that didn't happen at Johnson. I really think that the closeness of the space is what helped to do it.

The team found itself forced to deal with interpersonal problems rather than ignoring them:

> People began to address themselves to each other as a problem occurred. They didn't just run to the team leader and say, "What are you going to do about it?" For instance, there was a problem between Pearl Doyle and the team members. We dealt with it ourselves. It was getting to be a case of "Everybody picks on Pearl." So we sat down together and dealt with it; and now we know she thinks that some things a teacher is committed to sharing on a team are too personal. Since we gave the kids the right not to share if they didn't want to, we had to extend that right to ourselves as well. We also realized that if someone has to leave a team meeting early, it should be made clear whether that person

is willing to live with the decisions made in his absence or not. The team is more cohesive because we really dealt with these problems.

However, Mrs. Waters pointed out that, while the staff felt that they had gained a lot from the experience and had become more truly a team, the children did not feel the same way:

> "I think it was more a teacher-training kind of experience for us than it was anything for the children. The children are still leery about just what they got out of the AAI, except that they got to do some photography; they got to prepare a performance for their parents; they got out a newspaper."
>
> Question: "What exactly were the kids leery about?"
>
> Answer: "They just didn't know exactly what it was all about. And we haven't really dealt with that, because our team used the place in a different way, I think, from what Dr. Brown and John Wilder wanted. We did more with building self-esteem in the child than we did in terms of African curriculum. And I think the African curriculum was what they wanted to see developed. We did more in terms of self-esteem for kids. Teachers were spending a great deal of time with kids who needed it. Joanne worked an entire week with a child who needed some confidence built in him, and Marley took the rest of the class."

The Soul team's experience at AAI is an example of the unanticipated consequences of social action. The ends which were sought by sending this predominantly black team to the Afro-American Institute at the university were not reached. The difficulty was that each side was being asked to play a completely new role vis-à-vis the other, and neither knew how to begin. So they fell back on familiar patterns of role behavior. The university teachers tried to treat the Johnson teachers as if they were university students, there to master material as students did in their regular classes. The teachers vehemently rejected this role. On the other hand, the teachers expected that the AAI would hand them African material already shaped for use in elementary classrooms. This was the kind of curriculum guide elementary school teachers are familiar with, but which the AAI staff had no qualifications to make. The Africanists knew nothing about the developmental levels of elementary school children in general or Johnson's children in particular. Nor did they understand much about the kinds of discipline and activity which are typical of American classrooms.

On the other hand, Soul team members who had been teaching until then in self-enclosed classrooms, found that at the campus building, their mutual visibility in an open space forced them into intensive interaction which increased their cohesion. This result, which no one had foreseen, gave a positive cast to their experience, despite the failure to achieve the stated goals.

It was not at all clear at the end of the year how much had been learned from the experience at the Afro-American Center. Mr. Wilder not only planned to continue the program the following year, he planned to begin involving other schools in the district:

> Next year we want the district to pick up the program. We hope to be doing some public-relations type work, like getting teachers from other schools interested in and excited about it, and then hoping that they will involve other teachers from their schools, and perhaps inviting some of their classes to come up with our teams.

Mrs. Waters was to be the curriculum coordinator at the Afro-American Center during the second year. She had many functions to perform, only one of which was doing something about an African curriculum:

> I am going to be up at AAI next year. We're going to have to document what goes on. There will have to be someone to act as liaison between AAI and Johnson and the Board of Education. And we're going to have an African curriculum. I am going to do all of that.

Thus, again it seems that the effort planned for public relations was out of all proportion to the effort involved in developing the innovation itself—namely, creating an elementary school Afro-American curriculum. It was all puffery and little substance. Mrs. Waters was familiar with the difficulties, but as she said, "I like administrative work," and she was co-opted.

While the teachers' innovations were focused on improving pupils' academic skills, the principal's innovation was focused on raising their political consciousness. Mr. Wilder claimed that fostering a collective pride in their African heritage would raise the children's self-esteem.

Since he wanted to diffuse his innovation to all the black schools in the district, Mr. Wilder took care to locate it outside Johnson in a highly visible place. Part of his political ambition was for himself. If the elementary school Afro-American curriculum became a recognized program, he said, it would be the first of its kind in the country. As one teacher remarked, "Glory, glory, glory again."

The principal's innovation was also hardier than the teachers'. It got started despite considerable initial resistance from the Johnson staff. There were plans to continue and even expand it during a second year, despite the fact that the core of the project—the curriculum itself—had not even begun to be implemented during year one.

Why did the Board of Education and Centerville University permit the innovation to continue in spite of its apparent nonfeasibility? The answer was political. The black community resented the closing of Johnson-on-Campus. The Board of Education and the university felt it was necessary to assuage the resentment. Wilder convinced them that his program would perform this function.

Finally, the Afro-American studies project had one characteristic which is important, because we shall meet it again. It left it up to the teachers to translate a broad, vague mandate into a set of concrete materials and activities which could be called a curriculum—at the same time that they were expected to carry on all their other routine functions. The program gave the teachers virtually no organizational support. The university's Africanists had neither the time nor the skills to help them. They offered no materials the teachers could use without a major effort to transform them. These demands on the teachers were completely unrealistic. The reader will recall that the teachers themselves were highly skeptical about the possibility of working with the African specialists, after they were exposed to them at an orientation. But their fears were swept aside by Mr. Wilder and Dr. Brown. However, the teachers proved to be right. This innovation was initiated under conditions which made it impossible to carry it out. But there was no evidence that Wilder learned this lesson from the failures of the first semester, or if he did learn them, that he cared. He wanted to move ahead, involving other schools in the attempt to develop an Afro-American course of study, under exactly the same impractical conditions. It seemed more important to him that the idea be diffused, with his name attached to it, than that the curriculum itself be developed.

The District's Innovation

The Centerville school district had decided to experiment with an innovation called ILP (Individualized Learning Program) the year before our observations began. The program was developed by a foundation and has been introduced into networks of schools all over the country. The Centerville district sent one of its elementary school supervisors to the Midwest for several weeks of training as a change agent, and she, in turn, conducted a summer workshop for the teachers in Johnson and in Merrill, the two schools selected to introduce the innovation into Centerville. In addition, the foundation supplied an elaborate kit of booklets, records, and filmstrips intended to guide the innovation. Each of Johnson's seven team leaders received one of the kits, though they seldom so much as looked at them; they didn't have enough time.

ILP involved team teaching, differentiated staffing, and individualized instruction. Most Johnson teachers felt it was merely a systematization of what they had long been doing. They had had team teaching before; they had had differentiated staffing in the sense that there were team leaders, teachers, and paraprofessional aides. The teachers voted for the adoption of ILP largely because they expected it to bring them Title III funds and the many extras, in terms of materials, that such funds could buy.

While the teachers believed the innovation was not very new for them, the principal was privately unenthusiastic about it because, "Too much individualism is not where I'm coming from." However, he accepted ILP as a favor to the district office. He felt that he could ask for reciprocity later on in their support for the Afro-American curriculum.

Thus the adoption of ILP did not arise out of any felt need at the Johnson School. Both the teachers and the principal supported it for opportunistic reasons.[7]

As it turned out, the district's application for Title III ESEA funds was turned down. The city then agreed to fund the workshop for the change agent, the summer workshops for teachers, and the foundation's kit of materials. Beyond that, they refused to allocate any extra funds for implementing the innovation.

The Philosophy of Individualized Instruction

In its philosophy, ILP was like other schemes for individualizing instruction. The basic idea is that children learn at different rates and in different ways. The traditional classroom, which teaches everyone the same way and at the same rate, fails to take proper account of this fact. Individualized instruction, however, tries to take account of it first by diagnosing the child's skills and finding out what he really knows and is able to do. It also, in many of its versions, tries to find out what the child's "learning style" is: Does he do best by reading to gather information? Does he retain information better if he hears it? Is an activity mode the best medium of learning for him? Once the child has been diagnosed, the individualized instruction program seeks to meet him where he really is—not where he's supposed to be according to some set of norms—and to provide him with a curriculum which will carry him forward at his own rate and in his own style.

One basic tenet of individualized instruction is that no one should be labeled a "failure." Children are not compared with each other. Rather, a child's progress is measured against his own past achievement. By giving the child work which is well within his power to do, individualized instruction is supposed to develop a sense of mastery and self-esteem; in turn, self-esteem is supposed to increase objective mastery, so that a virtuous circle is set in motion.

The Organizational Structure of ILP

Team leaders, teaching teams, and paraprofessionals all had parts to play in the official version of ILP. In addition, it introduced one new structure and two new types of positions into the school. The structure was the IGC and the positions were those of "change agent" and "curriculum facilitator."

Team Leaders and the Instructional Guidance Committee

Team leaders were not new to Johnson, and teachers differed as to whether the position of team leader was beginning to acquire more authority and prestige than that of teacher. A relatively new teacher in the school thought it was:

One year he was part of the team, not in the leadership capacity. Then he became team leader, and people began to shy away from him because he was a team leader now. He was different. He was changing, and that created a whole different set-up around responsibilities. When people become team leaders, they get tight with other team leaders.

A teacher longer at Johnson disagreed:

Question: "Do you think that the position of team leader is becoming different from that of a teacher, in terms of authority or prestige?"

Answer: "Not necessarily. Because team leaders are teachers, so they are still teaching. It is a lot of extra work, so a teacher who is going to be a team leader has to be willing to take on that extra work. Not everyone is willing to do it. It doesn't necessarily bring prestige. Usually, it is an experienced teacher, so you know that if she is out of the classroom for an hour, the kids are not going to suffer."

The IGC consisted of the principal and the team leaders who met once a week to discuss overall school problems. At the meetings of the IGC, one could see the process of differentiation between teachers and team leaders beginning to occur. Team leaders were urged by the principal to exercise authority over paraprofessionals and teachers on their team. For instance, when several team leaders complained of paraprofessionals coming to school late, leaving early, and not doing their jobs, the principal said that team leaders had the authority to make schedules for paraprofessionals and to enforce them. Nearly all the team leaders had complaints about these aides:

Jaqueline Harris said, "My paraprofessionals told me that some on other teams had looked at their schedules and said, 'I would never do that.'" And she had responded to them, "Am I asking you to do something that you think you shouldn't do?" The answer she got was, "No, but other unit leaders should make their paraprofessionals do the same job."

Janet Carruthers said sometimes her paraprofessionals come into the room and ask for the kids they're supposed to work with, and the kids say they don't want to go, and the paraprofessional simply leaves the room and goes to have coffee. It should be noted that Janet did not feel able to insist that the paraprofessional take the child for the work.

Finally, Mr. Wilder said team leaders should tell the

paraprofessionals, "If the teacher has nothing for you to do, report back to me." Then, there should always be a follow-up so you know the aide is doing the work prescribed. If the aide is not doing the work, the team leader should report that fact to the principal. Aides are responsible for being in school until 3:30. They have to get here on time; they have to be more productive. In order to get them to do this, we should give them more voice in decision-making. We should tell them they're expected to participate in team meetings. Then we should say to them, "If you don't like my team, tell me, and you won't be on it." He suggested that if they didn't do their work, he would fire them and get new aides. "The market is on our side."

Far more difficult than assuming authority over paraprofessionals was assuming authority over other teachers. First, there is the traditional norm of equality of all teachers to be overcome. Second, team leaders were understandably reluctant to do anything that might create bad feelings, since the position of team leader rotated a good deal, and the following year they might well find themselves on the lower end of this step in the hierarchy of authority:

There came a delicate moment in the IGC meeting when there was a lot of play back and forth as to whether the team leaders would discuss among themselves difficulties they were having with teachers. It began with Cliff Wallace saying, "Maybe now we should talk about teachers." Then Mr. Wilder said, "Well, we have to talk about the Afro curriculum." But Jackie Harris put in, "It's time to talk about teachers." Wilder said, "Well, I have spoken to each of the team leaders individually about teachers." But the curriculum facilitator* for the primary teams was insistent on bringing up the case of a teacher on Mrs. Washington's team. She and Mrs. Washington alternated in bringing charges against this teacher. The curriculum facilitator said the teacher didn't come to meetings. If she did come, she left early. She wouldn't take children into her class whom she was asked to take. This morning, for instance, they brought a new child to the team, and Mrs. Washington assigned the child to her room. The teacher then arranged with another teacher to take the child, without consulting Mrs. Washington. Mr. Wilder, who had been taking notes, said, "We don't need to go any further

*"Curriculum facilitator" was a new position which was created along with the adoption of ILP. There was curriculum facilitator for the primary grade teams and one for the intermediate or upper elementary grade teams.

than that," as if that closed the case against the teacher. That was enough. He continued, "We have to put all of this in writing and have a conference with her, and she will get a warning."

Then Mrs. Washington said that she was afraid of the offending teacher and personally unable to confront her. Part of the reason for this was that the teacher was a member of the Johnson Cabinet and was also the school's representative to the Teachers' Union. Also, Mrs. Washington was unpopular with other teachers in the school for having reported their "improper behavior" to other principals in the past. Mr. Wilder said to Mrs. Washington, "If you could do it, that would be the best procedure. But if you cannot, that's what the principal's office is for." Then the curriculum facilitator said that the child would have to be given back to the teacher, and Wilder said, "That will have to be up to Mrs. Washington. The team leader has the authority to change a child from room to room within a team. We will talk to the teacher tomorrow, confront her with these statements, and when we finish that, Mrs. Washington, you need to say to her that the child must go back to her room. You must exercise your authority with her."

These two events from IGC meetings show how the role of the team leader, with authority over staff members of the team, was gradually being defined, even though some of the leaders were reluctant to assume authority. That was made easier by a decision later in the year that team leaders would remain in the position for the following year and that teams would be changed as little as possible.

Change Agent

The change agent charged with introducing ILP to the Johnson and Merrill Schools was also a district elementary supervisor. She said this created some role conflict for her. As change agent, she acted as a resource, particularly for team leaders, in implementing the innovation. But as supervisor, she had to evaluate teachers and sometimes give assistance to inexperienced, nontenured teachers who were in trouble:

> The dual role I play, which is a little difficult, is to be the ILP facilitator as well as really being an evaluator of the teachers' performances. I'm not sure the two should be in the same person, but they are this year. On one of the teams, I have had to work

directly with two teachers, and I've turned over the work on ILP to the curriculum facilitator.

Since she was the representative of ILP in two large elementary schools and supervisor for additional ones as well, the change agent was extremely busy. She was liked by everyone at Johnson who worked with her. Team leaders said her comments were always constructive. But they were fortunate if they saw her as often as twice a month. When she did visit Johnson, she took her cues from what the teachers were already doing on their own:

> If the teacher is attempting to provide a lot of individual independence or small group activities, and yet the room itself does not lend itself to this kind of activity, I would say to a teacher or a team leader, "I see you're really trying to provide small group experience and this is exciting. I wonder what kind of setting would lend itself best to helping children function well in small groups." And from this there would be a discussion on how furniture should be placed in the room; maybe the use of rugs or the use of quiet spots for individual activity—that kind of thing.
>
> Where I see a teacher trying to have children individualized only through the use of ditto sheets, I would encourage them to think of other teacher-made devices that would more readily and more interestingly for the child help them gain that particular skill.

Usually team leaders or whole teams took the initiative in approaching the change agent for help. It is, in general, a wise strategy for a change agent to wait until asked for help, and in this case, the fact that she was on the scene so infrequently made it almost imperative.

Curriculum Facilitators

A large part of the responsibility for implementing ILP in Johnson fell to the two "curriculum facilitators," one for the primary and one for the intermediate teams. The first step in implementation was assessment. Each child's skills were supposed to be diagnosed as a preliminary to prescribing curriculum appropriate to his needs. The primary teams' facilitator found one of her teams resistant to the demands of ILP assessment:

To individualize, you must know what each student is good in and what each child is bad in. Before you could do the other steps, you had to have an assessment. Most of the teachers said they made their assessments in their heads. I told them we had to have some way to assess on paper. ILP shows many different ways to assess. It may be the teacher's judgment or standardized tests, but it has to be written down. I left them with the statement that they should start an assessment program. I'm hearing that they are not doing it; they are waiting for the team leader to do the whole thing.

A major task undertaken by the curriculum facilitators was that of writing sequential curriculum objectives so that all the teachers would have a common understanding of what skills were to be taught and in what order. This was not called for by ILP, but it seemed to be needed in Johnson which had no district curriculum guides, and which had never quite recovered from having "thrown away the textbooks" under Dr. Phillips. Mr. Wilder had tried to return to an emphasis on the basic skills, but he knew nothing about curriculum and so was unable to help the teachers who needed guidance on it. The primary facilitator worked on this problem with whole teams:

> We sat around as a team, and I pooled some curriculum guides in reading from everywhere, even Pennsylvania. We pulled out the skills we felt kindergarten and first graders could meet. I wrote these down and formulated all of them, and then we went back through them to weed out anything that wasn't needed. Then I typed it up and gave it to each teacher in a folder.

The intermediate curriculum facilitator said:

> I am working with a math committee to develop a sequence of skills in the math area. Problem-solving, computation, basic operations, decimals, fractions, and geometry—the necessary things in terms of skill development.

She had similar committees in the area of science and social studies.

Curriculum *objectives* and curriculum itself are not the same thing. Teachers were supposed to be free to choose or write the curriculum they wanted to use, so long as it accomplished the objectives:

> We are not boxing anybody into a single approach to curriculum objectives. People can use any curriculum they want to use if it develops skills that can be measured by testers, by the city, by a teacher in another school.

Actually, as we pointed out earlier, the task of creating curriculum from scratch is a heavy burden for teachers. ILP compounded the burden by asking teachers to find or write curriculum appropriate for each individual child. Such a task is monumental, and it is not surprising that Johnson teachers could not do it, as we shall see below.

A final concern of the facilitators was to see to it that records were kept of each child's skill mastery so that continuity in his curriculum could be maintained when he changed teachers. This was crucial to coordinating an individualized program, but the intermediate facilitator said it wasn't being done:

> We are trying to set up a way of recording systematically throughout the school. Getting teachers responsible for recording skills and thus assuring that a continuation of the skills will occur—that's the whole bag. And it's not happening. This is your seventh year since Phillips came here, and it's just not happening.

A team leader bore her out on this:

> Each teacher keeps the cumulative folders of those kids she's responsible for and sticks in some information. but there isn't consistency and continuity between teams, which is what we need. We also need continuity between teachers on a team. This is why we are trying to get into assessment and record-keeping on our team. There just has never been that. Nobody checks up on it. Some kids don't even have folders.

Thus we see once more an innovation which makes heavy demands on teachers, but gives them minimal help in meeting them. The team leaders never had time to look at the large amount of ILP material they received. If they had looked at it, they would have found that they were supposed to diagnose pupils' skills, but they were not told which skills or how to diagnose. They were told to develop a course of study for each child, using small-group and large-group instruction and independent study, according to the pupil's "learning style," but they were not told what was meant by "learning style." There was no guidance as to how to relate the course of study to the diagnosis, or as to how to fit the individual programs together in order to have a manageable group.

Since the change agent was seldom present, and the curriculum facilitators knew little about ILP, each team pursued a course of action which was pretty much its own. Our next task is to look at how several of the teams translated ILP into action.

Chapter 4

Teaming for Individualized Instruction

We observed in Johnson in September and October of 1972 and returned in February and March of 1973.* In the second semester, we asked several administrators to name for us one team which had been relatively successful with ILP at the primary and intermediate levels and one which had been relatively unsuccessful at each of the two levels. There was high consensus among the change agent, the supervisor of student teachers, the principal, and the curriculum facilitators as to which four teams met these specifications. Each of us then observed two teams intensively for a month apiece. In our view, only one team in the school was successful in implementing ILP goals; one was partially successful. The other two were failures, though the failure differed in degree.

Our criteria for the success of a team in implementing ILP were divided into success in terms of staff, and success in terms of pupils. Success for the staff required that the members have a productive division of labor and high cohesion and morale. One premise of ILP is that individualized instruction requires more "output" from the teacher than does traditional whole-class teaching. Teachers are supposed to prescribe a learning program for each child, tailored to his needs. The product required of the teacher is thus quantitatively greater than it is where one lesson is given to twenty-five or thirty students. In order to attain this greater output, the team engages in specialization and division of labor. We also expected to see the individual classrooms giving way to a combination of large group, small group, and one-to-one instruction throughout the team. We expected to see both pupils and teachers identify increasingly with the team as a whole.

*Johnson was the largest school we studied, and we spent more time in it than in the other two.

Success so far as pupils were concerned required that instruction actually be moving toward individualization: a calculated "fit" between the child's diagnosed capacities and his prescribed curriculum. This "fit" is intended to guarantee that every child will experience success in his work. The abolition of failure is supposed to lead to a greater involvement of the children in their work and to a pleasant sense of increasing mastery, which in turn fosters the growth of objectively measured academic competence. We observed children closely while working with them and their teachers in classrooms, and we tried to understand how they felt about their daily work. We made no attempt to measure changes in achievement, but these measures were available from the district. We shall describe briefly each of the four teams studied and then analyze the reasons for differences in implementation.*

The Butterflies

A primary team led by Carla Young, the Butterflies, had 183 children aged five and six. This was named to us as a successful team at the primary level. The five-year-olds were kindergarteners who stayed only half a day in school, so that there were about 136 children present during each half of the day. The staff consisted of four full-fledged teachers, including the team leader, three Teacher Corps members, two Urban Teaching Interns, a paraprofessional teaching aide, a clerical aide, and a reading tutor. The team leader, two teachers, and both aides were black. Since the Teacher Corps members and the Urban Interns were treated by the teachers as equals and carried nearly full teaching loads, there was an effective ratio of teaching-adults to children of one-to-fifteen.

The team occupied six classrooms on two sides of a hallway. On one side were the three kindergarten homerooms and on the other side, the three first-grade homerooms. However, the children used their homerooms only to leave and collect their clothing, have snacks and lunch, and for a class meeting. The rest of the time the space was allocated to activities rather than

*The Butterflies and Giants were observed and written about in a first draft by Schorr. Soul and the Jets were observed and written about by the author. The final draft on all four teams was written by the author.

to classes. The kindergarten rooms, which had connecting doors, functioned as three "open"* classrooms filled with a variety of materials. The team was unusually rich in materials, compared with the rest of the school, because kindergarten is the one grade to which the Centerville School District allocates concrete learning materials. The "large muscle room" contained large- and medium-sized blocks for building; a basin and containers of various sizes for water play and measuring; a small balance beam for the children to walk across; a homemade "horse"; a play kitchen; Lincoln logs; tumbling mats; a set of small musical instruments; and plastic play figures of men, women, and children with which the pupils acted out stories. The "small muscle room" contained art materials: many kinds of paper, egg crates, scraps of fabric, an easel at which two children could paint, crayons, magic markers, sponges to paint with, newspapers and magazines to cut out, printing materials, collage materials, clay, and play dough; jigsaw puzzles; and a television set always tuned to the educational network. The "quiet study room" had a variety of mathematical games. There were poker chips, geometric shapes to classify, blocks to fit into the appropriately shaped holes, an abacus, geo-boards, a small library, a shell collection, two hamsters, a science experiment corner, and a music corner with a piano. All the children on the team spent the greater part of their day in these three rooms.

The rooms on the other side of the hall were devoted to small-group instruction. Every first grader was assigned to a reading group and a math group. Every kindergartener was in a "reading readiness" group in which he also received some math instruction. The groups were never larger than seven or eight; usually they contained four or five children. The assignments to groups were made on the basis of skill. Children's skill levels were tested three times during the year: at the beginning for grouping, in the middle of the year for regrouping, and at the end of the year to assess progress. The instructional groups were small, homogeneous ability groups. However, the fact that they were grouped by ability was not visible to the pupils, since the number of groups was large, and there were several at each

---

*These were not true open classrooms as open educators define that term. They were simply filled with manipulative materials, and the children were allowed to choose what they would do.

ability level. Furthermore, teachers used whatever basal readers and math books they individually preferred. That meant that groups at the same ability level used different materials.

The day was divided into thirty-minute periods. Each child met for a half-hour a day with his reading group and for a half-hour with his math group. Whenever a child was not in one of his instructional groups or with his homeroom class, he was in the open classrooms. At the beginning of each half-hour period, the teachers conducting small group instruction collected their groups from the open classrooms. The others supervised in these rooms. All teachers taught some reading and some math and did some open classroom supervising. The team leader had planned the allocation of space, time, and pupils:

> In room 111, Tania was working with four kids. They were reading sentences. Donna Valentine was working on DISTAR phonics with one girl alone. A boy was working alone on his math workbook. Three boys and Evelyn, who was a Teacher Corps intern, were reading words off a blackboard. There was so much activity going on, it seemed as if there were twenty people in this room, working in groups of three or four. Wherever I looked, there was a teacher working with a small group.

Sometimes the work was further individualized:

> On Friday, Sharon was working with a small group of children. She said she had a very individualized group. They read a little together at the beginning of the period, but then worked alone in the workbook, and they were all at different places. After they had worked in the workbook for a while, they were allowed to pick out a book to read from among ten which were available. Sharon said that this group was very advanced. They were reading above the norm for their age level.

In mathematics, as in reading, it was the top group on the team which was the most individualized:

> One boy was reading a whole book on the number ten. A girl asked the teacher, pointing to the place in her book, what was the difference between a number and a numeral. Another was confused by the word "nought," which appeared in her book instead of "zero."

A notable characteristic of this team was the consistency among teachers in the norms they held for pupils' behavior:

The observer asked Sharon why the children on the team worked so well. Why were they seemingly so self-sufficient? She said, "Well, everyone on the team has the same goals. This wasn't so two years ago on my team, where they would make a rule and one person would fail to enforce it with the children, and that would lead to an inconsistent standard of behavior for the children, which resulted in many activities falling apart."

Rewards and punishments were likewise uniform throughout the team:

I asked Carla if there were any special rewards or punishments. She said the teachers feel the work is its own reward, and they don't offer any special one. Punishment was isolation in the corner, a completely enclosed punishment structure with two curtained windows resembling a playhouse in which there was a single chair. In extreme cases, they get a spanking.

The consistency of norms within the team was due, in part, to the high rate of communication among team members. They met, not only in the three-hour Thursday afternoon sessions reserved for team meetings throughout the school, but also had lunch together every day in room 125; and they held an extra team meeting on any occasion when Carla felt one was necessary.

Another major cause of the normative consistency on this team was the way they used their space. Several teachers with small groups of children worked in the same room at the same time. This meant they were highly visible to one another and to pupils as they went about their daily work. Such mutual visibility makes normative inconsistency visible and produces a strain which the team resolves by agreeing on consistent rules:

Donna told the team the children were having trouble with the wooden horse, and she wanted to make a rule that they had to ask a teacher to get it out for them and to put it away again. Some teachers had been letting the kids handle it and some had been doing it themselves. They agreed that Donna's rule was needed and that they would all follow it.

Another source of high rates of communication on the team was a network of personal friendships. Carla and Felicia had known each other previously. Thelma and Sharon had been teaching together for a number of years, and both knew Helen from the previous year. Violet and Donna were roommates and close friends. Tania and Evelyn had been in the same teaching program together. The team members often went out together for a drink after school functions, had dinner at each others' homes, and met on weekends to work together. Since most of them were continuing their education at the university, three or four were enrolled in the same class which met three evenings a week. All but two members of the team enrolled in a "figure salon" together and attended in couples or groups.

The team showed special initiative in its relations with parents:

> Carla was explaining to Sharon a packet of materials she had developed so that parents could help their children to learn. This included a list of inexpensive but good educational games which were easily available. It told what skills the games taught, what age they were appropriate for, where they could be bought, and their prices. There was a three week TV program schedule for parents and children to watch and discuss together. There was also a vocabulary list for parents to go over.

The Butterflies held a "parent night" at which they presented, in summary form, the kinds of teaching employed on the team. They had a turnout of one hundred parents, representing over half of the children's families. It was by far the largest turnout that we saw during our stay at Johnson.

At team meetings, the Butterflies had high attendance and high participation:

> On this team, I still really can't tell who are the teachers and who are the Teacher Corps people and Urban Interns, because they are all treated like teachers and contribute as much as teachers. There seems to be no difference in the rate of participation.

The Butterflies was the only team in which the leader had been relieved of a homeroom class. While every other team leader in the school was subject to constant interruption of teaching activities to take care of team matters, Carla had a more rational schedule. She devoted part of her time to small group instruction, and part to helping other team teachers. Although there was no other permanent specialization on the team, each time there was a collective task to be accomplished, a temporary division of labor was organized:

> Carla split the team up into room committees to work on the revamping of each room. In room 103, Tania and Evelyn were

trying to dig up new materials, and Tania showed me two puppet sets she hadn't known she had. One was a large cardboard sheet the size of a young child, through which the child could poke his hands and face, with different drawings around them, and "role play." In another room, four teachers were sitting around trying to figure out new ways to arrange things so the children could be more self-directed. They decided to put up a board with different colored cards, each color designating an activity. When they came into the room, each child would have to take one of these "tickets" and keep it as long as he was doing that activity. This was also a way of preventing a pile-up of children around one or two popular activities.

The Butterflies team had become a thoroughly cohesive unit by February of the first academic year. The team leader indicated the excellent morale of the team when she said in an interview, "I am very excited about my team. I feel that we are working wonders with kids and with people." The other team members expressed similar gratification in their work.

The Butterflies also came closer than any of the remaining three teams to individualizing instruction:

> We tried to work with small groups. Some children are taught on a one-to-one basis. The grouping and regrouping that we have done through this year so far has gotten to a point where each child is learning with a group of kids who are about their level.

The fact is that "individualized instruction" usually turns out to be small-group instruction, in which the members of the group are as alike in skill level as resources make possible. In the school we shall discuss in Part II, homogeneous ability-grouping by classroom was deliberately abolished, only to creep back in this new guise. That the Butterflies were quite successful in matching the curriculum to the individual child seemed evident from the children's enthusiasm and involvement in their work. This was the only one of the teams observed in which we did not very frequently see children who were frustrated and "turned off" by the work they were given to do.

The Butterflies were rich in personnel and in materials. They made the most of both. They met our criteria for success at both the staff level and the pupil level. The team had high cohesion and morale. It had a division of labor between the team leader and other members. A temporary division of labor among teachers was established on occasions when it seemed necessary. Homeroom classes had given way to a combination of small instructional groups and larger open-classroom groups with an occasional child working independently. Most of the teachers had contact, at some point, with nearly every child on the team. The team was productive in the sense that it did several things no other team accomplished. It made an inventory of materials stashed away in closets which had been lying there, unused, since the 1960's. It involved parents in a very realistic way in the education of their children, and the parents responded with unusual enthusiasm. The very large number of small instructional groups achieved the fit between the child's capacities and the work given, which is called for by individualized instruction. The children were involved in their work and seemed happy.

Soul

The Soul team had 116 children at the intermediate level and was regarded by most administrators as the most successful team in the school. Seven of its thirteen staff members were black, including Karen Waters, the team leader. There were five teachers and four Teacher Corps members, who carried nearly a full teaching load. This made an effective teacher-to-pupil ratio of one-to-thirteen. In addition, the team had the part-time services of two reading tutors and the occasional services of two instructional aides. Soul was the most personnel-rich team in the school. It also had many materials in its resource room, but these were little used. The collection of books, cooking equipment, painting and carpentry materials, games, maps, scales, Cuisenaire rods, old magazines and newspapers had partly been bought the previous year out of a grant a teacher obtained, and was partly left over from the lush days of ESEA in the 1960's. Most of the materials in Soul's resource room remained in the closet. No one had an inventory of what there was or where it was.

Soul regarded its reputation as the best team in the school with some ambivalence. The team leader, who was an integrationist, suspected the principal of singling them out for praise because they were "the blackest team in the school." And she resented this, since she wanted Soul to be evaluated on its performance alone. But some black members of the team were closer to the principal on this point: "We're young, we're black, and we know where the kids are at, because we've been there."

Racial tension accounted for some unevenness of participation in Soul team meetings. Most of the input came from Mrs. Waters and two black women on the Teacher Corps. However, when it came to implementing decisions, everyone contributed willingly.

Soul had a division of labor for curriculum development. For instance, every child was assigned some work with concrete math materials each week, in addition to his regular arithmetic classes. One teacher was designated to find or develop the materials for each lab group. Similarly, another teacher sorted out the materials for the "self-esteem curriculum," which Soul used for social studies.

Every teacher on the team had a "back-up person." For four of them, this was a Teacher Corps member. The teachers and their back-ups covered for each other in all kinds of situations, major and minor. Sometimes the "covering" was not strictly according to Hoyle, but the administration condoned it so long as it was not forced on their attention. Team members said it was a great advantage to be able to stay out sick, leave early, or go downtown in the middle of the day on occasion, without having to cope with all of the red tape required to get official permission.

Another form of division of labor was the matching of children to teachers. Children who didn't get along with one homeroom teacher were switched to another who could handle them better. This escape valve was useful to both students and teachers. On one occasion, Jack Minelli (white) was asked to switch math groups with Paul Harris (black) because his group included some black boys considered serious discipline problems who would benefit from having a black male role model.

As it did on every team, individualization of instruction on Soul meant "regrouping" of homeroom classes for reading and mathematics. The dispersion of skills on the team ranged from nonreaders to readers who were achieving at seventh- and eighth-grade levels. The range of achievement by grade levels was greater among the older than among the younger children at

Johnson, as it is everywhere.* Because of this, regrouping was a more difficult task for the intermediate than for the primary teams.

Soul's procedure was to put their slowest children into homogeneous ability groups of seven to twelve members, while the remaining children, many of them also below grade level, but not so far below, remained in groups of eighteen to twenty which were scarcely less heterogeneous than the homerooms. Mrs. Waters' reading group, for instance, ranged from third to seventh grade in reading levels. For many of her assignments, she broke it into two subgroups which did different work, but even so, children who were several grade levels apart had the same work assigned to them.

In fact, the besetting sin of this team—and of most of the school—was that it gave many children work assignments which were too difficult for them. The children experienced repeated frustration and failure. This is precisely what individualization is supposed to avoid. The intention is to diagnose children's skills carefully and to give them work at which they are surely able to succeed. "Every child a winner," as one author puts it.[1] But most children on Soul were losers:

> I came across a group who were trying to answer questions about a passage they'd just "read." One question was, "What is your weather prediction for tomorrow?" They had trouble reading "weather," and they couldn't read "prediction." Nor did they know what it meant. I explained it to them. The next question was, "What is the basis for your prediction?" That left them completely floored. First, they didn't understand the question as it was worded, and I reworded it several ways before they got it. But then they couldn't think of an answer, which led me to suspect that they hadn't gotten much out of the reading assignment. This was the situation in many groups throughout the room. The children didn't understand the instructions for the

---

*Interindividual variance in measured achievement increases with age. For another example, see the dispersion of achievement at age eleven, among children who achieved the same scores at age eight, in Britain, shown in W. E. B. Douglas, *The Home and the School* (London: Macgibbon and Kee, 1964). In this case, the middle-class children also opened a widening gap between themselves and working-class children. Coleman et al., *Equality of Educational Opportunity*, shows analogous phenomena for American children, and for the gap between blacks and whites.

exercises, and when these were explained, they couldn't do the
the exercises. One exercise was very difficult for such a group.
There was a list of words out of a story. The directions were to
choose from this list of words one word which would serve in both
of the following sentences. It wouldn't sound the same or mean
the same thing, but it would look the same. "Mary wiped a
_____ from her eye. Jane did not _____ her paper." The
instructions completely confused the children. When I got a few
of them straightened out on that by giving them an analogous
problem along with the answer, they still couldn't find the answer
to this one, perhaps because they don't distinguish in pronuncia-
tion between the two words.

When I mentioned the situation to Mrs. Waters, she sighed and
said there were not enough workbooks for every skill level:

> I can't throw the books out, because I haven't time to write ma-
> terial. We haven't enough personnel here to completely indi-
> vidualize and do all the necessary planning. We also haven't
> enough money for better materials. We have to use what's on
> hand.

Paul Harris also gave the children tasks which were far beyond their capacity to perform:

> They were writing a composition about a famous black. On
> this particular day, they were all supposed to write about
> Benjamin Banneker. They had seen a filmstrip about him, and
> they were asked to answer the following questions, which were
> written on the blackboard: "(1) What inspired him to go into the
> field of work he selected? (2) Why do people feel he is worth re-
> membering? (3) What things did he believe in? (4) Tell whether
> you agree or disagree with what he believed in and why. (5) How
> did he contribute to the progress of his race?" On other days, the
> children each had a different book about a famous black. The
> questions, however, remained the same. In many cases, the book
> was way above the child's reading ability. For instance, Kirk, sit-
> ting near to me, had a 200-page book on Ralph Bunche. Had he
> been able to read the book or not, there wasn't time. Kirk was
> trying to get through a one-paragraph summary of Bunche's life
> in the front of the book. I talked with him about it, and dis-
> covered that there was scarcely a word in the paragraph which
> Kirk understood, though he could sound them out.
>   The next day, Paul showed a filmstrip on Robert Smalls, a
> slave who escaped and worked for the Northern side during the

Civil War as a navigator of warships. After the filmstrip ended, he took a big group of kids to the front of the room to discuss the film with them, because he knew they couldn't write. The other kids were left to answer the questions. One youngster asked me to help him to read the questions. They had been on the board for several days, but he couldn't read them. One child asked me what "field of work" meant. Several were puzzled by this phrase today, because they had caught from the film that Smalls was a house slave, not a field slave. Most of the children who were left to write spent the better part of their time copying the questions off the blackboard. Many of them had copied them more than once before, but they were copying them again rather than answering them. Even those who could read the questions had no idea how to answer them. The questions were too abstract for the children to understand.

When Paul became aware that the class was not doing the assignment, he tried to discuss the film with all of them. However, the discussion was thoroughly frustrating for both him and the children:

Paul said to the class, "Well, what did Robert Smalls do?" "He helped slaves. He freed some slaves." Paul asked, "Why?" and the kids said, "Because he was tired of working." Paul said, "We all have to work." Lisa said, "Because his pay went to his master." Paul said, "You pay income tax. What makes it different?" Kevin said, "He didn't know how to read or write until he was twenty-three." Then Paul said, "Let's go over some of the things that happened to him." The kids did recount the narrative to some extent. They did much better with that than with Paul's questions, but now he returned to the questions, "What about being a slave wouldn't you like?" The kids said, "Shining shoes, lighting lamps" (both things which Robert Smalls, the slave, had done). "But what about your relationship to other people?" asked Paul. There was complete silence. The kids were squelched. They didn't know what he wanted. Finally he said, "The thing I was getting at was the phrase 'sold on the auction block.' Some of his friends were sold. Would you like it if your mother, father, brothers were taken away. Wouldn't that make you want to do something about it?" The kids chorused, "Yes!" Then he said, "Suppose your brother, mother, sister walked out of the door and got beaten up, snatched up. How would that make you feel? He wanted to do something about them, so he did." Then Paul went on to question two, "Why is he worth remembering?" Dead silence. "Don't you think he was worth remembering?" One of the kids finally said, "He freed some of the others from slavery, and maybe you could have grown up and become a slave." Paul said, "Any other answers? Don't you think things like that are happening today? What are some of the things happening today that you feel are wrong?" Lisa, a white girl, said, "The Vietnamese are being bombed." And Paul said, "Yes." Then a black boy said, "People are stealing things." Paul, close to despair, said, "What about what Dr. King did? Are any of those things he did something about still happening today?" And Karen, a little white girl, said, "Some people won't sell their houses to black people." There were no other answers. Not a single civil-rights-oriented answer had come from the black children in the class. At 10:30 Paul gave up and turned to another assignment.

Thus, while the very lowest-skilled children on Soul were in reading and arithmetic groups small enough for individual attention, the majority were in groups of eighteen to twenty-five which were very heterogeneous in ability. The children in these groups were frequently given work which was very poorly suited to their capacity; it was way over their heads. Mrs. Waters said her greatest problem was "keeping the fastest children challenged," but it seemed to the observer that the problem affecting most of the children was the opposite: the academic challenge was beyond their ability to meet.

Since there were many obviously frustrated, unhappy, and withdrawn children on this team, and since the work was not tailored to their individual needs, we judged Soul a failure in terms of pupils. In terms of staff, it was a success, but it only became so after its stay at Centerville University. As we recounted above, the experience there welded the Soul team teachers into a unit with high morale and cohesion such as they had not had while in the Johnson building. It appears from this case that it is possible for a team of teachers to work well and contentedly together without any of the benefits they derive from this happy state being transferred to their pupils.

The Giants

The Giants were another intermediate team with pupils aged nine to eleven. They were judged a relative failure by the administrators of Johnson. There were five teachers and two

Urban Interns. In addition, there were two student teachers and two paraprofessional aides. Two of the teachers were white men. One female teacher and one female Urban Intern were black. The team leader, Janet Carruthers, and a male teacher, Curt Jenkin, were close friends. They were also the only experienced teachers on the team; the others were all new. Curt and the other male teacher were also somewhat friendly. But other than these friendships, there was no network of personal relations in the team. The members scattered to different places for lunch:

> As a team we formally socialize, you know, for three minutes during the course of the day. In other words, our team could very easily socialize, but doesn't at all except at team meetings or informally in the hall. But outside of that, there's very little.

Participation at team meetings was extremely uneven. The team leader and Curt Jenkin carried most of the burden of discussion and planning. Other members of the team were silently acquiescent.

The lack of cooperation from the two paraprofessional aides assigned to the team made enforcement of their duties awkward for the team leader. A good part of the time they came late, left early, or were not present for team meetings. When they were there, they said little or expressed negative reactions to work assigned to them:

> Mrs. Carruthers asked a paraprofessional to cover for a teacher while the latter was in the training session. The aide replied, "If I am able." Mrs. Carruthers assured her that there wouldn't be a whole lot to do and the student teacher would be there, too. The aide didn't look too happy about it, but she said she would be willing "if she were able."

The use of materials on the team was very sparse, but that did not mean that the Giants lacked these resources:

> I was sent to the book supply room, and there were over 300 books in there, lying idle. There are many sets of texts and also many single copies of books for reading which were not being used.

The team leader was aware of this situation:

> Janet mentioned that there were a lot of resources left lying idle. She said there is no one to dig up and coordinate what resources there are—books, in this case. She said that the curriculum facili-

tator at the primary level did a good job on this, but the facilitator for the intermediate level hadn't taken on the chore of cataloging books and other materials so as to make them accessible to the teams.

By the time the Giants were observed in January, they had regrouped only for language arts, which was taught for two hours of the day. Math was still taught in the homerooms. The curriculum was almost exclusively made up of these two subjects. There was only one science lesson over the month and a half they were observed,* and they were just beginning to work on a social studies curriculum. The Giants were a collection of homerooms rather than a team. One result was inconsistency in the norms of behavior which teachers demanded of pupils, an inconsistency which caused trouble when the children changed rooms:

> A Giants teacher said she sees problems in behavior when kids come into her room from other classes on the team. There is no consistency in the treatment of kids. Kids have no respect for other teachers on the team and feel they can ride roughshod over them, because they aren't "our" teachers. She said she wished the team would enforce some kind of standards of behavior for all children so that they would know that they have to behave in the same way in all rooms.

A related problem was the identification of the children with their homeroom teachers. They resisted going to other teachers on the team:

> One day a teacher became ill in the afternoon and went home. Her kids were assigned to different rooms for the rest of the day. They had to be chased all over the hall and physically pulled out of their classroom to go to the others. Two girls and a boy were crying, and one girl was so angry she slashed the pupil reassignment list with a knife. There was no other teacher on the team the kids wanted to go to.

One day the team leader's class berated her for not being in the room when they felt she should have been:

> At a class meeting at the end of the day, Harold asked Mrs. Carruthers, "Why weren't you here the other morning?" "Because I

---

*They had been observed for half a month during the fall semester, as well as for a month during the spring.

had a team leaders' meeting," she replied. (These meetings start at 7:30 A.M. and are supposed to end in time for team leaders to get to their rooms at 8:40 A.M., but sometimes they run overtime.) He said, "You weren't here when we came in. There was nobody here." The whole class joined in criticizing Janet Carruthers for not being there when they felt she should have been. They obviously felt very insecure without her in the room.

Part of the problem in inducing a team feeling in the children was that regrouping for reading had never been explained to them in terms they could understand. In September, the children knew they were going to switch classes for language arts, because they asked when it would happen. But no effort was made to provide them with a rationale for the exchange of pupils:

> There was a change-of-class rehearsal on Thursday. That is, the children had to change classes just to learn the procedures for maintaining a smooth flow of traffic in the hallway. The children were told where to go, but neither why they were going to that particular place nor why certain others were or were not going with them. They were split up in what seemed to them an arbitrary way. The result was a great deal of resentment and resistance on the part of the kids. They didn't understand it at all, and the ban on the use of the water fountain and bathroom during this change of rooms seemed unneccessary to them.

Giants was another team where, like Soul, the work had not been tailored to the children's level. This was particularly true in math, where there had not yet been regrouping:

> The math problems that the kids had been given involved some pretty complex verbal analysis. The problems are embedded in a one-paragraph story and the kids couldn't read them. I had to read every word to them. This assignment betrays a poor estimate of the children's abilities. They can't do their math problems because they can't read them. Most of the problems were not only difficult to read; they were rather complex in the conceptual demands they made of the children. Instead of just asking for the answer, they asked for the children to make up one addition equation and one subtraction equation. First, the children didn't understand that "addition" means "adding" and "subtraction" means "take-away," so you had to explain that. Then it involved making up their own equations, which about half of them couldn't do.

The class was supposed to be able to do one- and two-digit multiplication. I helped a boy with his multiplication. He couldn't do one-digit multiplication, and he didn't know the simplest multiplication tables. I had to sit there the whole time and do every problem with him.

The Giants never jelled as a team either at the staff or the pupil level. Except for language arts, they remained a collection of homerooms. Participation at team meetings was almost confined to the team leader and her friend, Mr. Jenkin. That the pupils had no feeling of identification with the team was shown by their resistance to changing rooms for language arts. They felt comfortable only with their homeroom teachers, with whom they closely identified. The staff had poor morale and little division of labor. The pupils experienced almost no individualization of instruction. By all our criteria, the team had failed to implement ILP.

The Jets

The Jets were doomed to failure as a team before they started. Jean Washington, the team leader, preferred a self-contained classroom to teaming, although she approved of individualized instruction. There were ninety-six, six- and seven-year-olds on the team, with five teachers, two student teachers, one paraprofessional aide, and one reading tutor. The team leader, one other teacher, and the aide were black. Since student teachers did not carry a full teaching load, as did Teacher Corps interns and Urban Interns, two student teachers could be counted roughly as the equivalent of one teacher, giving a teacher-to-pupil ratio of about one-to-sixteen.

Mrs. Washington claimed that she had been given all the "rejects"—teachers other teams didn't want. The team indeed had more than its share of uncooperative teachers. Two of the five had been the subject of discussion at IGC meetings and had been reprimanded by the administration.

The administration clearly thought of the Jets as the poorest team in the school, a fact of which Mrs. Washington was well aware. She had an equally poor opinion of the administration. She felt disliked by other teachers in the school, and she also felt that the Wilder administration mistreated her because she was outspokenly disapproving of the Afro-American curriculum.

Mrs. Washington was one of several teachers in the school who emphasized to us that the only way to raise the children's self-esteem was to raise their academic skills. Black studies of whatever kind she rated as much less important, if not quite superfluous:

> That's all we say:"Black is beautiful." And I say, this doesn't mean a darn thing; it's inside how you feel. Now, you teach this black kid to read as well as the white ones. Then that's self-esteem; that's when black is beautiful.

She said her own success in providing primary children with reading skill and the appreciation received for it from children and parents were the only things that enabled her to survive in the school:

> If you were at the covered dish supper in the fall, a number of parents were talking about how much the children had learned in my class. That's why I can walk around these halls proud. Otherwise, I would fall flat on my face and crawl like a snake from the way they treat me in this building, just the tone of it. That's all, for no reason whatsoever. Because I want the kids to learn.

By spring, the Jets had regrouped for reading instruction in a way which reduced the heterogeneity of skills in the classes to some extent. That was all they did on their own. Mrs. Washington gave the impression that she expected the individualization program to be given to her in the form of help from the outside. She didn't grasp, or was unwillingly to accept, the concept of the team itself individualizing instruction. At the first Jets meeting observed, there was something like a struggle between the team, which wanted the primary curriculum facilitator to set up "learning stations" for them, and the facilitator, who was trying to get the team to do this work itself:

> Maria Wilson, the primary curriculum facilitator, came to this meeting with the team. Mrs. Washington opened the meeting by saying, "Mrs. Wilson is here to talk with us about learning stations." This use of last names is unusually formal for Johnson, where, among the staff, nearly everyone is on first-name terms. Maria Wilson then said, "It was suggested on January 18 that I set up five learning stations in the phonics room. I spoke to

the change agent about the phonics room, and she said that five would be far too much. I would like to have a clarification in the minutes. I would like to set up just one learning station. If you want to set up more, I will help you, but I won't set up more than one. The type of learning station that we are trying to put up has never been done before, and it's going to be very complex. (It was on consonant blends.) The way I interpreted it was: I was going to gather the materials to put up a learning station, but that you were going to participate with me, and we were, in a way, going to do it together." One of the teachers said, "I understood you would set it up and show us how it worked." Maria answered, "You are going to have to set up learning stations in your own rooms. Will you be able to do that better if someone does it for you or if you participate? Afterwards, in any case, I am going to assign you one to do as a team, so wouldn't it be better if you participated?" Then she said she would go around the room and see whether people wanted her to do it or wanted to participate. However, she didn't do that. Instead, she pressed on, on the assumption they would participate. Mrs. Washington brought her up short. "Mrs. Wilson, you said you wanted to go around the room and see how we vote as to whether we wanted to participate or whether we wanted you to do it and show it to us. And we haven't done that." When the curriculum facilitator went around the room, all the teachers voted to participate, including Mrs. Washington the team leader. It was the power of the teachers to decide that the team leader had wanted to reaffirm.

The Jets had several members who were among the oldest teachers in the school and also the most traditional. At one team meeting, it came out that these traditional teachers believed that arithmetic instruction should consist of the rote memorization of "number facts." They seemed to have no sympathy for the idea that children should be helped to gain a conceptual understanding of mathematics:

A late teacher came into the meeting and said to the others, with a broad smile, "I was just at a math workshop, and the man who ran it, who had a Ph.D., said that modern math was not working. It was no good. It was out the window, and we're supposed to go back to the old way of teaching math." Mrs. Washington said, "Hooray, hooray," and another of the older teachers said something very similar. Then the latecomer went on: "He said modern math teachers get up there and teach the kids that three plus four equals four plus three when they don't even know that three plus four equals seven. Mrs. Washington said, "Isn't that wonderful? People are coming back to their senses." Then there was a discussion of how the children have to know their "number facts" and how they have to memorize them. One team member said, "I don't bother with concepts at all, and they don't teach concepts in junior high school either."

There was some dissent from younger members of the team. One of them said, "Well, I was taught traditionally, and I do think that maybe when you get to ninth grade and you hit algebra, you get into trouble. My kid sister who learned modern math just whizzed through algebra with no trouble at all, but I had trouble." An older teacher replied, "I think people have trouble with algebra just because it's algebra."

There was evidence on this team, as on Soul and the Giants, that children were assigned tasks beyond their capacity to do:

After some preparation on the concept of a map, Mrs. Washington told the class, "I'm going to take you on a walk through the hallway of the first floor, and when you come back to class, be ready to draw a map of everything you saw." So she took them through the whole first floor. It's very big and very complicated. As they went by various rooms, they were asked to notice the numbers and words like "Custodian," "Gymnasium," "Principal's Office," "Exit."These were second graders. By the time we got to the other end of the building, I was totally unable to remember where things were and could not have drawn a map. Mrs. Washington apparently realized it was a bit much to ask of the children because when they got back to their room, she never mentioned drawing the map. She had them put on their hats and coats and then sit and wait silently for twenty minutes until it was dismissal time.

The Jets were a team with much internal conflict, especially between the teachers' union representative and Mrs. Washington. We described the problem between these two in our account of the IGC. There was also conflict between the more traditionally oriented older teachers on the team, and the younger teachers, who were somewhat more favorably disposed toward modern teaching methods. The team leader was seriously alienated from the administration and from many of her colleagues. The team took the attitude that implementation of ILP was largely up to personnel outside the team. From their point of view, their constant complaints that they needed help and did not have time to do the work of individualization had some foundation, since other teams were better staffed numerically. But the Johnson administration viewed these complaints as resistance to the innovation, and there was truth in that as well.

The Relative Success of the Teams

The only team successful in implementing ILP, both in terms of staff and pupils, was the Butterflies. The staff of Soul became welded into a cohesive team in the university's open space building but Soul never succeeded in individualizing instruction. The Giants and the Jets failed at both the staff and pupil levels. What circumstances account for these differences?

There were a number of special conditions which contributed to the Butterflies' success. Personal friendships among the group before it became a team contributed to the cohesion which developed. No other team was similarly blessed, though the members of Soul became friends at the university center. Good personal relationships among the members seem to be essential to the success of teaming.

Another important factor in the situation was the use of space. We saw that the Soul team was forced into intensive interaction, into developing normative consistency, and into facing and solving their interpersonal problems when they worked under conditions which made them mutually visible in open space. The Butterflies' teachers were not *forced* by the Johnson building to use space so that they were mutually visible as they worked, but they *chose* to do so. Again, the result was intensive interaction, cohesion, and normative consistency.

There is research which shows that teachers who are not teamed, working in open-space schools, are perfectly capable of behaving as though there were walls around their classes. And our study shows that a team which meets together, but does its teaching as separate individuals, invisible to each other in self-enclosed classrooms, may never develop teamwide cohesion and team-wide norms. But the *combination* of teaming for instruction, and using space so that the members of the team are visible to each other as they work, seems to create a situation where cohesion and normative consistency must develop—or, alternatively perhaps, the team must break apart. It is easy to see how matters which cause no trouble when each teacher has her own classroom can become sources of conflict when space must be shared. On Soul, for instance, a somewhat sloppy teacher and a compulsively neat teacher had a lot of trouble with each other and were forced to negotiate matters which neither had thought about at all when she had her "own" room. Such conflicts are a potential threat to the team, but if they are successfully dealt with, the team ends up a more cohesive unit than it began. So our hypothesis is that teaming in open space leads either to high cohesion or to severe conflict and breakup of the team.[2] In the case of Butterflies and Soul, it led to cohesion.

Also contributing to the Butterflies' success were circumstances which were fortuitous. They had a good supply of kindergarten materials which they could also use with their first graders. They were the most materials-rich team in the school. In addition, the fact that the Butterflies had the youngest children in the school, including the kindergarteners, had two important consequences: first, they had the lowest dispersion of skills to deal with, and second, they were able to form many small instructional groups which met for an hour daily, leaving most of the pupils under the supervision of a few teachers in the open classrooms for most of the day. They could do this because it was considered "legitimate" for the youngest children to receive only a minimum of formal instruction each day. With these many small instructional groups, they were able to attain a close fit between the children's skills and the work they assigned them. Every team with older children had a wider dispersion of skills to cope with. And no team with older children could have formed so many small instructional groups, as the Butterflies did, because none of them could have gotten away with giving so little time to formal instruction. In the higher elementary grades "playing" most of the school day would have been considered illegitimate.*

The fact that their pupils spent a large part of the day "play-

*The community which Johnson served defined the activities of the Butterflies in their so-called "open classrooms" as "play" in a sense which makes it the opposite of work and learning, but many experts in child development understand play as an important mode of learning for children.

ing" in open classrooms not only gave the Butterflies maximum flexibility in grouping; it left them free to do such things as inventory the materials which had been lying in their closets for five years, to work on instructional packets to send home to parents, to stage a "parents' night," and to write a grant proposal. They were able to accomplish much more than other teams because of their special circumstances.

The Giants and the Jets never really became teams. The Giants had too many inexperienced, apathetic members who did not participate in team matters. The Jets had too much internal conflict. In addition, the Jets' leader, as well as some members, disapproved of the idea of teaming.

Finally, Soul, the Giants, and the Jets all failed completely to reach the main goal of ILP. None of them managed to tailor the academic work to the children's capacities in such a way as to guarantee the pupils' success at their tasks. On the contrary, as we have pointed out, they persistently gave children such difficult tasks as to guarantee their failure. In the next chapter, we must look more closely at this phenomenon.

Chapter 5

Goal-Defeating Behavior

The major goal of ILP was to meet each child where he actually was in terms of academic skill. The basic idea behind all individualized instruction is that the experience of mastering a task increases a child's sense of competence, and the growing sense of competence helps in the objective improvement of skill.

In view of Johnson's explicit commitment to this doctrine, we were surprised to find time and again in our observations that the children were given work far too difficult for them to succeed in doing. Situations of this kind occurred not only at the beginning of the school year but also after the teams had regrouped for reading and math, according to diagnosed achievement levels. All of the following observations were made *after* regrouping. Here is a math group on an intermediate team. It was the "multiplication group," which meant that the children were supposed to have mastered addition and subtraction:

> The teacher gave out ditto sheets with word problems. The children invariably find these more difficult than straight computation. They have had little conceptual training in mathematics. They know, to some extent, how to compute, but they have a hard time figuring out the mathematical strategy for attacking a word problem.
>
> The first problem said, "There are 365 days in an ordinary year. How many days are there in three years?" When I went around the room, I discovered that the children stumbled over the word "ordinary." Then they had difficulty with the strategy for solving the problem. Many of them thought the way to solve it was to add 365 to 3. Of the eleven pupils in the group, only two were able to figure out the strategy for the problems in multiplication. On the addition problems, some of them deduced that they had to add, but some of those didn't know how to add two-place numbers. Many still added by counting on their fingers.

Here is an experience of the top reading group on one of the primary teams:

They were given a picture of Charlie Brown and Snoopy. There was a piece of wood falling on Charlie Brown's feet, and there was a big word, "Cronk!" across it. Mrs. Washington asked the children to write a story about the picture. She told them that if they needed any words spelled, I would help them. The task of writing a story down was beyond them, except for Bill. He wrote a paragraph and then turned the paper over and drew his own cartoon strip of Charlie Brown and Snoopy with his own dialogue. Tony wrote one sentence by himself, with a little bit of help in spelling. Gene made up a good story with rather sophisticated vocabulary, but he couldn't write it at all. He told it to me, and I wrote it down for him. The other kids, too, needed nearly every single word they wanted to use spelled by me. That was time-consuming, so they came nowhere near to finishing.

Faced day after day with tasks they couldn't do, the children developed several profitless coping mechanisms. One was withdrawal. It took two forms. Either the child would stop his work and find some more exciting activity, like picking a fight, or he would sit sullenly in front of his work, making no attempt to do it and often refusing to speak. Behavior of this sort was very familiar to the teachers, who labeled such pupils "nonachievers." Predictably, the label became a self-fulfilling prophecy. Children who acquired it tended to be left alone by the teachers a good part of the time. However, the most striking and pervasive means that Johnson pupils used to deal with work too difficult for them was to engage in compulsive copying, which served as a substitute for doing the assigned task. The idea of copying as a form of academic work did not originate with the children. There was a good deal of teacher-assigned copying in the school. A text was written on the blackboard each morning for the children to copy as a handwriting exercise. Sometimes copying was intended to help the children learn to read, write, and spell:

> She asked the kids to give her some sentences about rats. She printed these on the board and also did them in cursive writing. The first sentence was, "Rats creep in holes." She said, "You can print it or write it." So they were copying again. After they got that sentence written down, she asked for another sentence from them. "Rats run around and eat garbage." They took quite a long time to copy that.

However, the children carried the copying into all sorts of academic situations. Children who could neither read what they copied, nor understand it if it were read to them, could frequently reproduce a paragraph from the blackboard or a book successfully, if laboriously. When assigned a task they couldn't do, they automatically retreated into copying:

> Marsha called five girls up to her desk. She gave each one of them a worksheet. They were to go to the library, choose a state, and find a reference book to discover the state flower, the state bird, the state motto, the number of people in the state, the capital of the state, its main industry, its agricultural products, and "the most interesting facts of its history." This was a group of girls who were supposed to read pretty well. I went to see how they were doing. They had gotten out a number of encyclopedias and tried to find the facts. They didn't all function very well. Two girls systematically put down the questions with the answers next to them. Two of them had just found the state in the encyclopedia and had begun to copy out the whole article. They had gotten stuck, because their particular encyclopedia didn't have "industry" and "agriculture" as headings, but instead had "manufacturing" and "farm products." They did not understand these as synonyms for the words in their assignment. Nor did they have any notion of how to select from the article the parts which might constitute answers to the questions.

On one occasion, a boy who was having great difficulty with a reading lesson threw his book across the room in a rage. He then pulled out of his desk a reference book on his favorite subject, fish, and began frenziedly copying the text, which he could neither read nor understand.

Children who were asked to draw a line from words in a left-hand column to synonyms in a right-hand column copied the two columns of words from the board with no connecting lines. They managed, in this way, to fill up the time period allotted for the task. Children who were asked to fill in the blanks in a comprehension exercise copied the exercise, leaving the blanks unfilled.

We saw the pattern of assigning work too difficult for large numbers of the children on every team we observed except the Butterflies, and, in each case, the children responded with some form of withdrawal. The question naturally arises. Why did so many teachers do something so contrary to their explicit goals?

Part of the answer lies in the difficulty of assigning appropriate work when skill levels are so heterogeneous. But another part lies in the reluctance of teachers to face up to the fact that many of their pupils were working well below grade level. Both the heterogeneity and the failure of the pupils were illustrated by the principal in an interview in January after the district achievement tests were given:

> Out of 136 children of first grade age, eighteen kids are on a reading-readiness level; twenty-seven are on a preprimer one; twenty-one are on a preprimer two; nineteen are on a preprimer three; thirty-one are on the first grade level, one-one; six are on the one-two level; seven on the two-one; and seven on two-two. Over half are below grade level already. This is really the second half of the year, so they should be on the one-two level.

> For the sixth graders, out of 109 kids, two of them are reading on the two-one level; three on the two-two; eight on the three-one; seven on the three-two; nine on the four-one; one on the four-two; ten on the five-one; seven on the five-two; twelve on the six-one; twenty on the six-two; and thirty children are reading over the sixth grade level. Only 43 percent are below grade level. Say, that isn't bad.

Teachers had several ways of handling the fact that so many of their pupils were failing. One was denial. The very fact that they persisted in assigning work at grade level, rather than work appropriate to the pupils' actual achievement levels, was the major form of denial. There were others as well. When large numbers of Mrs. Washington's children did poorly on the district math test, she insisted that they knew the material and proceeded to prove it:

> She said to them, "I don't know why you don't do it. When you do it with me, you know it perfectly." Then she put "3 + 4" on the blackboard. She said, "We are going to add these num-bers, three and four. On the test, it is written like this: $\begin{array}{r} 3 \\ +4 \\ \hline \end{array}$ and you put the answer *under* the line. Now what is the answer, class?" They chorussed, "Seven." That is, the most confident ones did. The less sure ones chimed in a split second later, and the least confident ones whispered. When she does the work with them that way, of course, she gives them all sorts of cues orally

that they don't have on the test. She tells them that the + sign means "add," which some of them didn't know when they took the test. She tells them that "$3 + 4 = ?$" is the same problem as "$\begin{array}{r} 3 \\ +4 \end{array}$," which some didn't know. And the chorus permits the ignorant to hide behind the others. Yet she said to me, "You see, they *do* know this material."

Paul Harris, who gave the unsuccessful black studies lessons we described in our account of the Soul team, explained in an interview that his students did poorly in these lessons because they were inattentive:

> You must have noticed in class that I have . . . I don't know what is the matter with them, but it seems as though they don't listen. They don't hear what I say. They can remember facts, but every time you ask them "Why?" they seem to turn off completely. They don't give any answers.

Karen Waters blamed the failure of some members of her reading group on the fact that she didn't have materials on an appropriate level for them and hadn't the time to develop such materials herself. She focused her attention on particular neighborhood children who had made notable gains:

> I think your test is going to be not with the total school, but with the individual children where you noticed a remarkable change, and it has all been due to the attitude of the teacher who has changed the child's attitude about learning. Ricky got a reading tutor because he was two years below his grade level. He was a fourth grader last year, and he was reading somewhere on a low third, and at the end of the year he was a high five, and now he is in one of the top reading groups, and that is making him feel even greater. So when he goes into that room, he really feels tops. He is going to keep achieving. Now, Clarence is one child who has just been permitted to slope along and "Don't hassle me." But when you start pointing out to him, "Look how well you've done here," and the right teacher comes along and mates up with that child, he starts zooming ahead.[1]

Some of the staff, like Paul, were simply poor teachers who did not know how to adapt their demands to the children's capacities. Some were new teachers who had not quite taken in how low the pupils' skills were. Others insisted that standardized tests were not sufficiently refined to catch the gains they saw children making. They may have been right. In a school like Johnson, a teacher must learn to be gratified by very small gains or suffer constantly from feelings of defeat.

Another way of coping with the situation was to falsify it. From the moment Dr. Phillips became principal, Johnson's almost instantaneous reputation as an innovative school had some negative effects on it. Both Phillips and Wilder felt themselves under constraint to give continuing evidence of "success," lest their flow of extra personnel and their privileged position of autonomy within the district be withdrawn. Both principals understood that "success" was at least partly to be measured in terms of improved achievement scores. Thus Dr. Phillips had proudly boasted of rising scores, which Mr. Wilder claimed did not apply to the neighborhood children. Similarly, Mr. Wilder showed us some district statistics which "proved," according to him, that the Johnson School's reading achievement had gone up over the years of *his* principalship. In fact, the statistics showed only random fluctuations. The Director of Elementary Instruction in the district told us that Johnson's scores on nationally standardized tests had remained unchanged for many years.

The pressure which the school felt to prove itself resulted in various kinds of tampering with test scores. Under Phillips, one member of the staff was so dedicated to him, and so convinced that the national tests were not reflecting improved achievement, that he actually erased scores and substituted higher ones—and was caught. Staff members at the junior high schools which received Johnson graduates told us that Johnson and one other elementary school in the city sent them students who consistently tested quite a bit lower than their elementary schools said they did. And, indeed, some falsification of city test scores was going on while we were in Johnson:

> While I was talking to the principal, a teacher stuck her head into the office. She asked, "What do I do about a kid who was on level eleven on the math test and went down to eight? Should I just report eleven and pray that he gets back up there by the end of the year?" Wilder first said, "Yes. Do that." But then—remembering my presence—he amended it to, "No, I guess you had better report the actual performance of the kid."

More widespread than outright falsification was the phenomenon of teaching to the test. Mrs. Washington gave the district test in math to her class several times. In between test administrations, she drilled the pupils on the problems they got wrong. As soon as a pupil scored on grade level, he was reported as having passed the test. Cliff Wallace, an intermediate team leader, said:

> As far as helping the kids, you know, and not following standard test procedures, I know one person on my team—I don't know if she even knows what she is doing. I mean, I came in there, and there she was practically reading the goddamn question to the kid. Now there's somebody that just wants so bad for the kid to do well. Now that's why I don't tend to believe statistics that come out of a school study unless I know who did it and how they did it. Because I know what teachers do, and they don't give objective tests. That's why nobody else who has been around schools believes it either, you know.

What we see here is a situation where much was out of joint. Bused-in children and neighborhood children were almost at opposite poles of the skill continuum. Even with all its personnel, Johnson did not have enough staff to form homogeneous ability groups for teaching reading and mathematics. Many children passed through the school making little or no progress. Intermediate team teachers had ten, eleven, and twelve year olds whose work was at a low primary level. They had to teach beginning reading to pupils who had been "taught" it several times before, but hadn't learned it. Every staff member had to make his own peace with this situation, while at the same time supporting, or at least not undermining, the public position that Johnson was a successfully innovative school.

The constraints of this situation produced dysfunctional behavior. Teachers persisted in giving children work too difficult for them to do, in the face of clear evidence that they were frustrating the children, and despite their professed goal of individualizing the work to fit the child. Pupils responded to frustration of their need for mastery by withdrawal, disruptive behavior, and by substituting a pattern of compulsive copying for performance of their academic tasks. Administrators and staff conspired almost unconsciously to make the public measures of academic performance look as good as possible.

The bused-in white children suffered in the opposite way in this situation. The work was far too easy to challenge these pupils from upper middle-class, often academic, families. Not only was the gap in achievement wide, the subcultural differences between lower-class blacks and upper middle-class whites, which are largely class differences rather than differences in racial subcultures, meant that the pupils of the two races largely segregated themselves from each other, because they did not understand the culture patterns of each other's social class. Compounding a difference in social class with a difference in race always makes integration more difficult.

Conclusion

Both Dr. Phillips and Mr. Wilder wanted to maintain their independence of the Centerville School District, since autonomy broadened their power to control the policies of Johnson. However, in order to keep that independence, they felt that they had to keep up the public-relations facade of Johnson as an innovative, achieving school. The need to preserve this facade intact made it impossible for the school to face its real problem: the low achievement of its pupils.

Under Phillips, many of the innovations were modish, but irrelevant to the improvement of basic skills. Under Wilder, none of the four innovations we saw was actually implemented. The teachers' innovations, which were specifically meant to help low performers, were quietly squelched before it could get out that a great many children needed them. Wilder's innovation, the Afro-American curriculum, was more a political gesture than a feasible program, given the lack of organizational resources to support it. ILP, which required enormous resources, was adopted without sufficient funding and proved impossible to implement in most of the school, for lack of personnel, materials, and time.

Thus Johnson continually adopted innovations without thinking through the requirements for implementing them. The burden of putting them into practice was invariably on the teachers. But the teachers were expected to effect great transformations in the classroom with no support system. There were never enough experts to show them how to perform their new functions. For instance, there was no one on the scene who could have shown the teachers how to transform university-level African materials into an elementary-level curriculum. And no provision was made to give the teachers time to work on this problem. Exactly how they were to accomplish this central task was never carefully considered.

Similarly, with ILP there was not enough assistance to permit vital routines to be carried on while new roles were developed. Teachers, having diagnosed their pupils, did not have time to search for curriculum materials suited to each in every subject or to write those materials. An appropriate support system would have done that for them.

We had it from the district office that achievement scores at Johnson had not changed since the initial increase which occurred when middle-class children were first bused in. So the constant adoption of innovations had had no effect on academic outcomes, possibly because the innovations were never actually implemented. The school's innovativeness did go along with a change to a more humane and progressive atmosphere than had prevailed in Pelham School. There was no doubt of that. But the lesson to be extracted is that such an atmosphere, while valuable in itself, is not enough to raise the achievement of children who are failing badly in school.

PART II

Southside: A School in a Complex Environment

Chapter 6

The Institutional Setting

At the second and third schools we studied, the innovation we came to see was the open classroom. However, when we arrived at Southside, we found another innovation in progress as well, and we studied both. Southside was located in Walton, a major metropolitan center. At the time we were there, the school had open classrooms in kindergarten through third grade, and it had an individualized reading program which was supposedly being implemented throughout the school.

The District

Unlike the autonomous Johnson School, Southside was embedded in Community School District 7, which constituted a complex politico-bureaucratic environment. Walton had decentralized its school system on the model of New York City. There were ten community school districts, each with an elected Community School Board representing parents. This Board had some power. It had less power than the parents had wanted and more than the Walton teachers' union had wished for. There was a continual struggle between these two groups over the power to hire, fire, and transfer school staff, and the fate of open education in the district was tied to the struggle. During the year prior to our observations, parents in Community School District 7 who supported open education had replaced teachers who had seniority with new teachers trained in open education and had carried the fight over their right to do so into the courts—where they lost. As a result, the district was required to pay both groups of teachers and the costs of the lawsuit out of the current year's budget. They were severely short of funds.

In addition to the organized parents and the organized teachers, other centers of power in the district were the superintendent's office, where much innovation originated, and the OCT (Open Classroom Teaming) Advisory, a group based in the local public university, which came into the schools and, for a fee, trained teachers to open up their classrooms.

The principals, who often hold important powers in their own schools, were weakened in District 7 by a city ruling which denied new appointees tenure as principals and put their appointments to the principalship on a yearly basis. Their lack of security in their posts undermined the new principals' bargaining strength and made them dependent on the good will of both parents and teachers. The principal of Southside, herself a new appointee, told us that this situation made principals extremely chary of change. They tried to be responsive to the demands of competing groups, but they dared not take initiatives which might step on the toes of any organized interest.

Some of the power relationships in Community School District 7 can be illustrated through our experience as researchers. In Centerville we gained entry to the Johnson School by obtaining the consent of the principal. That was all we needed. Officially, we should have had the consent of the district as well, but the principal forgot about that, or chose to ignore it. The issue came up when we finally came to interview Centerville district officials, and it proved to be a minor formality.

In Walton, we first got permission to work in Community School District 7 from the district superintendent. When we arrived to do our field work, he turned us over to the coordinator of innovation. After hearing our description of our project, the coordinator warned us that things were extremely tense in the district and that he could not guarantee us entry into any school; but he said that he would try to help. He warned us not to give any sort of achievement tests in any school and not to question administrators about such matters as the school's reading scores.

The school staffs were nervous about parental demands for accountability in areas such as reading. In the light of this, it is clear why the coordinator chose to send us first to the school which had the district's highest reading scores. He told us that it was entirely up to the principal whether or not we could work in the school. Fortunately, Mrs. Jones, principal of Southside, had no objection to our proposal. However, she, in turn, cleared the project with the two teachers whose classrooms we went to first, and she also cleared it with the school's PTA.

Mrs. Jones' receptivity was a surprise after what the coordinator had told us. However, at a later date, when we attempted to find another school in the district where we could make a few comparisons with Southside, we found out what the coordinator meant. Each principal said the study was all right with him, but that we would have to make a personal appearance before a meeting of the PTA to get their consent, and he would have to clear it with the teachers involved. In one school, we obtained the principal's consent and the PTA's consent, and the principal obtained the consent of the teachers. We also, at this principal's behest, obtained the consent of the deputy superintendent of the district (the superintendent had by then resigned), and the chairman of the Community School Board. On the day we were scheduled to begin work in the school, the principal withdrew his consent, because the director of the OCT Advisory had made clear to the parents that he did not want us to have further entry into any of the district's schools.[1] He said our research might interfere with on-going studies he was sponsoring. The district coordinator of innovation told us that no one from the OCT Advisory had any authority to say who could or could not do research in the district. That authority belonged to the superintendent's office, which had given its consent. However, the principal of Southside explained to us that the OCT Advisory provided schools with the services of two change agents, three times a week, for only $6,000 a year. This was a bargain which school principals would not risk sacrificing for two researchers with nothing comparable to offer. Thus, the director of the OCT Advisory had strong leverage—informally—on any group of parents or any principal who already used the Advisory's services, or thought they might be interested in using them at some future date. He exercised his influence to maintain *de facto* control over who studied open classrooms in District 7.

Our experience illuminates the peculiar combination of bureaucratic authority and professional autonomy which characterizes school districts. The district superintendent's consent to research was necessary, but his respect for the professional prerogatives of the principals meant this did not guarantee entry into any school. The consent of the principal did not guarantee entry into any particular classroom; for that, the teacher's consent was needed. In this particular district, where parent power was well organized and untenured principals were highly vulnerable to it, it was necessary to win the consent both of the local PTA and the Community School Board. To administer a test of any kind to pupils, one needed the consent of each parent. And, finally, the director of the OCT Advisory had the *de facto* power to prevent anyone from studying open classrooms in the district, by threatening to withdraw his services.

Another aspect of Southside's context was the political conflicts going on among the parents, their own elected Community School Board, and the teachers' union. These conflicts came out in our observations of two regular public meetings of the Community School Board, the first on October 30, 1972, and the second on December 4.

Here are our observations of the October meeting:

The meeting was scheduled for 7:30 P.M., but it didn't begin until past 8:30 P.M. because some of the Board members were delayed by other meetings elsewhere in town. It took place in a large school auditorium. The Community School Board sat up front facing the audience. They alone had the right to vote and conduct business, but anyone could attend the meeting, ask questions, and make comments. By the time the meeting was fully underway, there were about seventy-five people in attendance, and about one-third of the people present were either black or Hispanic. An agenda for a September meeting and this October meeting were distributed, and since the September meeting had not been held, we began with the September agenda.

I eavesdropped on some conversation before the meeting. I picked up, in a conversation between a couple of Spanish-speaking men, that two members of the Board, who have left, have been replaced through appointment by the present Board. According to the newspapers, a court ruling a couple of weeks ago held that this procedure was illegal in another community school district. Community school boards are supposed to be elected, and when members have to be replaced, there is supposed to be an election. So these two men were planning, when that item on the agenda was reached, to challenge the legality of this *whole* school board. As it happened, the item was not reached during the meeting and they were very frustrated at the end of the evening.

When the meeting opened at about 8:35 P.M., the secretary read the first item on the agenda in English and Spanish. The entire meeting was conducted in both languages. There were four whites and two blacks from the Community School Board present that night, and the district superintendent was present with some of his staff members.

They began with a debate on the appointment of an assistant principal to a junior high school. The principal of the school, who was a black man, got up and spoke in support of her appointment. The black woman on the Community School Board said, "How will our vote on this appointment have any effect? It will have no effect one way or the other." The point she was making all through the evening was that the Board, of which she was a member, had no power. In fact, one of the observations that ran through the evening was that the people in the audience were very hostile to the Board. Their hostility reached a pitch of intensity at about 9:45 P.M. and it continued until 11:00 P.M., when they adjourned. By that time, it was a real shouting match.

The next item that came up was about pairing two schools. This was a pairing to promote desegregation which was first set up five or six years ago. A woman who represented the PTA from those two schools, the principals of the two schools, and a woman who represented a special parents' council all spoke in support of this pairing. Speaking in opposition was a white male member of the Community School Board who said that he had received protests from parents of some of the young black children. The parents didn't want their children bused as far as they were being bused under this pairing plan, and so he would have to vote against it, he said. But all of the other members of the Board voted for it, and the pairing was continued.

Next, a Puerto Rican member of the audience said that there was a lot of "supplanting" in his child's school. "Supplanting" means using federal funds for regular expenditures, instead of the "extras" they were earmarked for under the federal law. He implied that the supplanting had deprived the Hispanic pupils' bilingual classes of teachers, and he wanted to know where were the federally funded teachers and where were the tax-levy teachers.* The district superintendent said that supplanting was illegal and it was a very serious charge: "If you can document it, I wish you would tell me about it, because we've been checking up on it. We have to stop schools from supplanting everywhere." A mother explained how supplanting came about in her child's school.

From the floor, a man claimed that he had found an error in the budget distributed to the audience. He questioned the accounting procedures in the district: "You know, if there are errors in the budget that you present to us, how can we have any confidence in your accounting procedures?" This started a debate on the budget. The budget was presented on a mimeographed page with the headings of the columns virtually illegible, because it was done on a terrible mimeographing machine. But even when the headings were explained by a member of the district staff, they were incomprehensible to the audience and to us, and the audience became very hostile. They said they didn't understand this budget. It was not what they wanted anyway. It was the projected budget for 1972–1973. What they wanted was the actual expenditures in each school as of last year, alongside the projected expenditures for this coming year. They also wanted last year's actual and projected expenditures alongside each other. If they could make those two sets of comparisons, they could make some sense out of the budget. As they kept calling for this, there was no response from the two district officials. The black female member of the Board said that in the black section of Walton not all the money which is budgeted to a school actually gets spent in the school. "It is quite a lot of money, and it has been lost to us for years," she said. Someone else said, of a junior high school, "We have ten people in out-of-classroom administrative positions, where we need remedial reading teachers. We've closed our industrial workshops, which we need open, and we need people in recreation." The district superintendent responded to that: "Those supervisors are not in offices—those out-of-classroom people—they are supervising the flow through the halls and the yards, and you are one of the people who talked about the need for that just a few years ago. I was down there this afternoon. Those supervisors are very active, and they're helping the flow of traffic through the school and keeping it from interfer-

---

*Paid for by city taxes rather than federal funds.

ing with the teaching program." Then a male black parent, who was very obstreperous throughout the meeting, got up and said, "When I finished high school, I went down to see the man, and he said to me, 'Boy, what can you do?' And I said, 'I can play and I can do shop,' and the man said to me, 'We haven't got any jobs for people who can play and do shop.'" The parent then began to yell, "We don't want shop and we don't want play. All the kids do in this district is play all day. We want education." As he walked down the aisle past me, he said, "Screw shop."

Next, there was a motion about the excessing rules. "Excessing" and "bumping" are two terms which need definition. When a school hasn't got enough money, a position can be declared "in excess," and the person occupying that position is dropped from that school. If the person has tenure, he or she is found an equivalent job elsewhere in the district, if there is one. The word "bump" means that if the person who is excessed in one school has greater seniority than somebody who has the same job—for instance, assistant principal—in another school, then the one with the greater seniority is transferred into the job, and the person already in the job is "bumped" out of it. A Puerto Rican man disputed that the excessing rules applied to paraprofessionals. He said, "We cannot accept this motion which says that we are subject to the excessing rules, because this would subject our paraprofessionals to being moved around to other schools." He advocated very strongly that the paraprofessionals should fight this motion. He said, "One hundred and thirty-six paraprofessionals have been excessed in this district. At the last meeting, we suggested an adjustment in the Title I budget to get back the paraprofessionals we lost. What have you done about this?" The district superintendent indicated that something had been done about it, but not so much as this gentleman had suggested.

A black woman who was the principal of a school in the black section of town indicated that she was angry because an assistant principal in her school had been excessed, and somebody else, who had seniority, and the right to the position under the rules, was coming in. She said, very aggressively, "Keep him at the district office. We don't want him in the school." She even said they would keep the door shut and wouldn't let him into the school. The superintendent tried to explain that the rules under which the man was coming in clearly gave him the right to the position, but the principal kept saying, "Why can't you keep him at the district office until our assistant principal [a woman] is reassigned?" The superintendent said, "He is entitled to the position, and he will have to serve beside her." The black principal angrily replied, "Keep that jackass down at the district office. I won't let him in my school." She said she would sue the Community School Board, if necessary, over the assistant principal issue. A white woman made the same kind of case for the assistant principal in her school. A number of people in the audience insisted that the community wanted the right to decide who should be the assistant principals in their schools. They started yelling from the floor that they would close down the schools if they didn't get this right. A black Baptist minister came to the microphone and said, "We will close the schools. If you force these people on us [meaning the new assistant principals], you are going to create havoc in the black neighborhoods. We are the parents. We want to control the personnel." He continued, "To the community I say, 'You have no power.' To the union I say, 'You knew when you drew up the contract that you were creating this bumping situation. You want to prevent paraprofessionals from getting jobs as teachers.' "

Another woman went up to the microphone and said, "We lost our best assistant principal and we lost seven of our best teachers due to the excessing situation. We took up the slack with paraprofessionals. Some paraprofessionals have been kicked out of their schools. Now you want us to bump our paraprofessionals and take those that have been driven out of other schools." She added, "If you think there is anything big going on in Belleville [a white neighborhood where parents were boycotting the schools because some black children had been assigned to them], wait until you see what you are going to have in the black neighborhoods if you bump our paraprofessionals."

A district official spent a great deal of time explaining that the Community School Board had done everything that it could legally do about the excessing situation. They had gone into court last year together with the NAACP to fight the law concerning excessing. They had lost the suit. Now it had been made clear to them by the Federal Department of Justice and by HEW [the Federal Department of Health, Education, and Welfare] that they were subject to the excessing rules which had been negotiated and contracted between the union and the Walton Board of Education. A black man yelled from the audience, "Well, you may be subject to the rules, but we parents will close the schools down." A woman shouted, "We're going to lose our assistant principals. We got told on Friday that we would get somebody else this coming Wednesday. We don't want the new principal.

We just don't want him. We want to keep the assistant principals we've got." It was getting close to 11:00 P.M., when the meeting officially closes, and the agenda was nowhere nearly finished. Apparently this happens regularly. They take up the unfinished agenda at the next meeting.

There were two things that stood out for us at this meeting. First, a lot of people around the city still cling to the idea of community control of the schools, but under the law which created the community school boards, there is not much power in the hands of these boards. There isn't anything approaching community control. And one of the things that the community people wanted most, namely, the right to hire and fire personnel in their own communities, is a power which was definitely *not* given to the community school boards under the law. What seems most likely to happen, according to some experts around Walton, is that the fights that have been going on will lead, at the next session of the city council, to a further weakening of the powers of the community school boards.

The second thing that was notable about the meeting was that the people in the audience were hostile to the Community School Board members whom they had elected. There are two ways of interpreting this, in our view, and they are not mutually exclusive. One is that parents believe there is some advantage to being on the Community School Board. There is some patronage. There are promotions. There are chances for upward mobility that one can get access to if one is on the Board. We would guess that many of the activists who attend these meetings regularly would like to be members of the Board themselves and are therefore hostile to the people who are now members.

The other possibility is that the parents are hostile essentially to the fact that the community school boards don't have much power. The fact that they don't is due to the way the law is written. But the activist parents feel the boards should *take* the power which is "legitimately," even if not legally, theirs. They're very angry that parents don't have the opportunity to run their "neighborhood schools."

This is a very complex issue. "Community control" cuts both ways, racially. An example at the time was the boycott in the white neighborhood where the parents were essentially saying, "OK, *they* [i.e., the blacks] want community control, and *they* want to say who can come to their schools and who can't. We want the same kind of community control, and we don't want their kids bused into our local community schools." There is a conflict between racial desegregation through busing and local community control of the schools. The two policies are mutually incompatible in some ways. If children are bused out of their home communities for the sake of school desegregation, the community in which their school is located no longer resembles, in its racial composition, the population of parents with children in the school. Community School District 7 had some parents who wanted desegregation—by busing if necessary—some who wanted community control, and some who wanted, and believed they could have, both.

At the December meeting, the teachers' union entered the picture. We have already seen that the parental advocates of community control were hostile to the union:

> There was a union representative at this meeting who defended the union position at several points. He said that, so far as excessing and bumping were concerned, the Community School Board should have taken the responsibility for making the decisions on a district-wide basis. He claimed that the Community School Board had ducked this responsibility. Some principals also said this. The members of the School Board mostly denied it, but the black female member agreed that the School Board had ducked the responsibility. The excessing rules are now in the union contract for teachers, but they are not in the contract of the Walton Supervisory Association.

Southside, then, was part of a highly complex school system with multiple levels of political, bureaucratic, and professional authority which were sometimes in open conflict with each other and sometimes working unknowingly at cross-purposes. We shall see below that this created problems for implementing innovations in the school.

Problems notwithstanding, District 7 was fairly bursting with innovations. OCT had been adopted by some classrooms in nearly half of the district's schools; often it coexisted in the same school with other innovations. There were bilingual programs for Spanish- and French-speaking pupils. There was the Individualized Reading Program (IRP). There was team teaching. In some buildings, teachers were experimenting with videotaping classroom sessions and were using the Flanders Rating Scale of teacher performance for mutual evaluation and training. Eventually, the district hoped to abolish local attendance lines and to give all parents a district-wide option as to where their child should go to school. The rationale behind this plan was to encourage schools to compete for students, stimulating innovativeness and responsiveness to parental demands. It was a variant of the voucher system.

So, just as it was a center of political struggle, District 7 was also a buzzing hive of innovative activities. Almost every innovation fashionable at one time or another in the 1960's and early 1070's had been or was being tried there. The district's policy was "Let a thousand flowers bloom."

The Composition of Southside

District 7 was drawn in such a way that it included a wide range of socio-economic groups, from upper middle-class whites to low-income Hispanic and black families. Every school in the district had enough low-income pupils to qualify for some assistance under title I of the ESEA.[2]

Southside as a school reflected the ethnic and socio-economic mix of the district. Out of 637 pupils in grades K through five, it had 102 blacks, 145 Puerto Ricans, 88 "other Hispanic" pupils, 15 Orientals, and 287 whites. The attendance area included luxury apartment houses, inexpensive tenements, and one condemned building, which for a while was occupied by black "squatters." The school was ethnically and socio-economically integrated.

The staff also reflected the mix of the neighborhood, including a black principal, two black teachers, five Hispanic teachers, and a Puerto Rican school-community coordinator. An important feature of Southside was its attempt to carry integration to the classroom level. Five years previously it had adopted a policy of making every class heterogeneous, both ethnically and with respect to ability.

Race and integration were not salient issues at Southside as they were at Johnson. The principal was apolitical and rather passive. The upper middle-class white mothers, who dominated the PTA, were political liberals who approved of racial integration. Presumably those upper middle-class whites who did *not* approve, had left the city or sent their children to private school. In the kindergarten through third grade classrooms which we observed at Southside, there was less ethnic self-segregation among pupils than we had seen at Johnson. The reason for this was probably that the gap in skills between minority and white children was not so great. The principal pointed out to us that most black and Hispanic families in the neighborhood were upwardly mobile. This seemed credible since it must have taken determination and know-how to locate the rare combination of low-rent housing and high-quality schooling that the Southside attendance district offered. Parents who go to so much trouble to find a good school for their child in a neighborhood they can afford are the kinds of people who plan for the future, and try to maintain active control over the course of their lives. In social-psychological theory this is called "high fate control," and parents who have this complex of attitudes tend to pass them on to their children. Coleman's famous study showed that high fate control among pupils was strongly correlated with high scores on achievement tests.[3]

The staff of Southside included twenty-six full-time teachers. Five staff members were called "other teaching professionals." In theory, they consisted of two reading specialists, a music specialist, and a library specialist, paid out of Title I funds to "enrich" the school. In fact, as the principal explained to us, they were teachers with tenure who could not be fired, but who were considered so bad in the classroom that they were used only to relieve other teachers during their preparation periods.

Professional staff members were supplemented by a rich variety of paid and volunteer assistants. There were three school aides, all of them middle-class white mothers who had worked in Southside for many years. They ran dittos for the teachers and cared for the textbook supply room. There were also ten paraprofessionals, mostly Hispanic mothers recently hired under Title I funds, who guarded entrances, patrolled the lunchroom, gave hearing tests, and helped in classrooms. A group of parent volunteers came in several mornings a week to do remedial reading on a one-to-one basis with children who needed extra help. There were also many parent volunteers who came in more or less regularly to help in their children's open classrooms. Many classrooms also had student teachers.

The Parent-Teachers Association was active, but it consisted almost exclusively of a small group of upper middle-class white mothers. It had a personnel committee which advised the principal on new staff. The principal found this helpful rather than threatening. She said if a new appointee "bombed," the parents had to share the blame.

The principal had just succeeded to her post and so came under the new "no tenure" rule. Some teachers complained that, compared to the previous principal who had had tenure, she exerted little leadership and gave them little support. Others said she was busy lining up a faction of supporters within the faculty. She did spend considerable time observing and evaluating teachers who were coming up for tenure. In particular, she gave a lot of help to a black male teacher who, she said, had certain great strengths in the classroom, but also serious weaknesses which she hoped to help him overcome. This kind of constructive assistance was the only course of action open to her, Mrs. Jones said, since the union grievance procedure made it virtually impossible to get rid of an incompetent teacher—even one who did not yet have tenure.

Mrs. Jones portrayed her own position as one of weakness. She was caught between the teachers' union and the parent organizations, with very little room to move on her own. It was all she could do to keep both groups reasonably content. In a nearby school, the parents had demanded the right to enter classrooms and to make their own evaluations of teachers up for tenure. The union had told the teachers that if any parent group of that nature showed up, they should walk out of the classroom. "Thank God," said Mrs. Jones, "nothing like that has happened here—yet."

Southside had the highest reading scores in District 7 and ranked among the top 25 percent of the city's schools in reading. Its reputation was definitely that of a "good" school.

The district context in which Southside functioned was very different from that of Johnson. Johnson was able to keep the district headquarters at a distance, whereas Southside was not able to do this. Johnson's principal controlled the parents' association. Southside's principal was deeply concerned to maintain their good opinion. Johnson did not have to deal with a strong teachers' union. Southside did. Thus, Southside was far more vulnerable than Johnson to pressures from outside the school. They could come from the district headquarters, from the parents, or from the teachers' union. One strong pressure, while we were there, was an order from the district superintendent's office to implement the district's Individualized Reading Program (IRP).

Chapter 7

The District's Innovation: Individualized Reading

The Individualized Reading Program was adopted by the top officials of District 7 for implementation by all of the district's elementary schools. The superintendent and his aides gave it the very highest priority. They told the principals that their reappointment would depend in no small measure on how well they carried it out. Yet the innovation failed completely to be implemented at Southside. In this section, we must consider why this was so.

IRP contained several steps. First, a group diagnostic reading test was given in grades three through six. Grades one and two were not tested. Instead, their teachers received a long check list of behaviorally defined skills for each child, on which they were to mark three times a year which skills the child had mastered.

In the second phase, a nationally known textbook firm processed the tests and returned to the teachers a printout, giving the child's stanine rank in several reading skills. From these data, the teachers were supposed to group the children for skills instruction and find or write the appropriate curriculum for building the needed skills.

The principals attended meetings with a consultant from the textbook firm, who gave them guidance on methods of grouping and demonstration lessons in the kinds of curriculum needed. The principals were then supposed to hold workshops with their teachers to transmit what they learned from these sessions.

We attended one such principals' meeting, at which the district superintendent presided. He was disturbed because he felt the principals were not implementing the program, despite the urgency with which he pressed it on them. He said:

"The process is not being filtered down to the teachers. They are not aware of the sample lessons. They haven't read the material. They have had no orientation on the procedure in some schools, in others they have." A principal said, "It takes time for all the teachers to absorb this." The superintendent replied, "The public is not willing to give us time. The public wants results. This diagnostic and prescription approach is sweeping the country. The judgment of your leadership as principals will be based on how well you're implementing this effort. If we cannot implement a program like this, it will be our undoing as professionals."

Following the superintendent's speech, the consultant demonstrated a test for determining whether children's reading comprehension was at a "literal level," an "inference level," or a "level of critical evaluation." Principals kept drifting out of the auditorium all through this presentation, and the district coordinator of innovations expressed doubt that many would return to the session after lunch. He said:

"The principals' jobs depend on this, and this has a very, very high priority as far as we're concerned. It's been decided that this has to be done, and it just simply has to be done. But it's falling apart."

During subsequent weeks at Southside, we learned why the innovation was indeed falling apart. First, there was insufficient time during which principals could orient teachers as to how the innovation worked. Mrs. Jones explained:

"I have one staff meeting a month which I devote to reading and one grade level meeting a month which I devote to reading. Everything else which we can devote to this program is voluntary time on the part of the teachers, and no one will stay after school." I asked about using 'prep' periods. Mrs. Jones said, "The union contract provides that the 'prep' period is to be used by the teacher for any professional purpose she chooses, and all of the teachers use it to prepare their lesson plans. The only time I can hold workshops is to take twenty-five minutes out of their lunch period, and that will have to be voluntary. Under union rules, I can't force them to do it."

In fact, attendance at Mrs. Jones' voluntary clinics was very low. The district coordinator of innovation was aware of the problem, but glossed over it. He said teachers would attend voluntarily if they thought the clinics would really help them in the classroom. However, the district did nothing to convince the teachers that the clinics would be helpful. It delegated to the principal the responsibility for transmitting a large amount of information and for motivating teachers to learn it and use it, but it gave the principals no support of any kind.

The teachers at Southside not only did not perceive the clinics as helpful, they were quite resistant to the innovation. They saw it in a context which seemed to them threatening. During the previous year, and again in the autumn of the current academic year, they had received a district circular concerning their "accountability" for achieving certain reading goals. They perceived this circular as part and parcel of IRP. The goals were formulated quantitatively: "Eighty-five percent of the children should have mastered 75 percent of the following skills by the end of grade three." The teachers were not certain how seriously to take their "accountability" for these results. Some were quite sure it was unenforceable:

> I think the teachers are being very foolish to be scared by that. I don't understand why they are insecure. Nobody is going to enforce those goals. They can't enforce them. If the kids don't reach the goals, what are they going to do—get 10,000 new teachers for District 7? Nobody is going to teach Manuel to read on a third-grade level this year. It can't be done. He'll learn a lot, and perhaps he'll overcome his dislike of being in school. I'll be happy if I accomplish that.

Other teachers were apprehensive:

> I don't know what they'll do to us if we don't reach the goals, but it makes me nervous.

Still others felt that accountability was unjust:

> If Gino is not reading by the end of the year, it's because he's not ready to read. There's no reason for me to feel guilty as a teacher because he's not reading. And the same is true of some of the other children.

Since teachers did not attend the voluntary clinics, Mrs. Jones assigned one of her assistant principals to meet with them individually, at a time when their rooms could be covered by someone else, to help them with the grouping of their pupils.

The assistant principal explained to us that grouping was very difficult, since children who scored alike on one skill often scored very differently on others. It was almost as though one needed a different set of groups for each skill. The consultants had not really made clear what was to be done about that. So she worked out her own rough system and then helped each teacher to form groups based on her printout.

But that was not the end of the problem. The printouts reported stanine ranks for each child in such areas as "consonant blends," "auditory discrimination," and "reading comprehension," but not the precise problems of auditory discrimination the child had. That specific information was needed in order to write a curriculum prescription for the pupil, but it could only be obtained either from the tests themselves or by retesting each child in his weak areas. The assistant principal said they had requested the return of the tests, but she supposed she'd be a great-grandmother before they came. The teachers were bitterly disappointed when they learned the only feedback they were going to get from the tests was the relatively uninformative stanine ranks.

Furthermore, assuming the teacher did retest the children in their weak areas, she still had the burden of finding appropriate curriculum material in the books available at Southside, or of writing the curriculum herself. The teachers were told that they were supposed to devise an individual curriculum "prescription" for each child. As the principal pointed out, this was an inefficient use of time:

> I do not see why, if we're going to do this individualization, the local school board at the district level can't prepare the materials for the teachers. We're going to get these profiles, and they're going to show that certain kids are deficient in certain skills. Those kids are all going to need similar materials. Why doesn't the district prepare all those materials, instead of expecting the teachers to spend their time preparing it? It is terribly time-consuming to have thirty-two kids and thirty-two different prescriptions to do.

Most of the teachers did not plan to undertake this demanding task:

> I had my lunch in the teachers' room, where there was a discussion of the individualized reading program by teachers from the third, fourth, and fifth grades. Janice Hunter asked another

teacher what she was doing with the results of the diagnostic tests. "I'm not going to do anything. It's useless," she said. Janice replied "I think it's useful. I'm the only one who thinks so. The results tell me what to work on with each kid. I'm going to make three groups." Then she indicated she had been doing whole-class teaching in reading and now she was going to break it into groups. Bella said to her, "You are supposed to write an individualized prescription for each child." Janice replied, "That's horseshit. Don't be so chicken. They [the district officials] are not coming around. Don't do it. Don't do anything that doesn't help the children." She made a speech about this. She's an informal opinion leader among the teachers. She said they shouldn't be afraid of the district office. Then several of the other teachers sitting there declared that they absolutely would not write individual prescriptions. Janice said, "As it is, I have about eight hours of school work I have to do this weekend." And she enumerated the things she had to do.

First- and second-grade open classroom teachers felt the behaviorally formulated reading skills instrument they were supposed to fill out for IRP was completely out of keeping with the philosophy of open education. The Open Classroom Teaming advisers agreed with them, and eventually the Advisory negotiated with district officials for a more "appropriate" instrument. In the meantime, the open classroom teachers were obliged to fill out the skills sheets—a task which was meaningless and frustrating for them.

One day, in the corridor, we heard a teacher tell the principal she had no intention of writing individualized prescriptions. The principal, who herself thought this an unfair demand, simply did not reply. There must have been other incidents like this, and they meant the teachers were getting a message that the principal's support for IRP was weak. That, of course, strengthened their own resistance.

Finally, as if to underline the complete lack of realism in the efforts to implement IRP, the superintendent's office, after threats to check up on what principals were doing and promises to send in "master teachers" to help, followed through on neither their threats nor their promises.

District 7's reading innovation is a classic example of poor planning and poor administration. The innovation itself was faulty in much the same way as the ILP program at Johnson had been. It provided neither a sufficiently specific diagnosis for the teachers' grouping needs nor sufficient assistance to teachers in finding appropriate curriculum for each child. The teachers were expected to undertake a completely unrealistic workload for the sake of a program handed down from on high to which they had no commitment.

District officials were insufficiently aware of the problems with IRP, because teachers had no opportunity to communicate with them about it. All communication was filtered through the principals. The teachers' opinions were asked neither at the inception of the program nor while they were supposedly implementing it. The only direct communication they received from district headquarters was the one concerning their accountability, which they perceived as a threat.

The district did not take the trouble to make sure that such matters as grouping procedures were clear to the principals, who had to explain them to teachers. They did not return the diagnostic tests to the teachers who needed them for curriculum prescription. They did not send around the "master teachers" who were supposed to help with implementation.

In short, IRP violated all the rules for successful implementation of an innovation. The principals and, most of all, the teachers, who had to carry it out, had played no part in the decision to adopt it.[1] Many of them actively disliked it. Furthermore, even if they had wanted to implement it, the support system was grossly inadequate. Filtering information from the change agent through the principal to the teachers was very inefficient. The teachers needed to be exposed to the change agent directly to avoid the loss of information and the distortion which occurs in such a two-step process. But that was logistically impossible, since every elementary teacher in the district was involved. So, the district headquarters simply commissioned the principals and teachers to carry out an impossible task and, worst of all, backed up this commission with threats. The principals were threatened with loss of their untenured positions, and the teachers felt threatened with some unknown sanctions should they fail to live up to their "accountability" goals. On the whole, the school staff believed that the district would not carry out its threats. But even if they had thought otherwise, an innovation implemented out of fear of sanctions could not possibly be implemented well.

Chapter 8

Walton University's Innovation: Open Classroom Teaming

The innovation which had originally interested us in Southside was Open Classroom Teaming (OCT), and since open classrooms were also the chief innovation at the third school we studied, it is well to begin by outlining the philosophy of open education as it is practiced in the United States.[1] Since it is well known, we shall treat it only briefly, following the exposition of Roland Barth, which is the best in the literature.[2]

As Barth points out in *Open Education and the American School*, practice has frequently preceded theory. Open educators often cite the psychology of Piaget, Froebel, Isaacs, and Dewey as authorities, but one cannot demonstrate that open-classroom practices derive in any rigorous way from the theories of these writers; they are connected only suggestively. Open education is best described as a *movement* consisting of certain classroom practices together with a philosophy which has grown up around them. The philosophy emphasizes learning and de-emphasizes teaching. Here are its main assumptions, partly quoted and partly paraphrased from Barth's book:

1. Children are naturally exploratory and necessarily the agents of their own learning. To teach something does not mean it will be learned.

2. "Play is not distinguished from work as the predominant mode of learning in early childhood" (p. 24).

3. "Intellectual growth and development takes place through a sequence of concrete experiences followed by abstractions" (p.33). Since cognitive development proceeds from the concrete to the abstract, " . . . children will learn best in an environment which offers a wide array of manipulative materials" (p. 23).

115

4. "Children will be likely to learn if they are given considerable choice in the selection of the materials they wish to work with and in the choice of questions they wish to pursue" (p. 26).

5. Left to themselves, children will often work collaboratively and learn from each other.

6. Each child learns at his own pace and in his own style, though all go through an identical sequence of developmental stages.

7. Objective measurement of performance may have a negative effect, since it tends to make the child seek extrinsic rewards (high grades) rather than the intrinsic reward of learning itself.

8. Children should never be compared with each other. Competition should be discouraged and cooperation fostered.

9. A child's self-esteem derives most importantly from his own experience of having mastered something. Social approval is not unimportant, but it is secondary.

10. The best, if not the only, way to evaluate a child's learning is to observe it over a long period of time. Open educators dislike achievement tests, since they feel these do not measure important aspects of learning, such as creativity.

11. "There is no particular body of knowledge which it is essential to know" (p. 46). "Curriculum is a joint responsibility, guided by the adult through the selection and construction of materials and determined by the child through his individual response to materials" (p. 50).

It follows from these assumptions that the teacher's role in an open classroom is not so much to teach as to facilitate the child's learning. She must provide an environment rich in exciting materials. She must give the children considerable freedom to choose what they will do. She must create an environment of warmth, trust, and openness about one's feelings. She helps the child with his work by showing him how he can extend his own explorations.

Open educators believe in "the integrated day." This concept owes a good deal to Dewey's "project method." It states that the traditional separation of academic subjects into language arts, mathematics, science, social studies, etc., is undesirable. It is preferable for a child to be engaged in an inquiry of his own devising and to acquire the skills he needs and the information he requires as a natural outgrowth of the demands of the project.

Open educators claim that the child will learn to read if he needs to for some purpose of his own; he will learn to measure and calculate the same way. As Barth points out, the acquisition of basic reading and mathematical skills are considered very important by most parents and educators, ". . . but open educators have been somewhat evasive, offering few specific guidelines which would help a teacher help a child learn to read. The child reads because others do, because he needs information, or because it is fun. Provide the child with sufficient materials which involve looking at words, talking, listening, writing, and reading, and they will somehow evolve their own best individualized reading 'programs'; they will learn how to read" (pp. 36–37).

Finally, open educators believe that human groups should be egalitarian, not hierarchical. This last point is not made by Barth, but it appears elsewhere in the literature. In our interview with the director of the OCT Advisory, he emphasized it:

> At our workshops, we all work together and are treated alike. You can't tell the teachers from the paraprofessionals.

Open educators proclaim the superior humaneness of the open classroom as its chief virtue. Even if achievement is no greater than in the traditional class,[3] the children are happier, and that is sufficient justification for adopting it. Clearly, the moral values embodied in open education philosophy are more important to its supporters than cognitive skills. As so often in educational history, the battle between open and traditional education does not concern pedagogical methods so much as it does the question of what values should be internalized by children. It is the conflict over values which heats up the debate.

The Adoption of Open Classrooms and the Problem of Voluntarism

Open classrooms came to Southside through a process of diffusion. A parent had observed them at another school and was very enthusiastic about them. She managed to interest some other upper middle-class Southside parents, who got together and asked Samuel Wylie, Director of the OCT Advisory at

Walton University, to show a film and give a talk about it at the school. The film aroused further interest among parents and staff. At the request of the core group of mothers, Professor Wylie began to explore the possibility of introducing OCT in Southside. He met separately with administrators, teachers, and parents—and finally with all three groups together. To the teachers, he stressed that OCT required far more work than traditional whole-class teaching. They would have to devote prep periods, lunch hours, and after-school time to meetings and workshops. He did not believe they should try OCT unless they found themselves dissatisfied with what they were presently doing and eager to invest heavy effort in change. To the administrators, he stressed that the OCT teachers would have to be located close to each other in the building so that they could gradually come to work as a team. To the parents, he stressed that their support and help in the classroom would be needed.

Wylie's official policy was that no school should embark on opening up its classrooms unless teachers, parents, and administrators were all eager to do so. He believed that, without strong motivation from all three groups, the innovation could not succeed. In most schools where OCT was introduced, there was a policy of maintaining at least one traditional classroom at each grade level for parents and teachers who preferred to stay with that style of education. But no option was left at Southside, ostensibly because the innovation had the overwhelming support of both groups as well as the principal. When the second grade went OCT in the second year, and the third grade in the third year, the balloting of parents and discussions with teachers were said to have shown that OCT had such wide support that there were not enough children to set up a traditional class. The assistant principal said that almost all third-grade parents had returned their ballots, and only seven were against OCT.

Nevertheless, in our interviews, we uncovered evidence that participation in OCT was not so voluntary as it might have seemed. One teacher, an enthusiastic supporter of OCT herself, told us:

> We really have no choice about OCT. We were simply told that OCT was coming to our grade level. I was told, "Either you accept OCT or you will be moved to a different grade level. If there

isn't an opening, you would have to switch schools." A lot of people like this school or like its location, so there really is strong pressure on you to go along with it.

There was also evidence that parents' support was less than overwhelming:

> One of the OCT advisers said that the parents had had a choice as to whether their children should have open classrooms or not. But a teacher said that wasn't true. She said she had had a meeting with the parents of her class and asked them how many of them had voted for open classrooms, and only one raised her hand.

The leading parent activist, the one who had first mobilized parents for open classrooms, was not sure that there had actually been a ballot the first year:

> Question: "What about the parents? Do you think a large majority of them support OCT?"
> Parent: "Well, part of it is the fact that it could have been loaded the first year. We didn't want to wait so no one was asked; it just went."
> Question: "You mean the parents were not really asked?"
> Parent: "No, it just went. Now we're having problems with that. What I'm beginning to find is that I heard the vocal people *for*, but I didn't hear the vocal *against*. I think the first year it was done administratively, not through the parent body. They say here the Spanish people would not opt to take it, but I don't know anymore; I really don't."

And still another pro-OCT parent said:

> I still think parents do not understand what it is all about. I've spoken to so many mothers. People have started coming to me and saying, "What's this whole business of open classroom? I think it stinks." Or, "My kids are completely out of control; the teacher has no control in the classroom."
> I think the parents, some of them, didn't understand what the ballot was all about. Mrs. Rivera [the school's Puerto Rican community coordinator] made a statement with respect to the referendum that even if you translated the ballot into Spanish, many parents are illiterate in Spanish, and they will not understand what this is about. Then I began to wonder about the ballot on open classrooms. It's hard for me to believe that only seven parents were against it in the third grade. And that they got

nearly all the ballots back—because I find such tremendous apathy among parents in returning *anything* to school. I wonder whether the Hispanic parents really understood what was going on. If they really knew what they were doing, I don't think that— only seven against—I don't think that could happen.

And one Puerto Rican parent made clear that she personally did not approve:

> Open classroom is good, but not for our children. We bring up our children to be obedient and to do what we tell them to do. Then they go to school and the teacher says, "What do you want to do?" Then they start trying to act that way at home. It's confusing to our children.

This situation raised a potentially serious difficulty for Southside. The activist, upper middle-class, white parents wanted to mount a campaign to inform Hispanic and black parents about OCT and gain their participation in the program. As matters stood, there was virtually no participation from mothers of those two groups. However, an educational campaign might not have had the intended effect. If it turned out that the minority parents actually preferred the traditional classroom, the introduction of an option at each grade level would have led to ethnic segregation of the classes—the white children in OCT rooms and the Hispanic and black children in the traditional rooms. The alternative would have been that some parents' choices could not be honored. This possibility was raised by the principal at a PTA meeting, which discussed instituting an option. She said that, in order to maintain ethnic heterogeneity in every room, it might become necessary to assign some children whose families preferred OCT to traditional rooms, and vice versa. One of the white parents, in an interview later, said that she understood the problem, but that if her child were ever assigned to a traditional room, she would leave the city for the suburbs, where open classrooms were easy to find.

Thus there was a conflict between two desired goals. It might not prove possible to give all parents and teachers their choice of program and, at the same time, maintain the heterogeneous classrooms which both district and OCT policy demanded. There was some evidence to suggest that the system had worked so far only because most minority parents, and some white parents as well, did not understand the choice before them, were apathetic about it, or believed in leaving such matters to the superior wisdom of the educators. Helping them to make their choice in the light of more information and understanding might have brought the goal conflict to a head.

The dilemma is also an illustration of the larger problem of voluntarism in school innovations. Most authors emphasize the importance of gaining a strong commitment to the innovation from all parties who will be involved in implementing it. Professor Wylie believed that voluntarism all around was absolutely necessary and made strong efforts to abide by this principle. Yet it is no easy task to gain consensus on a radical change from a large group of parents, teachers, and administrators. A certain amount of dissensus is to be expected. Wylie's solution was to leave open an alternative for the dissenters—a traditional classroom at each grade level. This kind of situation, where two modes of teaching based on conflicting assumptions coexist in the same school, creates its own problems, as we shall see when we look at the Coolidge School in Part III. But at Southside, no alternative was provided. There was disagreement among the Advisory, the principal, the parents, and the teachers as to how unanimous parental support for open classrooms actually was.

Flaws in the Support System

The OCT Advisory at Walton University furnished a wide variety of workshops, displays, resource materials, and lectures on open classrooms for parents and teachers, scheduled for their convenience. Its most important service, however, was the provision of two advisers who visited the school three days each week to work with OCT teachers in their classrooms, and to hold discussion meetings with them. Dr. Wylie said his advisers would take a willing teacher at "whatever point she is at" and help her to move, at her own pace, toward the goals of the open classroom.

It seemed to us that the OCT on-site training was an excellent resource for the Southside teachers. Yet, as we came to know the teachers' views, we found that not one of the five we observed felt the advisers were useful. A first-grade teacher said they were a help during the first year, because they had a lot of foundation money and brought in wonderful materials. But aside from that, she hadn't much respect for them:

> I really feel that the only person that's given me any worthwhile help was Professor Wylie, when he came. It's incredible to see him sit down and work with a child. I get so much out of that. The people he hired to work in his guidance service are people who never taught open classrooms—just went to some of his summer workshops that they were interested in, and he picked a few and made them trainers. Some of us would like to see them take a class for a whole day. We had several come in last year who were just awful. One of them made me so nervous; she didn't do a thing. She really didn't know. I think that if someone is going to help you that they really should be a trained person. And that's the kind of help I would really like and that I don't see at all from our advisers.

A second-grade teacher said the advisers were "no use at all":

> One day I asked her [one of the advisers] what I could do with this art corner. She went off on a marvelous explanation of the things I could do, but they all involved materials I don't have and have no way of getting. So I said to her, "Look, this is what I've got. What can I do with it?" She was no help on that.

With respect to one of the two advisers, the teachers actually believed that she had never had any teaching experience. This was untrue. The adviser was an experienced teacher and had had considerable training at the OCT Advisory as well. Nevertheless, the teachers perceived her as deficient in classroom expertise.

Sometimes there was overt friction between teachers and advisers. One such occasion was a conference between an adviser and a second-grade teacher. The adviser had brought three first-grade children to visit this teacher's room, in an attempt to increase the flow of children between classes. One of the second graders had proudly shown a first-grade visitor his new math book, only to be told, "Oh, I finished that a long time ago"—a remark which upset the second-grade child. The adviser commented that it was necessary to investigate why the first-grade child made such competitive remarks. But the teacher burst out, "No! I will not have that child in my room again. My job is to protect my children. Don't bring him back!" And she walked away.

On another occasion, at a meeting of OCT teachers, the advisers were trying to suggest some movement toward the "integrated day." The teachers resisted. They hadn't enough help to teach that way. They hadn't enough time to plan for it. As matters stood, Mrs. Davis said, they were giving up prep periods and lunch periods, which was not legally required of them. At that point one of the advisers said:

> You are treading on dangerous ground. You volunteered for this program. We know that you are not legally required to give a lunch period to it, but you committed yourself to do that when you volunteered for the program. It's not required of you legally, but it comes out of your commitment. In other schools, they stay after dismissal until 4:00.

This response infuriated the teachers, who shared their feelings afterward with all the other teachers in the lunchroom.

One of the OCT kindergarten teachers told us that the weekly formal meetings called by the advisers had destroyed the practice of *informal* luncheon meetings among OCT teachers, which existed before the advisers came to the school:

> I think there's a tendency toward a "close your door" kind of thing, partly due to the fact that there are so many meetings. One is giving up so much free time that many of the teachers are just tired of it. Where we used to lunch together and discuss open-classroom activities, we don't do that any more because the meetings are above and beyond this lunch gathering. We used to gather informally and have our lunch in one of the rooms, but we don't any more, because we had to have meetings in addition to that, so it just dissolved. Nobody said anything but it just ceased.

This teacher thought the informal meetings were more productive than the formal ones. At informal meetings, the teachers could talk about specific children and how to treat them. At the formal meetings, they were constantly forced to translate such problems to a higher level of generality and that was "uncomfortable":

> When you meet informally, there's a tendency to very often go off on a tangent. In formal meetings, if you do that, you're usually brought back to the main topic of conversation, and somehow I find that this tends to block people. They're no longer comfortable. Even though you could say what you want to say, you're somehow stopped. Many people feel that tangents are very rele-

vant. You go into a meeting, and invariably if you're dealing with individuals: "Well, I have so and so in my class and he is . . . ." Well, the advisers may not be interested in that. They want you to generalize. And this tends to make people uncomfortable. How can we generalize when we do have individual problems? I think this is the difference between the informal and the formal gathering.

This suggests that the advisers were not skilled at leading discussions. They did not seem to know how to deal with the individual problems which concerned the teachers and move from there to the more general implications of those problems.

The kindergarten teacher was also confused as to whether attendance at the meetings called by the advisers was compulsory or voluntary. Actually, it was expected that a teacher in the OCT program would attend these meetings unless there was a good reason for her absence. But, as we have already seen, that was neither fully understood nor fully accepted by the teachers. The kindergarten teacher believed that the ambiguity about attendance at meetings called by the advisers, prevented those who did attend from speaking freely:

> I think it always works better when it's a more informal group, for the simple reason that, although you say to a teacher, "We are having an OCT meeting at lunch time on Monday," the teacher knows it's voluntary, but the question comes up, "Just how voluntary is it?" What are the repercussions if one doesn't show up week after week? Do they look down and say, "Well, she really isn't interested in the OCT program?"—which is inevitably what happens! If you don't show up, you show a lack of interest, but this may not necessarily be the case. It's just that some people feel lunch time is their free time. So they feel a pressure, and each of us feels a different degree of the pressure. I mean, I will go sometimes; sometimes I won't go. But what bothers us is when the advisers come in and say, "Don't forget you have a meeting today." They may say it twice or three times just to remind people. But you don't know if not attending the meetings is being held against you. So there's a tendency to try to avoid as much of that as possible. When you meet informally, you know you really don't have to be there. You don't feel any kind of pressure if you don't show up. I think that's the difference. So that during informal meetings, people are more apt to say what they feel.

Here the teacher expresses plainly the constraint which the OCT teachers at Southside felt in the presence of the advisers. Although the advisers were supposed never to act as supervisors or evaluators of teachers, but rather to behave always as status-equals, in reality they had some authority over the teachers. They could and did invade a teacher's room with unwanted visitors from another room. They could and did compel attendance at weekly meetings. By calling these meetings, they unknowingly killed off the informal luncheon meetings the teachers had been holding to share their problems. Had the advisers really been perceived as status equals, they probably would have been told about these informal meetings, and they could have joined them as resources for information and advice. However, the teachers' resentment of the advisers' power, together with their lack of respect for their expertise, resulted in their never mentioning the informal luncheon meetings to the advisers. Formal meetings with compulsory attendance were instituted, and were very probably less productive than the informal ones, where people were more apt to say what they felt.

The small core of activist parents had a very different view of the advisers than the teachers held. They thought they were doing a wonderful job:

> They're just so fantastic with finding fun and exciting games and equipment for children to use as a learning experience. And the workshops that they've been running I think are very helpful to the teachers, getting them to come out and see the kind of equipment that they can make or get for their classrooms.

Several of the parents made a major point of the fact that the advisers were beginning to get the teachers to work in teams. We shall see below that there were very different understandings about this among teachers, advisers, and parents:

> I think without the advisers I don't know how we could do it at all. Because, as far as I'm concerned, part of the whole open education thing is not only interaction among children, but interaction among staff, parents, teachers, administrators, all working together. I think it's one of the most difficult things that a teacher has to understand; that she's not the autonomous person in the classroom, that maybe two people working together can make life more exciting for children. I think the natural thing

> would be to struggle on by yourself. The advisory helps them to come out—not all, but some.

And another mother said:

> I think both of them are unbelievably important. One of the most basic things they do is getting the teachers together, even if it's only that once a week they meet with them at lunch time or prep period and just talk about what has been going on or what you would like to see happen—just having teachers talk *together*. Once they talk together, other things come out of it. I mean, you could be banging your head against the wall for months and months, thinking of how to solve a problem, and suddenly somebody, just by talking about it, comes up with a solution.

During the period of our observation, the OCT advisers, the Southside administrators, and the activist parents made a misstep which raised the apprehensions of the OCT teachers. They met to discuss the teachers behind the teachers' backs. The topics of discussion were the emotional difficulties of one teacher, the presumed lack of commitment of another, and the general failure of the OCT teachers to work in teams. Here is how one parent described the meeting:

> A parent came in with specific problems within her child's classroom. The teacher was having emotional problems, and the question was, how can we suppport her? We didn't want to lose her. Then the other problem is that someone came into the OCT program saying she wanted it, and nothing was happening in her room. And this was being allowed by the administration, having a room that was devoid of any kind of materials, any kind of life or life of children in it. It was sterile, and the administration wasn't doing anything about it. These are the kind of problems.
> The other problem is that teaming is a philosophy, and I don't think it comes through osmosis. It is a family kind of thing. You work with other teachers. You open your doors. And I don't know if everyone understands that. There are teachers who are not functioning well in our school.

It was decided to set up an evening meeting of parents, advisers, administrators, and OCT teachers to broach these problems with the teachers. However, news of the secret meeting leaked out, and the teachers became very concerned that the parents would attack them at the evening meeting for not being "open" enough.

As it happened, the meeting brought out friction among all the groups and also brought to the surface many of the problems of implementation that we had been observing.

The first topic discussed at the meeting was teaming. It was evident that the advisers and parents had already talked it over and come to some consensus about persuading the teachers to try it:

> A parent said, "Is teaming going on in this school? I'd like to see more doors open. I'm not aware that we really have open classroom *teaming* here."
>
> Then one of the advisers said, "Of course, there are problems. There are large registers in the classes and very little help with them." Another parent chimed in, "If three teachers could work together as a community, we wouldn't have these problems. Could teachers choose at the beginning of the year who would be together in a community and have their preps together?" The principal told her that second- and third-grade teachers all had at least one common prep period a week.
>
> The second adviser then explained, "Open classroom and OCT are not the same thing. An open classroom uses the same principles, but it's a self-contained classroom. We have been trying to build a community of classrooms. That's what we are working for in this school." At this point, a teacher burst out with some irritation, "If you're working for a community of classrooms, we certainly have heard nothing about it at our weekly meetings." The adviser responded, "We can't impose this on you. It has to come from you, and then we'll help you do it." Another teacher supported the first, "You say you want to promote it, but you have not spent one of the meetings we've been having weekly discussing it yet. We have these meetings at lunch time once a week, and nothing has been said about it." Whereupon the adviser replied, "The teachers have to do it together."

The advisers' position was anomalous. On the one hand, they often made suggestions to teachers and even pressed them to do things differently in their classrooms. But here they were insisting that the initiative for teaming had somehow to come spontaneously from the teachers, even as they asserted it as their own major goal. It is also interesting that the advisers thought there was not enough help in the classrooms even though the adult-to-child ratio in the rooms was unusually high. This speaks to the fact that open classrooms are expensive, since so much adult assistance is required to make them run smoothly. And finally, the parent's comments indicated that she had close familiarity with the school, probably because she spent a considerable amount of volunteer time there. And she took it for granted that parents had a legitimate input into such educational policy matters as whether there should be open classroom teaming or not.

Another delicate matter came up at this meeting, and that was parents passing judgment on a specific teacher. Parents have always had the right to complain about teachers to the principal, of course. And teachers have always expected the principal to support them in the presence of the parents—whatever she might say to them in private. But to attack a teacher by name in an open meeting like this one was a different matter, an unusual exercise of parental influence. Two parents did so. The first said:

> "Mrs. Davis doesn't go along with open classroom." Mrs. Davis replied, "No, that isn't true. I don't go along with the community thing, but I believe in the philosophy of open education." One of the advisers interjected, "Those teachers who are interested in creating a community have our services to call on." Then another parent said. "The teachers don't seem to have decided whether they want teaming. We [the parents] said we wanted it, but it isn't set up."

The second attack on Mrs. Davis was based on her attitude toward teaming:

> Mrs. Davis said she was willing to try teaming, but she sounds opposed to it.

At this point, the teachers' union representative became very angry:

> I represent the teachers of this school to the union. The teachers in this school are very cooperative. They give up lunch hours. They stay after school. And legally they don't have to do this. How much more dedication do you want from them?

It was an impasse. After a brief silence, a parent took another tack. Again she was addressing a complaint to the teachers:

Why do you have the feeling that you have to know where kids are, or that somebody has to supervise their movement from room to room? Why can't they just move freely from one room to another?

This comment left teachers, administrators, and advisers aghast, since they all knew the school was not secure against dangerous intruders—every entrance was guarded by a paraprofessional— and that they were legally responsible for the children's safety in school. But a first-grade teacher was disturbed by the comment on other grounds as well. She said:

"You can't just have chaos. Open classroom has to be organized and planned." The mother said, "Why? What sometimes you don't think is purposeful for a kid is purposeful. Sometimes he just wants to do nothing." A kindergarten teacher said, "That's fine, but some kids will do nothing day after day, if you let them."

This exchange illustrates that some of the activist parents were more radical than the teachers in their open education philosophy.

Finally, a parent suggested that there was opposition to open classroom among parents, even though the reports they received concerning parent balloting seemed to indicate otherwise. The reports did not square with her personal experience in talking with parents:

I have a feeling some of the parents are only half committed to open education and others are opposed to it. The ones who are opposed aren't here tonight. Every year we give birth to new open classrooms, and we don't really know who supports it and who doesn't.

The principal said that, if they were going to have more evening meetings of the four groups together, there would have to be a higher parent turnout. Only eight parents were present. Finally, after some discussion, they decided to have another meeting to talk over whether there should be an option between open classrooms, and open classroom teaming.

The meeting left some of the participants with resentments and anxieties. A first-grade teacher said the next day that she had been very much disturbed by it:

I don't think that parents and teachers should be up in arms against each other. We really need each other. It's a shame and it bothered me a lot last night. I think the program is doing well here. You have to accept people according to their philosophy, and I don't think you can push anyone one way or the other. I think it's horrible that people picked on Mrs. Davis the way they did. Let her be in the program the way she wants to be in it.

A parent said she had come to the conclusion that they made an initial mistake at Southside. There ought to be an option between open and nonopen classrooms:

> I think we've done something wrong at Southside. I don't think we can change the world. There are people who have attitudes that are very open, but I think we haven't yet come to the point where some people can be that free and open about their attitudes toward children and their learning. Maybe what we should think of for the future at Southside is an alternative. It sounds impossible when someone says that the ballots came back and all but seven or eight parents wanted OCT. I can't believe it because I think teachers are a good reflection of what society is thinking and doing, and if teachers can't all feel comfortable in it, how can all parents feel comfortable in it? I can't understand that. I think for some teachers, it's just not their thing. Maybe they don't know it themselves, but it's just not their thing, and I think it cannot be the thing for everybody at this point.

Mrs. Davis was so incensed at the attack on her at the meeting that she complained to a teachers' union representative that OCT was illegally encroaching on teachers' time. After some discussion, she backed off from making formal charges. Her colleagues shared her reservations about the advisers and her feeling that the program was not entirely voluntary for them, but they respected Professor Wylie and they believed in the philosophy of open education. Furthermore, it was a time of teacher surplus and there was fear of the consequences of "rocking the boat."

Thus the implementation of OCT at Southside lacked some ingredients which were crucial according to OCT's own philosophy. Apparently large numbers of parents, especially minority parents, did not understand what was going on at the school. Had they understood, many might have opted for the traditional classroom.

From the teachers' perspective, the advisory system was not so egalitarian as Professor Wylie claimed. They saw Wylie at the top of the hierarchy, the advisers at the next level, and themselves at the bottom. Therefore, even when they had opportunities to talk with Wylie personally, they did not feel able to go over the advisers' heads to complain about them to him. They were unsure how receptive Wylie would be to such criticism, and they feared repercussions from the advisers themselves. Wylie lost out because nearly all that he knew about the program at Southside, he heard from the advisers, who were a biased and limited source of information. They themselves were either unaware or unwilling to admit to the nature of the teachers' sentiments toward them. In our interviews with them, they interpreted all of the teachers' hostile gestures toward themselves as resistance to open education, which was natural, they said, coming from novices.

Wylie was quite out of touch with the teachers' views. In our interview with him, he heaped the highest praise on one of the Southside advisers. There was no sign that he had any inkling of what the teachers thought of her. Wylie needed some direct and frank feedback from teachers, and the teachers needed some way to make their problems with advisers known to him. But no direct channel of communication between Wylie and the teachers existed.[4]

So, despite attempts to insure voluntary participation on all sides and equal status among all participants, the OCT program at Southside failed to achieve these two goals.

Chapter 9

Open Classrooms: Variability in Implementation

It is a commonplace of educational research that differences among teachers are often more potent than differences among teaching methods. When studies attempt to compare experimentally the outcomes of various teaching methods, it often turns out that their effects are smaller than the effects of variation among teachers using the same method. The large differences among teachers constitute a problem for implementing educational innovations. An innovation which is programed in detail, like DISTAR,[1] is the kind most likely to be implemented in a uniform way. An observer not briefed in advance would hardly fail to distinguish between a teacher using DISTAR and a teacher not using it.

In the case of a far more complex innovation, like open education, teachers implement it in widely differing ways. Walberg and Thomas developed an observational scale which enabled unbriefed observers to distinguish validly between classrooms intended to be open and classrooms not so intended, in Britain and the United States.[2] Nonetheless, the open classrooms we observed differed widely among themselves. We observed five classrooms in the OCT program at Southside for two and a half weeks each. The rooms we saw included one which we judged as quite highly structured and one which seemed to us very unstructured. The other three fell somewhere between. A trainer of open-classroom teachers who read our field notes,* independently identified these two classrooms as the extremes on a continuum of structure, and also said that they exemplified the two most common ways that open education is being implemented in the United States. For this reason, we shall describe these two classrooms in some detail.

*This was Professor Diane Levin of Lesley College, who was a member of the seminar mentioned in the Introduction. I draw heavily on her seminar paper in this chapter.

A Structured Open Classroom

Natalie Roseman's first-grade class had twenty-two children, twelve boys and ten girls. Two of the pupils were black, five were Hispanic, and the rest were native-born white. Most of the white children came from upper middle-class homes; the minority children were considerably poorer. There was some correlation between ethnicity and academic skills (though not necessarily ability); none of the highly verbal and quantitatively sophisticated pupils in the classroom was a minority child. On the other hand, no child in the room was on such a low level of skill as we saw very often at the Johnson School.[3]

Two student teachers were doing their practice-teaching with Miss Roseman, and one or the other of them was present nearly all the time. In addition, there was a volunteer mother, who also happened to be a teacher-in-training, who came in four mornings a week. This meant there was nearly always an adult-to-child ratio in this room of one-to-eleven, and sometimes of one-to-seven. Furthermore, the helping adults had training in teaching skills. Miss Roseman felt she needed every bit of this assistance. She repeatedly said, "You need a lot of adults around to run this kind of program." On this point she was at variance with Professor Wylie, who thought that one teacher plus an aide was about right for an open classroom with twenty-five children. More adults than that, he felt, tended to undermine the children's independence. Even this recommended ratio of about one-to-twelve is higher than one finds in conventional class-rooms. The open classroom teachers at Southside nearly all agreed with Miss Roseman rather than Professor Wylie. They claimed that "slow children" and children with a short attention span could not work independently and required constant adult supervision.

The Environment: Space and Materials

Natalie's classroom was attractive, cheerful, and very tidy. All the materials had a "right place" to be stored and the children knew these places. In an open classroom, children must be taught to put materials away carefully, in good shape, ready to be taken out and used by the next child who wants them. The importance of this basic organizational principle can hardly be exaggerated. Part of the theory is that "materials teach" without the teacher. But if children are to use materials freely, they must be able to find them promptly and the materials must be in condition for use. If children don't put materials back where they belong, and if they don't care for materials to see that they don't get broken and that parts don't get lost, the classroom becomes disorganized; children waste much time searching for misplaced things and lost parts. Miss Roseman spent a considerable part of numerous class meetings discussing with the children the need to be careful with materials. She emphasized that all the materials in the room belonged to all of them, so that everyone was responsible for their good condition.

Children's work was on display in the room, but perhaps to lesser extent than in other open classrooms in the school. The teacher's work was relatively more conspicuous in this room: Natalie's chart of the Cuisenaire rods, their colors and letter labels; her chart of the concepts "shorter and taller," "littler and bigger." But there were also children's paintings, their dictated stories, their rhyming books, and their dancing pumpkins for Halloween.

Basically, the materials were arranged around the four sides of the room, while the center space contained several tables and chairs where children worked. Along the wall to the right of the door was a blackboard and a peg board. The peg board had round tags with the names of the children and stickers with the names of the room "areas." The children were supposed to hang their name tags under the areas they were at. Next came a small stove, pots, and other cooking utensils. The children cooked about once a week. Next to that was the "listening area," equipped with a recordplayer and earphones, a library of records, and books which went with them. These were stories which children could listen to and look at at the same time.

On the left-hand wall were the children's and teacher's clothing closets and the children's storage cubbies. The door of one closet had a chart of the children's reading groups. There were six groups: one had six children in it, one had five, one had four, one had three, and two had two.

In front of the closets was the "math area." It was a table with a lot of materials: geo boards, tape measures, counting books, small- and medium-sized blocks of different shapes, colored cubes, a peg board on which you could put from one to ten rings on a peg, a chart of simple geometric shapes with their names, a number line, Cuisenaire rods with a box of task cards, and some dittoed sheets with tasks to do.

On the window side of the room was the "art area." It consisted of a long work table covered with attractive oilcloth. In clear plastic boxes on the window sill, each neatly labeled, were ribbon, foam bits, yarn, macaroni, wooden pieces, beans, buttons, clay, fabric, magazines, scissors, crayons, a ruler, colored paper, and flour for making paste. There were also easels. The paints and brushes were in a closet. Next along this wall, separated from art by an unused piano, came the "language arts area." It had some very big building blocks in it. It also had a closet jammed with letter, word, and math games of all kinds—some bought, many made by the teacher.

On the right-hand wall, there was a box marked "Children's Day Books" containing books which the children had made. Several of them were filled with drawings and labels—some crude, some sophisticated. There was also a box marked "Math Work Books," one marked "Story Books," and one marked "Coloring Books." There was a little bookcase which contained part of the class library. In the corner, covered with plants, was the teacher's desk. She hardly ever sat at it. Instead, she used a filing cabinet backed up against the side of the piano where she kept her records and plans. Finally, toward the middle of the room there was a "science area." It had two of the inevitable gerbils, some autumn leaves, a pumpkin, a book on rocks and minerals, and a box of cards with "things to do" written on them. Natalie felt that science activities were the weakest part of her program—and by comparison with other open classrooms we saw, we would agree. She also felt that her room was very poor in materials, but that too is a relative matter. Compared to many classrooms at Johnson it was very rich in materials. Compared to some open classrooms we have seen in wealthy private schools it was less impressive, but hardly describable as "poor in materials."

Schedule and Content

In theory, the open classroom structures space strongly, as Natalie's room did, but destructures time. Children are not supposed to move from reading to arithmetic by the clock, but to work at an "activity" as long as it absorbs them. This ideal is seldom fully realized; most open classrooms have some kind of time schedule, albeit a flexible one. Natalie's room ran on quite a regular schedule. The day began with a class meeting to discuss news, the weather, upcoming holidays, or whatever else the children wanted to talk about. The teacher used the meeting to tell the children about any special activities of the day and to give instructions to the reading groups. Then the children broke up into their ability-homogeneous reading groups. The most advanced group worked alone with programed SRA[4] materials. The teachers worked with the slower groups. Occasionally children were assigned to a language game during this period or given individual help. Natalie and a student teacher had decided one day that "Joseph has broken the phonics code, but he doesn't understand what he's reading"; the next morning Joseph was taken by a student teacher for special help with reading comprehension.

The reading groups were a source of some friction between Natalie and her OCT adviser. The adviser thought there should be more emphasis on "experiential reading" and less on formal teaching of reading. An example of "experiential reading" is to have a child dictate to the teacher an account of something he has done; he then learns to read the account which the teacher has printed for him. Natalie had such stories on display in the room. However, she told us that she had made clear when she volunteered for the program three years previously, that she would not give up her reading groups. She was irritated by "the pressure" from the adviser to modify her methods of teaching reading.

When the children finished their reading assignments, they were free to choose another activity. The great bulk of the "free activities" in this room, however, were games, books, or records which reinforced basic reading and math skills. There were only a few more "open-ended" activities—painting, building with blocks, and modelling with clay.

In the late morning there was another class meeting, and this was a time when children who had signed up to do so, "shared" something with the class. Natalie saw to it that all the children participated. For instance, one morning she called on a boy to read his primer, which he had just completed. He did so a little haltingly. She commended him and suggested that he might like to help someone else to read that book later in the day.

After the meeting, Natalie took the children to the playground for a recess. Then they went to lunch in the school cafeteria which was under the supervision of the principal, the assistant principal, and aides. Natalie ate her lunch in the classroom and worked right through the lunch period. Lunch time was when she recorded the children's progress in reading, made anecdotal notes on what kind of work they needed next, and set up the classroom for the afternoon's activities.

After lunch there was another class meeting. Sometimes Natalie read the children a story, but on several days of the week this was her "prep" period. Then the school's language arts, music, or library teacher took over the class. These specialty teachers were the OTPs (Other Teaching Professionals) the principal had told us about: tenured teachers who were confined to covering classes during teachers' prep periods "to minimize the damage they can do."

We could see what the principal meant. Natalie's well-behaved class, to whom she never raised her voice, fell apart when Mrs. Katz came in to do "language arts." Mrs. Katz could not hold the children's attention, and when they began to converse with each other, or to wander off into an activity area, she said harsh things to them in something close to a shriek. The other OTPs were equally ineffective, and equally out of tune with the methods and spirit of the open classroom. They intruded a completely incongruous note into the children's week. The OCT teachers felt guilty about leaving their children with these "specialists"—but they needed their prep periods.

A frequent early afternoon activity for Natalie's class was phonics—another formally taught program for which they were divided into two groups. Sometimes the class did mathematics in the afternoon. Some engaged in simple counting activities; some worked with Cuisenaire rods, beginning to develop arithmetic concepts; and some worked at various points in programed math workbooks. Natalie took great care to see that she had taught the children the concepts they needed in order to do the problems in the workbooks; she always told the child where to stop and bring the workbook back to her for checking.

When math or phonics was finished, the children had the

rest of the afternoon for free activities. Not infrequently, a mother came into the room for an hour during the day to cook with a group of children, to show them how to make hooked rugs, and so on. Almost anything a mother thought she might like to do with the children was accepted with gratitude.

Relationships

The social climate in Natalie's room was warm, relaxed, and cooperative. Children conversed with each other freely and often worked together by choice or by assignment. They gave and received help with their work, and Natalie encouraged this. She treated all the children alike although, like any teacher, she had her private preferences among them. Natalie's biggest complaint was about the upper middle-class children. At a meeting with the OCT advisers she said that she was hearing more than ever from these children that they "didn't want to do" what she asked them to. She mentioned somewhat defensively that an English headmaster from an open school had said in a talk that there was nothing wrong with telling children what to do when necessary. She said these children were "spoiled" at home, and she found them a bit tiresome.

Natalie did all she could in class meetings and in working with the children to encourage cooperativeness. She never set a child in competition with another. Yet the children brought their competitiveness from home—and while it was not a prominent feature of their interaction, they did sometimes make remarks like, "I'm ahead of you in that workbook."

The children's groupings in this room seemed, during observation, to be quite fluid. We were unable to distinguish any firmly established peer groups. The only line of segregation was between the sexes. Ironically, when children are left to group themselves, there is more sex segregation than in teacher-made groups. The children in this class did not seem to group themselves either by ethnicity or by ability. There was one interesting example of "peer effect." Helen Fuentes was a black Puerto Rican girl who barely spoke a word to the teacher during the first month and a half of school. She pretended not to know English, but Natalie could tell that she understood a great deal. Helen had an attractive personality, however, and other children in the room frequently sought her company. Sometime in October she was adopted as a "special friend" by a white, upper middle-class girl named Betsy, who was an exceptionally able pupil. The two girls visited each other's homes and spent much time together in school. Suddenly, Helen began to speak English with other children, to adults, and even at class meetings. She volunteered for special activities, became more and more extroverted, more successful at her work, and apparently much happier. Natalie attributed Helen Fuentes' rapid progress to her friendship with Betsy, and all that it implied in terms of exposure to an attractive, English-speaking milieu.

Analysis

Natalie Roseman's classroom conformed to open education philosophy in some respects and departed from it in others. If one follows her daily schedule, it immediately becomes apparent that the greatest emphasis was given to academic skills and above all, to reading and mathematics. Social studies and science received hardly any attention. In addition, most of the children's time was spent doing teacher-determined and directed activities. Within the appointed tasks, children sometimes worked independently and in flexible ways, but because there were nearly always two, or even three teaching adults in the classroom, teachers could and did oversee nearly all the children's activity. Pupils had only a small part of the day in which to make their own decisions about what they would do.

We have already pointed out that Natalie insisted on keeping her reading groups. In her interview, she insisted as well on the absolute necessity of didactic teaching:

> I think definitely that teaching is necessary. I mean, that's it! I *don't* believe that kids can acquire things out of the air or from materials. If they're learning sounds or words or whatever, when they've finished with that, and with certain instructions, I like to give them a game they can play well that reinforces that kind of skill. But they have to learn it first. I don't think they're going to learn it through the game or doing an activity or something like that. I think doing that is frustrating to the child.

Here Natalie rejected a key portion of open classroom doctrine. From the open educator's point of view, her classroom was also deficient in that there were no continuing projects, based on the pupil's interests, which would have posed new problems and challenged the children to find solutions. Projects of this kind are relied on to stimulate the children's creativity and their analytic capacities. Other open classrooms at Southside did have such projects. One, for instance, took several walks around the school's block with a parent, noting everything they saw, making rubbings of manhole covers, taking snapshots. Then they dictated essays about what they had seen, which the teacher printed, and which became material for learning to read. They were also working on a scale model of the block, which involved some simple arithmatic calculations needed to keep things roughly in their proper size relationships. When nearly all of the class work is organized around such projects, open educators call it "the integrated day." Natalie's adviser was urging her to move in this direction, but again Natalie rejected the suggestion. She told us that the adviser was unrealistic about what could be done in a first-grade classroom because she had never been a teacher herself.* To Natalie, the key tasks of the first grade were to learn reading and beginning arithmetic. Projects were trimmings:

> Maybe later these kids will be ready for an integrated day. But right now, I don't think they are and there aren't enough people around to handle that. I feel that if some kids are doing a science experiment and some are doing a math experiment, it's fine. We do that too, but I think in the beginning they need the structure of beginning reading. Once they got into routines and were reading better, then I wouldn't care so much if they were doing a science thing all day or working on a construction project for two or three days. That's what happened at the end of my first grade two years ago. At the beginning there was much more of this scheduled work.

Thus Natalie showed that she did not trust a considerable part of what open education asserts as true. She did not believe that pupils would learn basic reading and arithmetic in the natural course of problem-solving on projects. Unlike open educators, she thought it was necessary for the children to learn to read as soon as they could—as a prerequisite to other kinds of work.

On the other hand, there were substantial parts of the doctrine which Natalie accepted and practiced. She did not believe in whole-class teaching. Most of the work was done in small

---

*As we explained above, the adviser was, in fact, an experienced teacher.

groups, which took account of the children's rate of development; frequently it was individualized to meet some particular child's needs. Natalie kept careful records of what skills the children mastered and gave much thought to what work she should present each child with next. Group meetings were an important part of the daily schedule. Not only did they serve to enhance communication skills, they provided an opportunity for the children to share interests and to develop an increased social awareness. Their collective responsibility for the state of the room which "belonged to them" was emphasized. In no situation were children invidiously compared with each other. There was actually little competition in the classroom and what little there was clearly came from home. For the most part, the children were mutually friendly and helpful.

Here we see a well-respected teacher (professors of education were eager to have their students do their practice teaching with her), in her third year in the OCT program, with a classroom which was "open" only to a rather limited degree. Further, she was firmly resistant to the advisers' suggestions that she move toward what they defined as more openness. From their standpoint, the most they could hope for was that she would initiate some "projects" during the last part of the academic year. It was most unlikely that Natalie would abandon her firm belief that reading and arithmetic had to be taught as subjects in their own right, rather than as instruments for accomplishing the goals of a project—in the face of contrary suggestions from advisers for whom she had little professional respect.

An Unstructured Open Classroom

Abe Winner's second-grade class had twenty-six children, sixteen boys and ten girls. Six were black, six Hispanic, and fourteen white. As in Natalie's room, the white children were from comfortable, upper middle-class homes with college-educated parents, while the minority children came from homes of much lower income and educational background. When Abe rank-ordered his children for us in terms of reading skill, all the white children, save one, ranked above all the minority children. However, as we noted above, skill and ability are not the same thing. Abe pointed out to us several of his minority children who were poor readers but who, he said, were "exceptionally intelligent" or "ingenious."

Abe welcomed the observer into the class as an "extra hand," because he had virtually no help. The paraprofessional aide assigned to him didn't do her job. He had not seen her in weeks and she did not appear in the classroom while we were observing. Two volunteer mothers each gave a few hours a week, but one of them spoke little English and could only help in limited ways.

Just as Natalie's room reflected her views, Abe's reflected his. He told us that he "wouldn't be caught dead" with reading or math groups because having to perform in front of peers was a "threatening and punishing" experience for a child. He believed that all learning was individual. He also said, "The teacher is peripheral"; children must learn from materials and activities. "The few minutes they spend with me individually is more important than a longer time spent in groups where they would pass a great deal of the time in listening passively, just waiting for their turns."

Abe's room had the reputation of being the noisiest, most disorderly OCT class in the school. Other OCT teachers and the assistant principal, who was on his floor, complained that some of his children ran shouting up and down the corridors and in and out of other classrooms, disturbing everyone. Natalie, who was on the floor below, said, "There are some OCT rooms I certainly wouldn't send my children to visit. They'd come back to me *flying!*" These two had a mutual disrespect for each other's philosophies and practices.

The Environment: Space and Materials

As one entered Abe's classroom, it gave an immediate impression of messiness. There was trash and litter all over the tables and floor. There was also a lot of movement and noise. Children chased each other excitedly around the furniture. The mess was bright and gay, however. Children's paintings were strung diagonally overhead on a clothesline. There were a lot of animals: guinea pigs, mice, gerbils, hamsters, fish, and a rabbit. There was a workbench with tools and material for woodwork. There was a math table with much the same equipment as in Natalie's room, but, except for the balance scale, it was unused during the period of observation. There was also a science table with coral, some plants, a fossil, and some coal—all neatly labeled and also unused.

The room had two playhouses which were used incessantly. One, a rectangle at least six feet high, had openings for door and windows. Nearby in a closet were dress-up clothes for dramatic play. The other house was on the floor underneath the tables, and children crawled in and out of it. There was a closet filled with books and games. The right-hand side of the room as one entered was carpeted and partly partitioned off by a blanket hanging from a clothesline. This was the area for class meetings. The teacher's desk was there, too, invisible under the clutter. Like Natalie, the teacher never sat at it. At the front of the room, the alphabet and a number line were above the blackboard. A peace flag hung there and a motto: "I do and I understand."

The room was not clearly divided into areas for specific activities. Reading could take place anywhere. The left-hand wall had the clothing closets, children's cubbies, and math table. Woodwork was sometimes in the corridor, sometimes in the room. Books and the fish tank were at the back, under the windows. The rest of the animals and the science table were up front. In the center of the room were tables and chairs which the children used for whatever they happened to be doing.

Schedule and Content

The day and the week were no more clearly structured than the space. Perhaps the only routine was that the class usually held three meetings: one the first thing in the morning, one after lunch, and one at the end of the day. The early-morning meeting opened with children reciting the day, the month, and the year. This was often followed by a discussion. The day after Halloween, for instance, Abe asked, "What did you do last night?":

> Robert and Tim said, "We got money. We stole it. And we got all kinds of candy." Another one of the boys said, "I went trick-or-mugging." Manuel reported almost being mugged while he was "trick-or-treating." Frank said some kids pulled a knife on them and asked for their money, and they said "No" and ran.

Here is some real experience which seemed to demand that the teacher respond to it in some way, but Abe ignored it; he said nothing. On one other occasion, when the children talked with great excitement about violence seen on television and in the neighborhood, he got them to admit that they would not like to be on the receiving end of violence. But they continued to talk about violence done to others in tones of pleasurable thrill, and Abe did not succeed in bringing the two sentiments into relation with one another.

Class meeting was also used for story-telling. After lunch Abe sometimes read from *Charlotte's Web*, which was over the heads of many of the children. They occupied their time making faces at each other and fussing with their hair. Frequently Abe used the class meeting as an occasion to teach:

> The children handed him on little sheets of paper guesses as to how much the Halloween pumpkin weighed. He took out the scale and said, "Now I'm going to set the scale so that when I stand on it I weigh two hundred pounds." He had several children check to see that he did. Then he took the pumpkin and he stood on the scale with it and said, "Now I want you to see what the scale says." The children had trouble reading the weight, but finally said it was 241 pounds. So Abe began to go through the papers to see whose guess had been closest. The prize was a lollipop. But many of the children didn't understand what was going on. They kept shouting, "Weigh the pumpkin! Weigh the pumpkin!" Finally Abe did and it was forty-one pounds, but I'm sure the point of the exercise did not get through to many of them. Abe didn't elucidate. This was another manifestation of his disbelief in didactic teaching.

After class meeting Abe said to the children, "Now you may go to your morning activities." On one morning, no more atypical than any other, the children scattered in all directions. Some were doing woodwork. They sawed up pieces of wood, glued them together into "abstract" constructions, and painted them. Other children went and got animals to handle and play with. A few children were building with blocks. Several others were playing in the big cardboard house. One pair was playing a game of chess with quite a group of spectators.

Abe approached individual children and worked with each for a few minutes on a math or reading workbook. Occasionally, a child whom he asked to bring a workbook up to him, didn't do it, and Abe didn't seem to notice.

As we worked with children in their workbooks, we found that often they had gone a dozen pages beyond the point where they understood the concepts needed or the task to be done, and they had done the work randomly. For instance, on a page where the instructions were to draw a line connecting objects whose names rhymed, a child had simply connected every object with another at random. We asked Abe about this, since Natalie was very clear about not allowing it to happen—but his view was different. He said he didn't mind if they went ahead on their own for a bit. "There is always an increment of learning."

Abe had another belief: that a child's errors should always be ignored, rather than corrected, unless the child was exceptionally able and had a strong ego. Apparently there was no such child in the class, because Abe never corrected errors. He gave only positive feedback concerning work, and he carried this to such an extreme that—as he told me—some of the children didn't believe he was a teacher. (It is not clear what they thought he was.) As an illustration, one morning he asked Robert to play a high note and a low note on the recorder he had brought into school. Robert played a high note and called it low, and vice versa. Abe laughed, but made no comment. On another occasion, we were caught correcting the spelling of a word by one of the "faster" children, and Abe admonished us never to correct anything a child had done, and never to give help unless asked for it.

The help that Abe gave when he was asked was often inadequate. One morning Claude came to him wanting to know how to solve the problem: "? − 2 = 4." Abe sent him for the abacus and told him that he must find a number such that, when he took two away from it, there were four left. Then he waved Claude away and turned to another child. Claude looked puzzled. We decided to see what would happen if we helped him. "Take a guess," we suggested. He guessed ten, took two away, and saw that he had the wrong answer. "Take another guess." He guessed five and got the wrong answer again. We plunged in boldly, "Ten was too big and five was too small. What do you think you should do now?" "I'll take something in between." Luckily he chose six and beamed when the answer was right. Then he went on to do some analagous problems using the same strategy.

On another day, we found Nan, one of the brightest children in the class, looking bewildered at a page in her math book which asked her to make up some addition and subtraction equations using the numbers one, four, and five. Nan knew how to add and subtract, and she had seen the problems in equation form earlier in the book. But she was not quite aware of what the "=" sign meant, and she didn't know what an equation was. It took us five minutes to explain it to her, and then she became so absorbed in making up equations that she was reluctant to stop when cleanup time came. Abe did not explain the meaning of the "=" to anyone in the class until two weeks later. Since he insisted on working on a one-to-one basis, and since he had little help in his classroom, there was always a long wait for children to get help from him—just as long and frustrating, we would suspect, as that of children in a group awaiting their "turns."

Here is another example of what Abe's children experienced with their workbooks:

> Verna and Claude were each working in a phonics book doing an exercise I had seen Natalie's children do. They were given endings like "et" and "ot" and asked to put consonants in front of them to make words. Neither Claude nor Verna had any grasp of the endings. Not only could they not distinguish between "et" and "ot," sometimes they went so far as to confuse them with "ing." They did not know what a consonant was. They didn't seem to know the difference between a real word and a nonsense word. In short, they had no phonics skills whatsoever. Within five minutes, they put their workbooks away and went off to sing "The Yellow Submarine" with some other children.

Abe had assigned those two children to those pages, so he evidently had a misconception of their level of skill. We never saw him teach reading skills. He told us that the only way nonreaders would learn to read was "experientially." To that end, he occasionally had us take down two or three sentence "stories" which children dictated and which they were supposed to be highly motivated to learn to read, since it was their own product. Again, Abe rarely had the time to do this himself with his nonreaders, so they either did almost no work at all on reading, or they floundered aimlessly through their workbooks. It seemed to us that, from the children's viewpoint, their failure to gain any mastery—which they were well aware of—was a "punishing" experience.

Abe did not teach the children to care for materials and that, too, made for frustration in his room. Pencils and rubber bands vanished. Equipment was broken. Pieces of puzzles got lost. Children were constantly telling Abe that they couldn't find things they needed, and he invariably replied, "Well then, you'll have to look for it." Very often the children didn't bother since the room was so littered that finding anything would have been difficult. A good many lost things turned up at cleanup time toward the end of the day.

Abe had the virtues of his faults. He was always ready to take advantage of a learning opportunity which spontaneously presented itself. One day when he was reading the class a story with his back to the animals, the children said, "Look at the rabbit!" The rabbit had gotten out of its cage and dug up part of a plant and then gone back in to eat. Abe said, "Let's see what the rabbit is doing." "It's eating dirt." "No, it's eating the plant." "No, it's eating the roots." They finally agreed it was eating the roots and had a talk about what rabbits eat. They decided to try feeding it various things to find out. Abe did not comment on the fact that someone had left the cage open.

On another day, Abe found that some voting machines had been installed in the basement for Election Day. He got permission to show the children how they worked, and that became the basis for a discussion of what elections were.

One project and one on-going activity occurred in Abe's room while we observed it. A clique of upper middle-class white boys worked for several days building a maze for the gerbils. They designed it themselves, and it was very successful. The same group of boys carried on a chess tournament, which was watched with interest by the children who understood chess. The minority children in the room did not understand chess, nor did they seem to take any interest in the construction project.

Abe was eager to organize a rather ambitious project involving the whole class—he wanted to build a boat. But he said that to carry that out he needed the collaboration of another adult and lots of materials he didn't have. The following year, when we had lunch with him, he told us that his class was actually building a boat—without another teacher's help and with materials he had bought himself.

Relationships

Like Natalie, Abe had a warm, personal relationship with his pupils. He often shouted at them at the top of his very strong voice, but not angrily. He was extraordinarily patient with a paranoid, disruptive child in the room whom many teachers would not have been able to tolerate. On the playground, he engaged in a lot of horseplay with the boys, which they enjoyed very much.

Abe was a political radical who wanted to promote cooperativeness and mutual respect in his class and to abolish competitiveness on political grounds. However, his methods sometimes produced a result he didn't like. Consistent with his lack of structure in other areas, Abe let peer groups, at work or play, form freely. He never took the initiative in grouping children together to perform a task. In his classroom, there was a fairly clear-cut division of peer groups, not only by sex, but by ethnicity and ability as well. The white boys associated mainly with each other and so did the white girls, with the exception of a low-skilled one who was an isolate. Black and Hispanic boys intermingled and so did black and Hispanic girls. They formed several cliques, more or less divided along ability lines, as Abe estimated ability. The lowest-skilled boys spent most of their time fighting and playing games which involved a chase. The girls played house and "dress-up" and groomed their own and each others' hair. Abe was not happy about the composition of the peer groups—which he recognized—but he attributed it to the children's associations with each other outside of school.

Analysis

Abe subscribed more wholeheartedly to open education philosophy than Natalie did:

> "It's my belief that the teacher's role in the children's learning is really very minimal. The teacher should observe the children carefully. You learn a lot about them that way. You never spend more than a very few minutes with any one child, but they interact a great deal with one another and with materials, and that's what they do their learning from. They don't learn from the teacher. Anything a child does, which the child feels is a worthwhile activity, you should let him do."

He pointed out that Julio had been in a traditional classroom for two years and hadn't learned to read "because he got yelled at every day. My goal for Julio this year is that he should come to like school. He's really a very bright child."

Here is Julio's account, given at an end-of-day class meeting, of what he had done that day:

> "I had a fight with Manuel in the morning and then I had a fight with Luis. Then I went to recess and I had a fight with Roberto. Then I had lunch. Then I came upstairs and I had another fight with Luis, and he hit me in the eye. Then I played house for a while. Then I had a fight with Manuel and that's all."
>
> Abe laughed and said, "Mrs. Edmond* would be very angry if she heard you say that was all you did today. Was that *all* you did?" And Julio answered, "Yes."

Abe's theory that Julio, though very intelligent, was not "ready" for any kind of academic learning was a self-fulfilling prophecy, because Abe didn't give him any work. But Julio was only an extreme case. Although Abe subscribed to the belief that there was no distinction between work and play in a child's learning, work and play were sharply dichotomized in his room. The play had little or no cognitive content and the work was confined to his occasional whole-class teaching at class meetings, and to workbooks. Abe adhered rather rigidly to some of the more extreme beliefs often found among free school teachers. Children's errors should never be corrected; they should get only positive feedback concerning their work. The teacher should seldom teach and then only when asked for help. Small group instruction is "punishing" to the child who must perform in front of his peers. Basic reading and arithmetic skills can best be acquired by the child through experiential processes and through materials.

Abe seemed to have confused the freedom for children he so passionately believed in, with a lack of structure. Children could not find materials because the materials were in disarray. And the children with short attention spans could hardly have been helped by the absence of routine and predictability in the school day. The little learning which took place in Abe's room took place largely by chance.

In justice, we should say that this was only Abe's second

---

*An assistant principal.

year as an open classroom teacher, and he had been assigned his class on such short notice that he had very little time to prepare the environment. When we saw him informally a year later, his account of his class sounded as though he had adopted the "integrated day"—around building the boat. He was only able to do it, however, by spending a rather large sum of his own money, which he confessed he felt guilty about diverting from his family's needs.

Abe's experiences illustrate the hazards of "on-the-job" training. Abe did not understand that open classrooms have their own kind of structure. He might have been brought to understand this eventually, with the help of an adviser he respected, but in the meantime, his pupils were paying a price for his inexperience. Some parents who did not think open classroom was going well at Southside pinpointed the on-the-job training of previously unprepared teachers as a problem:

> That's one of the things I've been pressing the administration on. Ellen will be leaving shortly. I told them that I would not want to see another on-the-job training. I would want someone who had some previous experience with and practical involvement with OCT, somebody who is already trained to do it.

Finally, we should say that Abe's room was not the most chaotic that could be found in District 7. Natalie assured us that there were some in other schools which were completely out of control. Abe's personal qualities were surely beneficial to his pupils. He was intelligent, warm, and patient. The children loved him and that kept the class in control.

From the standpoint of an open educator, Natalie's classroom was overstructured and Abe's had insufficient structure. Natalie did not have enough "open-ended" materials in her room. She did not permit the children enough freedom of choice. She did not trust the children to learn to read "experientially," but insisted on teaching phonics and comprehension systematically. She refused to adopt the integrated day.

Abe's room on the other hand, didn't have enough structure. Abe took literally those parts of open education philosophy which de-emphasized teaching; he taught very little. Many things were amiss in his room. Neither space nor time was organized so that children could develop stable expectations about their world. His math and science materials were not used because he never suggested to the children how they might begin to use them. The minority children in his class spent their time playing house and dress-up, chasing each other, and fighting. The middle-class children used their readers and workbooks some and played chess. Both groups of children were bored. As one boy said, "Ain't nothin' to do in this room. We done it all."

Abe was alone with his twenty-six children most of the time. Given that circumstance, his insistence on one-to-one teaching, when he taught at all, meant he got to each child only a few times a week. Abe believed that nonreaders, of whom he had several, could only learn to read from their own dictated stories. But he had no time to take this dictation, so the nonreaders received no reading instruction. One girl spent 100 percent of her time drawing pictures, undisturbed. A few children made some headway in their books on their own, but others did dozens of pages in their workbooks incorrectly. We did not see how Abe—with his refusal to correct errors—handled this situation, if and when he caught up with it.

Of the two deviations from an ideal open classroom, Abe, who subscribed more closely to open education philosophy, conducted the less desirable classroom. Natalie's children were learning; Abe's were not.

Sources of Variability in Implementation

These two classrooms illustrate the variability in implementation of open education. One source of these variations is the vagueness of open education philosophy. There are not many clear formulations of it, because its early proponents took the position that all knowledge is idiosyncratic and cannot be communicated. That included knowledge about open education. Others took a position which explicitly promoted variation in practice:

> the "philosophy" under consideration is one particularly partial to pluralism; it supports flexibility in application and encourages individual interpretation of its tenets. . . . Indeed practitioners are particularly wary of any conceptualization that suggest there is an unchanging or transplantable methodology. . . . In summary it must be asserted that Open Education does *not* operate directly from theory.[5]

The other source of variation is the personalities of the teachers. Natalie's class probably reflected her need to be in control of her room. If this is a basic trait of her character, it might prove impossible for her to allow "open-ended" learning situations, which would place unpredictable demands on her, to develop. Conversely, Abe, and teachers like him, may find it very hard to be directive and that, too, could be difficult to overcome.

That character traits help determine how teachers play their roles is not a new idea. In one of the first systematic sociological examinations of the school, Willard Waller talked about the link between teachers' personalities and the authority of the teacher's role.[6] Roland Barth made an analogous suggestion about character traits and the role of the open education teacher:

> Open education is attracting many who find the facilitator-of-learning mantle a comfortable cloak under which to hide—a place where they do not have to reveal themselves or be assertive or directive. Many advocates of open education appear not to have resolved their own authority problems and are unwilling to be, if not incapable of being, authorities themselves. Safe under the aegis of the open educator's role, they resist either becoming directive when necessary or probing into their own difficulties with authority; they identify with the children and see themselves as colleagues in the war against the oppressive administration and less-enlightened teachers.[7]

Of course, many organizations which are engaged in changing people, rather than things—such as mental health clinics, prisons, and schools—are subject to nonuniformity in "treatments" which are supposed to be the same. Nonuniformity occurs because the treatments themselves are usually complex and because both the professional "treaters" and their subjects, being human, respond differently to the same stimuli.

However, open education is especially vulnerable to nonuniformity in practice. Its philosophy is at once vague and encouraging to individual interpretation. On the important dimension of the teacher's authority, it permits readings which vary from suggesting a fairly teacher-directed room to suggesting one where the teacher has abdicated all directiveness.

An innovation which lacks clear-cut characteristics and a clear-cut rationale eventually lends its name to all manner of practices and loses its identity. Open education is particularly susceptible of being interpreted as "let the children do what they please." Abe's classroom came close to that interpretation and so did some rooms in the next school we shall consider. That particular distortion was bound to give open education a bad name—and has.

Chapter 10

Innovation in a Complex Environment

We have recounted in detail the problems faced by two specific innovations which were introduced into Southside. But there are structural reasons why it is difficult to introduce *any* innovation into politico-bureaucratic systems as complex as Walton's school districts. There are many centers of power and authority in the district, and each has some capacity to resist the others. Here are seven examples of such resistance which we have discussed:

1. The first- and second-grade OCT teachers used the OCT advisers to help them get out of the requirement for filling out the district's diagnostic language instrument.

2. The teachers used their rights under the union contract to escape attending individualized reading clinics.

3. The OCT advisers used the implicit threat of expulsion from the program (and probably transfer out of the school) to compel attendance at the meetings they called.

4. The OCT Advisory also used the implicit threat of withdrawal of its services to prevent our entry into another school in the district, after we had obtained permission from all the line authorities as well as the parents' association and Community School Board.

5. The activist parents used their power over personnel to bypass the school administration, and to attack an OCT teacher whose performance they didn't like at an open meeting of teachers, advisers, parents, and administrators.

6. The principal passively resisted the district's Individualized Reading Program. She conformed outwardly at a minimum level, but she did not use sanctions against teachers who openly refused to write individualized curriculum prescriptions.

7. In a nearby school, parents claimed the right to observe and to evaluate teachers up for tenure. The union told the teachers to walk out of the room if a parents' group came to observe them.

With so many centers of influence potentially able to veto policies they don't like, it is far easier to stop an initiative introduced into the system, than it is to start one and keep it going. The district superintendent's attempt to implement a system-wide reading innovation from the top down failed because the principals and teachers were hostile to it and passively resisted it. The district's response to this passive resistance was threats which—given the near unanimity of the negative response—could not possibly be carried out.

OCT was introduced into Southside far more intelligently. The director, Professor Wylie, sought the support of all the major participants. The university-based Advisory gave the teachers access to all its rich resources and provided as well the services of two on-site trainers. Nevertheless, many things went wrong, as we have seen. We were never able to disentangle the contradictory accounts we were given of parental ballots, but—as two of the leading parent activists said—it is hard to believe that all the black and Hispanic parents both voted for OCT and understood what they were voting for. However, these parents largely stayed away from the school and left the field of "parent power" to the upper middle-class white mothers.

We have detailed the problems which the teachers had with the so-called "voluntarism" of their participation in OCT and the hostility of the teachers toward the OCT advisers. We saw how a coalition of advisers and parent-activists was formed and used against the teachers. Instead of mutual cooperation among parents, advisers, and school staff, there was conflict between the teachers, on the one hand, and the adviser-parent coalition, on the other. The principal was somewhere in between, but unable to play the traditional role of defending teachers vis-à-vis parents in public because of the power parents had over her. It was also partly because they knew the advisers were so close to influential parents that the teachers feared them.

While the OCT teachers at Southside were not precisely "closely supervised," they came under the observation of status superiors far more than is typical for elementary school teachers, whose classrooms are usually their castles. The advisers were regularly in the classrooms, and whatever their role was *supposed* to be, they were occasionally judgmental and occasionally pushed hard to get teachers to modify their classroom practices. An example of this was the adviser's attempt to persuade a first-grade teacher to de-emphasize her reading groups and use more "experiential reading." The activist parents were also frequently in the classrooms as volunteer helpers. The teachers said they needed and wanted help. But these upper middle-class white mothers were their status superiors, and also had some power in matters of personnel. The frequent presence in their rooms of status superiors, who had some power over their professional careers, made the OCT teachers understandably tense. That was an unintended consequence of OCT implementation procedures.

Given this difficult situation, we must end our account of OCT at Southside by saying it was remarkable that it was doing so well. Many of the teachers believed strongly in open education philosophy, or parts of it. They used the rich resources of the Advisory at Walton University to keep them supplied with inspiration and new ideas. Of the five classes we observed in grades one, two, and three, all save one were definitely open classrooms, however varied in quality and degree of openness. Due to the genuine commitment of most of the teachers, the innovation had not merely been adopted; it was slowly being implemented.

The facts of this case lead us to infer that the two most important factors in implementing an innovation in elementary school are real commitment from the teachers, and access by them to an adequate support system. For Southside, the on-site advisers did not supply that support system, but the Walton University Advisory did.

PART III

Coolidge: An Upper Middle-Class White Suburban School

Chapter 11

Professional Teachers, Powerful Parents, and Misbehaving Pupils

Setting

Coolidge School is located in Sundale, a residential suburb of an Eastern metropolis. Its population includes some fairly affluent families headed by skilled workers, and some upper-class Protestant families who send their children to private schools. However, it is predominantly upper middle-class Protestant, Catholic, and Jewish. The parents are successful businessmen and professionals. Nearly all the fathers and mothers of Coolidge pupils are college graduates, often from prestigeful schools, and many have degrees beyond the B.A. A good percentage of them live in Sundale because its school system has an excellent reputation.

Coolidge, like the district, is nearly 100 percent white. It has about 440 pupils, which makes it the smallest of the three schools we studied. However, in Sundale it is regarded as a "large" school. The school building is old and far from luxurious. It has a library and a gymnasium, but no auditorium or swimming pool. Despite the town's wealth, the school was unable to

157

get funds to have the classrooms painted. Instead, they received funds for the paint and held a Saturday "paint-in" where parents and teachers painted the inside of every classroom.

The teacher-to-pupil ratio at Coolidge was about one-to-twenty-five, but the prestige of the district attracted a great many student teachers, so the adult-to-child ratio in the classrooms was more like one-to-twelve.

Role Relationships

The Principal as Professional Leader

Coolidge was known in Sundale as a "graveyard of principals." The principal before the last had been transferred, because, according to several informants, the parents did not find him "polished" enough. The last principal had been transferred out of the school due to pressure on the district from the faculty, who claimed she was having an emotional breakdown. Dr. Alan Williams was only in his second year as principal and, not surprisingly, was apprehensive, especially about his relations with the community.

Unlike the principals of Johnson and Southside, Dr. Williams was an instructional leader. Whereas elementary school teachers usually feel that their principal's observations of them are too brief to be more than superficial, the teachers at Coolidge felt that Dr. Williams' observations were keen and the feedback he gave them was valuable. For most teachers in the school, the feedback was positive and supportive:

> He often says what a good job he thinks I'm doing. He comes in and watches things going on. He seems pleased; he reads the things the kids write. You know, he just does get involved in what's going on. He has a feeling for the classroom, and he's expressed his approval of what we're doing.

In the few cases where he thought a classroom was not well-run, Dr. Williams gave critical feedback. He told the teachers of the fifth-sixth-grade open classroom team that their rooms needed more structure, that he wanted skills directly taught, and wanted reports on children's progress in the skills. He also wanted the anecdotal reports to the parents to contain more discussion of skills.

Dr. Williams delegated considerable authority to his faculty. He created many committees, and every faculty member was on at least one of them. He appointed two teachers, respectively, as the Coordinator of Primary Grades and Coordinator of Intermediate Grades. Faculty meetings carried on full and frank discussions of important issues:

> If he wants to make a policy decision on something, he'll set up a committee or bring it up and let people volunteer to form a committee. A lot of the decisions he doesn't feel he has to make alone. He is not power hungry in any way. I think he basically trusts teachers; he basically likes the teachers and feels a lot of confidence in them.

The teacher who said this added, "But he does also make major decisions." Dr. Williams took the responsibility for the decisions he alone had the authority to make, like firing an untenured teacher.

Williams told us he felt that the professional development of teachers was his most important job. He encouraged talented teachers to go to workshops, to develop their administrative bent, and to leave for greener pastures whenever they had the opportunity, even though their leaving was a loss to the school. Coolidge could always replace even a superb teacher, he said. The teachers emphasized that this was a very unusual role for a principal to play vis-à-vis his staff:

> He also, within this school, keeps teachers informed professionally in a way which I have never seen a principal do. If an interesting workshop comes up—he knows I am interested in going to workshops—he will send it to me. If he comes in contact with someone who needs a workshop done in one of my areas, he will mention me. Then they ask me to come and do it for them because of his recommendation. He has exposed me to a lot of people who have made my life more interesting, which is very rare, I think, for a principal within a school. So he is professionally very helpful to teachers.

In one respect, Dr. Williams was an enigma to some members of the staff. He had written several widely read articles on open education, and many people who had heard of the articles, but had not read them, perceived him as an all-out advocate of open classrooms. He was not. Not only was his writing critical of many aspects of open education, he tried to make clear in the school his view that there are good and bad open classrooms, as well as good and bad classrooms of other types. On one occasion, he distributed a reprint of an article making this point, to every teacher in the school. He told the teachers that he wanted Coolidge to have a diversity of classrooms, and that he wanted them delabeled. He also tried to make the parents perceive each classroom as unique. However, many teachers and parents, who either wanted the school to go all-out for open classrooms or feared that possibility, didn't "hear" the message. They were puzzled by Dr. Williams' behavior. He warmly supported some open classrooms and was critical of others; and he supported equally strongly many classrooms in the school which were not "open." This appeared contradictory to those who didn't understand his views.

Dr. Williams opened up the school to parents in a way that his immediate predecessor had not. The PTA was reactivated. The school published an informative *Blue Bulletin* which went to parents monthly. Parent volunteers came into the school to help in the library. Small groups of parents and teachers met in school each week for informal conversation over brown-bag lunches.

At the same time, Dr. Williams had to spend a large portion of his day in his office talking with individual parents who had complaints. They came in a steady stream, and this was a source of anxiety for him.

Professional Teachers

Sundale's reputation for excellent schools meant that it was able to select its teachers from among large numbers of highly qualified applicants. As a result, it had an excellent staff. In the same spirit that Dr. Williams showed, Sundale district administrators treated their teachers like professionals. For instance, the district developed curricula in many fields and at all grade levels, but it did not require that these curricula be used:

> We don't have a set-up that says to teachers, "These are the things you must do. Come June this is what you're supposed to have covered." No. We don't do this. We never have. But there are things *available* for teachers to use. And they use them according to what they feel is best for the group of youngsters they

are working with. The schools are quite different from one another. In some buildings the kinds of curriculum materials they use may be very different from what is used in other buildings.

In a sense, this failure to prescribe curriculum produced a problem of continuity like that we observed in Johnson. However, at Coolidge the problem was not thought serious because the teachers were so skilled, and because the students were, in general, at a high level of achievement. Every teacher was considered competent to choose curriculum appropriate for her class. Even if a topic were repeated, the child would be doing it at a new level, and it would not be redundant. Dr. Williams said:

> My feeling is, if each teacher really is capable of observing kids and getting a lot of information from that, and providing something definitely in advance of where the kid is, that's the best we can do. You would think there would be problems, for instance, with one teacher doing a unit on water in the first grade, and then again, two years later, someone else is doing a unit on water. There is a lot of revisiting of topics going on around here, but I haven't heard complaints from kids or teachers. And I'm getting less and less from parents. I think they feel confident that the child's teacher knows what to do and is doing it well.

The Sundale district recognized its teachers' professionalism in many ways. Each teacher received an instructional budget of $300 annually to spend as she saw fit. Each teacher also got three "professional days" off a year to use for professional self-development. The district had an annual budget of $22,000 to make small grants to teachers who wanted to experiment with something.

Coolidge teachers had, in the past, played a major role in changes of school policy. For instance, they had an important role in the abandonment of the old report card which graded students as "above average," "average," and "below average" on a list of academic and social skills. The checklist was replaced by a written anecdotal report to the parents, the contents of which was decided by the teacher:

> We had to check off "above average," "average," "below average." "Above average" compared to *what* was the issue. And

nobody could seem to agree. Was it above average compared to
other kids his age? Or kids in his grade? Or kids in Sundale? Or
kids in the state? Or national percentile? Or what? It didn't mean
anything. And lots of us thought there had to be a better way. So
we had a committee work on it—what we could do to change our
evaluation system. We had several meetings with parents. Small
groups got together and talked about the system that was in effect. Then we had a large meeting at one of the other schools in
Sundale. It was in their auditorium that the faculty presented its
findings about what we would like to see. Some parents were opposed to eliminating grades. But we decided on a parent-teacher
conference as the report mechanism. We got approval from the
School Committee. After the first year, the parents expressed a
lot of concern that they wanted to see something in writing. So
we began writing the conference report and sending one copy
home. That's how it all came about.

On another occasion, it was the teachers who decided to
give up homogeneous ability grouping. Since the IQ's in the
school ranged roughly between 118 and 145, ability grouping
meant that "children who were above average regarded themselves as dummies." Besides, the teachers said, they researched
the issue and discovered that homogeneous ability grouping did
not yield better results, according to the best existing research,
than heterogeneous grouping. That being the case, there was no
justification for keeping it.

A third policy decision made largely by the teachers was to
drop the formal teaching of grammar:

We had a meeting which was a very hot debate about the teaching of grammar in the elementary school. It sounds like a boring
subject, but it brought out a great deal of anxiety and hostility on
the part of the parents who felt we were neglecting something
very basic. But we had speakers to present the points of view—
really of the teachers who have dropped teaching grammar.
There are one or two who still do it. I don't know how many
parents we influenced. But regardless of the meeting, nothing
was changed so far as policy went. The policy of not teaching
grammar in any formal way was *explained* at that meeting rather
than decided.

Thus, not only did each teacher have a great deal of autonomy in the conduct of her class, teachers at Coolidge had a
lot to say collectively about the pedagogical policies of the

school. Both the Sundale district officials and the principals of Coolidge treated the teaching staff like professionals.

Pupils: Upper Middle-Class Misbehavior

We have already mentioned the high IQ test scores of Coolidge children. They were a homogeneously high-achieving group. This did not mean that the teachers considered them ideal pupils. On the contrary, most of the teachers found that the students engaged in a lot of distasteful behavior. For one thing, they were rude to the faculty:

> Elizabeth Trudeau said she'd been in the school nine years and the rudeness was not new. She said that from what she observed, the pattern of rudeness was established at home, where the kids push around the domestic help in the absence of the parents. She was saying that the children treat the teachers like domestic help in the home.

A student teacher who was working in an open classroom and favored its philosophy nonetheless felt it bred rudeness in the children:

> I think there comes a point where the amount of flak that you are willing and able to take from kids begins to outweigh the benefits of the open classroom. At first, the rudeness, the disrespect with which the kids treat the teacher starts to grate on your sensibilities. You're thinking that these kids are spoiled, but I think it also starts to wear away on the classroom itself. Those kids are so rude that it makes it difficult for me to care about them. I think the open classroom is a breeding ground for rudeness. I think that when we tell children, whether we tell it to their faces or whether they feel it from the classroom environment, where we tell them that, "We think you are important. We respect you. We respect your opinions. We respect your capabilities. We think you have the capacity to decide for yourself what you want to do"—what we're basically saying is, "You are equal to us." But, in fact, they are *not* equal to us. There's no question about it. They're not equal to us in size. They are not equal to us in knowledge. And there are ways that they try to make themselves feel equal, when we tell them they are, when, in fact, they are not. And one of these is by being rude and flaunting their own attempts to be equal. That rudeness probably comes very much from home, but I still think it's a valid point to say the open classroom breeds it.

Another problem was that the children had no respect for property. They vandalized and stole both school's and each others' property:

> The children went down to the library. A volunteer mother came over and told them that the chessboards and the record player and a lot of the games that the children had enjoyed had had to be removed because a small minority vandalized them and stole them. She said, "Until all the children in the school learn to handle materials properly, we are going to have to take them away from you."

A second example of stealing from our field notes:

> While I was in the coatroom next door, it seemed someone in the class had had some money stolen from her. This resulted in a lot of accusations and innuendoes all around the room as to who stole what. A lot of children were demanding that everyone be searched, and the children were really trying to pin the blame on others. Later, the teacher told me that a lot of stolen money was returned to her in the course of the day.

The children were often cruel to each other. They engaged in less physical aggression than pupils at Johnson, although fighting among boys, especially after school, was not infrequent. More often, their aggression was verbal and entailed social exclusion, which was very painful to those excluded:

> A teacher said the kids can be vicious to each other. She told me a story of a kid who had been trying to break into a clique. One day he tried to join them at a table. They addressed themselves to each other, saying things like, "I don't see any room for another person here, do you?" She said the kid stayed home for about three weeks after that. The children were very clever and articulate, and it made them doubly poisonous when they attacked someone.

Another complaint by the teachers was that the children were "unappreciative" of the many special advantages which the school made available to them:

> A student teacher claimed the kids should have been excited about the presentation they saw on Renaissance musical instruments. She was very disturbed that they weren't. Beverly Rose tried to explain to her that they come from an environment which is culturally very rich. They go to concerts, and some of their

parents play musical instruments. They have a lot of records at home. So this was not a novel experience for them, which explains why they didn't get excited.

Most teachers in the school held a negative assessment of their pupils: They were arrogant, dishonest, aggressive, and blasé. A few teachers attributed these negative qualities to the fact that so many of the students were Jewish. The teaching staff was predominantly gentile, and it shared in some small degree the genteel anti-Semitism which the old, upperclass, Protestant residents of the community felt, and expressed by sending their children to private schools, and excluding Jews from their clubs.

However, there was a minority of teachers who dissented from the negative view:

> What those teachers said is not my opinion. I have never seen any more motivated kids. I've never seen kids work harder. I've never seen more intelligent kids, more education-desiring kids. I've worked with thousands of children in my life. I've been working with kids since I was fourteen. I've never seen a group of kids like this. The school is crawling with talent.

The Power of the Parents

The parents of Coolidge pupils had a history of dissatisfaction with the school which ran through several administrations. They were noted for the fact that they frequently took their complaints over the head of the principal directly to the superintendent or the School Committee:

> Of course, it's an old thing with Coolidge School. The parents around here—the minute anything happens, it's a crisis, and they run right away to the school superintendent or the School Committee. There are other schools around that have all the problems we have, the same problems, and the school district never hears about them. But these parents are always raising Cain, and it's been that way for a long, long time.

That Dr. Williams was sensitive to this reputation is illustrated by the events connected with a sex-education program. The PTA had voted for a sex-education program and had a committee which was working on it. At the same time, Mrs. Stuart, the fifth-grade open classroom teacher, was attending workshops in sex education. She was one of two teachers who was to run the program for the fifth and sixth grades. Sometime during the year, Dr. Williams was informed by a horrified member of the PTA committee that Mrs. Stuart had spoken approvingly of a workshop where the leader said that masturbation was all right. Dr. Williams told us:

> The handwriting was on the wall. The parent committee really didn't have confidence in the personnel who were going to do it. And they weren't sure about the program either. I figured if they, as advocates of sex education, weren't sure that these were competent teachers to talk with their children about masturbation or whatever, I was sure as hell the rest of them weren't. So it was a situation where a number of the parents clearly wanted no sex-education meddling of any sort. Others wanted just a sort of plumbing and nuts and bolts on anatomy. And others wanted a lot of affective counseling and stuff. And there is no line there to walk. I talked with a couple of School Committee people, and I said, "What will you do when 10 percent of Coolidge parents blitz the School Committee on this matter?" They said, "Well, maybe you should wait another year before you try that." That's all I needed to hear.

So Dr. Williams announced that there would be no sex-education program for that year. The teachers would give factual answers to questions pupils asked, but for the rest, the school would leave sex education to the homes.

The teachers, too, were constantly apprehensive about what parents would think. At one faculty meeting, there was a discussion as to whether the cast of *The Mikado* should be automatically released from their classrooms for rehearsals on Friday afternoons. The teacher-director asked his colleagues to release them. Some said they would. Some said they would, only on condition that the child was not behind in work assignments. Several suggested that they should telephone the parents of each member of the cast, to find out whether they wanted their child to be released from the classroom to go to rehearsal. Dr. Williams vetoed this, saying, "Let's not make a big issue out of this with the parents. Let's settle it ourselves."

A third illustration of parent power had to do with a fourth-grade teacher of the previous year who conducted an open classroom which was described by most people as "far out." He taught no skills such as reading and mathematics, unless children asked him to. This behavior is a part of "free school" doctrine going back to Summerhill. By October, so many of the parents with children in his room had asked that they be transferred, that the teacher would have been left without a class, and other fourth-grade rooms would have been overcrowded. Dr. Williams told the parents he couldn't make the transfers, but he fired the teacher at the end of the year.

Unlike the district officials and the principal, the more aggressive Coolidge parents were *not* respectful of the teachers' professionalism. As one teacher said:

> The parents around here think they know all about elementary education. They don't know anything about it, but they hassle us all the time about what we're doing.

And another recounted a put-down at a PTA meeting:

> Parents feel very free to come in here and challenge our credentials. I was called a civil servant and told I was not qualified to teach math. At which point, having tenure, I said, "I find that offensive," and walked away. I wouldn't have done that four years ago. I probably would have cried.

Yet, although he walked away on this occasion, the same teacher told us on another occasion how he accommodated to parent pressure concerning his teaching of math:

> The kids know a lot of math conceptually. They know all about place value and number systems, base ten and base eight, and some with different bases. And they end up liking math very much. But we don't force them to memorize the times tables and so on. They would eventually get that by osmosis from the math games they play. But the parents come around and say, "Yes, yes, but what about the basics?" So now I'm having them memorize the tables to satisfy the parents.

Dr. Williams summed up the power of the parents in a fairly strong statement. He said, "I really think the parents have *de facto* veto power over policy and personnel in the school."

In sum, the staff of the Coolidge School was the most competent of the three staffs we observed, and probably among the most competent in the country. The administration of Sundale School District and the principal of Coolidge treated them like professionals. They had more autonomy in their work than school teachers are usually granted. More striking, it was they—the teachers—who often initiated changes in policies which had to do with questions of pedagogy.

On the other hand, the school's clientele consisted of highly educated parents who did not believe that elementary education required any special expertise. They did not hesitate to pass judgment on it. They could and did bring pressure to bear to get rid of a principal or a teacher. They could and did get rid of a proposed curriculum unit, like the sex-education program. They could pressure a teacher into changing the way he taught math, against his better judgment. Their power also had some indirect effects. It led the teachers to put up with more rudeness from their pupils than they might have accepted from the children of families which were poorer and less politically powerful in the community.

In short, the best, most professional staff of teachers in our study were found in a community which also had the most powerful, educationally involved parents. And the power of the parents was the major threat to the teachers' professionalism.

In their study of school-community relationships, Litwak and Meyer have discussed the need for a balance in the relations between school and community which allows for community input, but does not threaten the staff's expertise.[1] Often the problem is that the parents are almost completely out of contact with the school, and the school must make intensive efforts to involve them. Litwak and Meyer don't say so, but it is well-established that this most often happens in the case of low-status parents who are intimidated by the school staff.

The opposite problem is one of too much intrusion into the school, by parents who want to take over some of the staff's professional prerogatives. This is most likely to be true of parents of high status, such as those in the constituency of Coolidge and some of those at Southside. In a case like this, it is an error, according to Litwak and Meyer, for the school to cultivate linkages with the community which bring the parents into very close relationship with the school:

> In some suburbs where parents are closely involved with the school and tend to disrupt professional activities by their too close scrutiny of the teacher, the use of communication via mass media may create a more distant and better balanced relationship.[2]

If Litwak and Meyer are right, Dr. Williams made a strategic error. He revived the PTA; he instituted the brown-bag, faculty-parent lunches; and he encouraged the use of parent volunteers. Thereby, he brought parents who were already intensely involved in their children's education, into a still closer relationship with the school. We shall see in Chapter 13 below that the parents managed to take over some of the faculty's prerogatives, and this caused great tension inside Coolidge.

Chapter 12

Innovation at Coolidge: Open Classrooms

The Innovational Input

The Sundale school district was very receptive to innovation. For more than twenty years, it had been in the avant-garde of educational change. Here is a description of those years from an interview with an assistant superintendent:

> I think I can go back to the early 1950's. I think Sundale was a rather comfortable place in which to teach. There wasn't the pressure there is now. Then, with Sputnik, we shifted into new math, the new sciences, and so forth. As a matter of fact, we designed a new social studies program, too. As I look back on it, we were sort of caught up in the various academic disciplines in this period. But Sundale was very much involved in the new— everything. That went on for about seven or eight years. There was a real start of a movement toward open classrooms beginning in the mid 1960's, then a real jump into affective education, then a sloughing off of the cognitive, I think, really frankly, in the late 1960's; and all through this tumultuous period, when we proliferated the student choices, we were more concerned about how humane the atmosphere of the school was. And now we're in another phase. I don't think any of us know what is really happening. I think we're beginning to turn back to a little more concern with what kids are actually learning and what they should be learning, and maybe moving off from the romantic push we were in.

The initiative for open education in Sundale came at first from teachers, who began opening up their classrooms on their own. The district was quick to respond to the teachers' new interests. As an administrator in Program Development described it:

> It really came from the teachers. Teachers began doing things in their classrooms or listening or reading or getting involved in

studies outside the system, taking workshops or what not. Some of the new teachers were coming out of school with open education training or at least some exposure. Then we started offering workshops ourselves because of the teachers' concern for this kind of classroom.

From the first, open education was a highly charged issue in Sundale:

Open education really came into the foreground about three or four years ago. People began to talk about it a lot. Some people became excited about it. Some people became very frightened.

Because the Sundale district never required its faculty to teach in any particular way, the personnel director said she was just about certain that no teacher was conducting an open classroom who didn't genuinely want to. However, even under these circumstances, an element of perceived, if not real, coercion might creep in:

Teachers are not pressured into having open classrooms, but you might find them *feeling* that they are. About half the primary rooms are now open. There's a lot of it going on, and when something spreads to such a point, teachers seem to get the feeling that they're under pressure from the district or their principal to do it.

Introduction of Open Classrooms into Coolidge

Open education was introduced into the Coolidge School in the way typical for the district. One primary teacher became interested in it at the school where she took her Master of Arts in Teaching. She first tried to implement what she had learned on her own:

The first year I was here, there were three classes in this room (formerly the auditorium), but for the first half of the year, each of us ran her own traditional classroom. It turned out that two of us were very much interested in open education, but the third girl was not at all. By February the two of us changed the room around in such a way that we shared the space and began to set up learning centers on a very limited basis. We had a little money, which we spent on things we felt were vital, like sand and water. We made a lot of our own materials and all our games.

> When we went into individualized reading, we bought the books
> with our own money, because the money we were given was not
> enough.

Later, she got help from the Sundale workshops:

> That spring Sundale put on its own workshop in open education.
> They gave it for fifty teachers, and provided substitutes in our
> classrooms so we could have a whole week off to do it. The two of
> us participated. Then that summer there was a follow-up work-
> shop. Then the following year, by choice, we had a kindergarten
> and two first grades in here because we wanted a K–1* grouping.
> By the middle of the year, we had changed the room around in
> such a way that there was one center for everything. There was
> one art area, one science area, one reading area. It worked very
> well.

Despite the fact that it worked well from the teachers' point of
view, there was opposition from the parents and the previous
principal:

> The first year we did it the parents had a great deal of apprehen-
> sion that the children were never going to learn to read. We got
> called all sorts of names, like a "zoo" and a "barnyard." The prin-
> cipal we had then was against it, but we just stuck it out. Then
> Dr. Williams came, and he has supported us all the way. Now we
> have a K–1–2.

Dr. Williams supported both open classrooms and classrooms which were more teacher-directed. He hired both kinds
of teachers. One young faculty member hired by him came to
Coolidge with good training in open education. She taught a
second-third-grade class. The fourth grade had had two open
classroom teachers the year before we were in Coolidge.
However, as we have already mentioned, one of them was fired
at the end of the year due to parents' complaints. The other, an
Englishman trained in open education in Britain, had also been

*Combining grade levels, as into a kindergarten and first grade, or a kin-
dergarten, first, and second grade, is called "family grouping." The practice is a
part of open education in England. It is a kind of limited nongrading which
permits children to move ahead at their own pace and also allows for a great deal
of teaching and learning to occur between children. In a K–1–2, only one third of
the group changes each year. The "old-timers" in the classroom give the teachers
a lot of assistance in socializing the newcomers into the way things are done.

severely criticized by parents and had "closed up" his room to protect his job. Of the two members of the fifth-sixth-grade open team, Nancy Stuart had had some open classroom training at the teachers' college where she took her Master's degree. Her young teammate, Manny Levine, had had no open education training of any sort. He said he just "made it up as I went along."

At Coolidge, when we observed, there was one open classroom at every grade level except the fourth—and at least two classrooms at each grade level which were not open. This pattern of organization, which might seem ideal in the light of our discussion of Southside, where no choice was provided for parents or teachers, actually caused great difficulty. The next chapter discusses these problems. This chapter takes a closer look at Coolidge's self-designated open classrooms. We already know from both Johnson and Southside that the same label can be attached to very different classes or teams. Again at Coolidge, we found variability in the implementation of open classroom doctrine. But more important, we found something which we had not noted at Southside, possibly because we were now more experienced observers of these kinds of classes. Open classrooms at Coolidge usually did not maintain social fluidity. Rather, they developed peer groups with strong boundaries, the more so the older the children were. The same thing happens in the "traditional" classroom, but in them the functions of the peer groups are more nearly confined to the extra-curriculum. In open classrooms, where children are permitted to choose their own associates for most activities, the peer groups often become the task groups as well. They take over many of the functions of the "traditional" teacher; for instance, deciding what work to do and how much of it. The results are first, the emergence of interpersonal skill as the main basis of peer leadership, second, a "hidden curriculum" which makes popularity with one's peers the highest value of the pupils in the day-to-day functioning of the class, and third, peer-determined norms which limit the output of academic work.

While the second-third-grade classroom and the fifth-sixth-grade team we shall describe differed widely in their conformity to open classroom doctrine—the second-third-grade classroom was a much better example of the type—both classes were strongly affected by the concerns of their pupil peer groups.

Carol Stone's Multiaged Second- and Third-Grade Class*

Carol Stone and her two student teachers[1] had a class of twenty-four pupils, disproportionately made up of the children of doctors and psychiatrists. There were only two children in the room who were not upper middle-class. One of them was the daughter of a domestic servant, who was so embarrassed by that fact, that she met her mother at the end of each day in front of the post office to avoid having her appear at the school grounds.

The classroom contained a rich variety of materials. Its space was divided into clearly defined areas, each used for specific activities. The children's work was kept in folders on the teacher's desk. Cuisenaire rods, Dienes blocks, math and language arts games, science and art materials all had definite places where they were stored. The walls, ceiling, and windows were used to exhibit children's work. There was an exhibit on American Indians, another on gerbils, a picture of Pegasus with a story to go with it, displays of the children's paintings and mobiles, and a window with their straw dolls pasted to it.

The physical arrangement of the room took into account the fact that small children do not like to sit in chairs all day. There are really only a few activities for which tables are required. Thus there were only a couple of tables to work at. There were three carpeted areas with dividers. One was for the class library. Another was the place where the children used math "manipulatives" and math games, as well as checkers and chess. The rugged areas were protected enough to keep children from disturbing each other's activities as they moved through the room. The traffic patterns had been carefully thought out. There was also a large, three-sided, painted box, with the open side facing a wall, where one to four children could sit isolated and protected from the rest of the groups. It provided an opportunity for being alone and out of sight of the teacher.

Carol had no consistent daily schedule, but there were a few regularities which provided continuity and prdictability for the children. As is common in open classrooms, a class meeting

*This classroom was observed by Laura Schorr and described in a first draft by Diane Levin. The final writing was done by the author, partly from Levin's paper, and partly from Schorr's field notes.

was held at the start of each morning to discuss the day's activities, class problems, and special events. For example, Carol might use this time to explain some new materials and how they worked. Another meeting was held after recess to help the children focus again on classroom activities after the excitement of the playground.

The other consistent element running through the schedule was the weekly work assignments. Every Monday, assignments for the week were distributed in folders to each child. Carol made up the assignments individually, no two pupils being assigned exactly the same work. The amount of work, type of work, and level of work were determined by Carol's conception of the child's ability and emotional needs. Children who had a hard time doing academic work had less assigned to them than those who did it easily. The work included math, reading, language arts, and projects. Children had until Friday to complete their assignments, and were themselves responsible for arranging their time so it would be completed by then. Part of the idea behind this procedure was that the children should learn to budget their time.

However, the system did not work altogether smoothly. One difficulty was that about seven children—nearly a third of the class—were unable to work independently or with other children. A few could work for a while with an adult, but others seemed unable to work at all. Carol explained that these children came from problem homes and had emotional difficulties. She tried to take such difficulties into account in assigning work to them. However, this created the danger of a self-fulfilling prophecy. Carol gave less work to children who were either less able academically than others, or under emotional pressure, and by thus expressing her expectation that they couldn't do much work, she actually made it harder for them to experiment with how much they could accomplish.[2]

The open education teacher is supposed to "diagnose" what level of work a child is ready for by observing the child. There was evidence that Carol made several errors of diagnosis. She gave some children work that was too hard for them and others work that was too easy:

> The pages showed different amounts of dollars and cents. Jack was supposed to count them out and write them down. He went through it very fast. Actually the work wasn't up to his capacity.

> He was doing it so rapidly and easily that it was clear he could have handled much more difficult material. He seemed bored by it, but the teacher said he had to do two pages.

And on the other hand:

> Some of the children have been given "Reading for Concepts" books, and they have just dropped them because they couldn't do them. I have heard them say several times, "Well, I don't know how to use it, so I just don't use it any more."

One very bright child told the observer that he did his work very slowly over the course of the week, because if he finished early, he'd be given more work. On the other hand, one of the girls in the class completed her week's work in two days by doing some of it at home, and then luxuriated in having the rest of the week free for activities of her own choosing.

On Friday, the folders were collected. Children who had not finished were not permitted to do anything but their assignments until they were completed. Nevertheless, when we looked through the folders there were some enormous differences in the amounts of work they contained. Some were crammed with work, others had less, and some had almost nothing in them.

Carol's schedule allowed for flexibility so that special activities could occur without disrupting the children's work. And Carol provided a lot of special activities. There were frequent films. Visitors came in to share some expertise with the children; for instance, a mime, a clarinetist, and an architect. Children went on field trips to learn about some current topic. On one occasion, they went to the computer center of a nearby university.

While Carol's class was given constant exposure to the academic skills considered important for second and third graders, no single teaching method was employed. Children got a wide variety of language arts experiences ranging from comprehension readers and phonics activities to creative writing, dramatics, and charades. A very frequent activity was to have the children dictate stories which one of the adults in the room wrote down. (In addition to the student teachers, there were frequently volunteer mothers in the classroom.) Because of this diversity, children had a wide variety of ways to gain a specific academic skill. This is in keeping with open education theory: children learn best when the same skill or concept is reinforced in many different ways.

Carol helped the children explore many topics in small groups or individually. These might be called interest groups. Thus, some children explored Greek mythology; others observed the changes in a tree outside the school, recording them through photographs; still others studied musical instruments. One girl did a project on moss. Two boys did one on different types of slingshots as weapons. Carol tried to integrate science, math, reading, and art into each of these projects. Children were encouraged to observe, question, and explore. Carol understood open education as helping children to formulate questions about the world, which they then tried to answer.

Carol spent a lot of her time moving around the room acting as a "facilitator" of learning: telling a child or small group how to use a particular material appropriately, suggesting a new activity with some material, giving new information, asking questions, teaching a new skill. She constantly brought in new materials and offered new starting points for skills and projects. For instance, she brought in seeds for the children to plant and at the same time, put up an exhibit on the structure of seeds which included cards for the children to write down what they had done and what was happening to their growing plants.

Carol believed that children also learn when the teacher is not directly teaching. However, she did not feel it was all right for a child to spend all of his or her time on one kind of activity for a long period. Rather, she thought children needed a wide variety of experiences, and she tried to see that they got them. Carol was helped in doing this and in making up her individualized assignments by the careful records she kept. For each child, she had "academic" record sheets where she wrote down what the child had done in math, language arts, social studies, and science; and "social-emotional" record sheets in which she took down observations of the child's social behavior. These records, combined with the child's folder containing his work, gave her a picture of every individual pupil.

In the realm of interpersonal relationships, Carol encouraged collaboration among the children. Children often taught each other. There was no stigma attached to a child's not knowing a skill. Rather, the norm was that children who knew something had the responsibility of teaching it to those who didn't. This is one of the important aspects of the multiage classroom. The teacher utilizes the children's wide range of skills to have them teach each other.

If this were a full account of this class, it would seem an excellent example of the open classroom, except for the large proportion of pupils who were doing no work. However, it is not a full account. All through the period of observation, the children were carrying on an underground life of their own, largely on the playground, but also in the classroom, which preoccupied them at least as much, and probably more, than the "official" activities. It was a life filled with competition and aggression, both verbal and physical. There was an intense struggle for control of a "fort" which the boys had built on the playground. They would not let "outsiders" in. Outsiders included all girls, everyone not in their class, and some boys in the class who were unpopular with the others:

> The fort consists of pieces of wood leaning against each other like a lean-to, with hay all across the top, like a house, and rocks along the side. Then there is an opening for children to crawl in. Actually, by the time other classes came out, there were about ten boys working on it, and there is only room for two or three inside. It has great symbolic value for the boys building it. Connie was totally ignored, and she was really angry. She said, "It is not fair that the girls are not allowed on this territory. It is not their territory. It is the school grounds, and anyone should be able to go there." I saw Lenny conferring with Sam. Lenny plays up to Sam a lot. Lenny was telling them, "Remember, we built up the fort and the fourth graders wrecked it. Now they think the fort we are building is theirs. We are going to attack them." Jimmy said, "Well, I'm ready to beat up anyone who comes over." They were really spoiling for a fight. Then John came and said, "Can I see Sam about joining the fort?" Lenny said, "You can't see Sam without an appointment." Connie threw a fit. "That's really crazy. You have to have an appointment to get into this fort." A group of fourth-graders came over and a fourth-grade boy said, "You wrecked our fort, so we are going to wreck yours." The boys in the class said, "No, we didn't wreck yours; it was ruined by the rain." The fourth grader persisted, "We are going to come back and wreck your fort." Carol's boys were very upset for a while.

The fort was the center of many episodes. Girls who tried to gain entry on one day were physically attacked by the boys, knocked to the ground, and had their coats torn off—in winter weather. The teacher in charge of supervising the playground at the time did not interfere. She said the girls enjoyed having the boys chase them. But the observer felt that many of them were frightened and some were physically hurt by these attacks.

A competing fort, built by a challenger for the leadership of the boys, caused a great many quarrels about the stealing of building materials and accusations about deliberate destruction of each others' handiwork.

Carol did not seem to be fully aware of the complex peer-group ramifications involved in the struggle for possession and leadership of the fort. She did know, however, that the children had taken exclusive possession of a part of the playground which belonged to the whole school. Several of the children pointed out that this was not "fair." Carol's style, in playing the role of the teacher, was never to give orders but always to discuss, explain, and persuade. She used these techniques to try to correct the situation, but to no avail. And she seemed incapable of simply asserting her authority to do what needed to be done. Instead, she allowed these aggressive children to keep their exclusive fort, taking advantage of the whole school, until the wind and the rain finally blew it down, and the children became absorbed in something else. This is the kind of teacher, extraordinarily reluctant, and even incapable of asserting authority, who, as Roland Barth pointed out, is disproportionately attracted to open classroom teaching.[3]

Another observation we made about this class was that popularity with peers and working hard academically were negatively associated:

> Sam does very, very little work, even though he is the most popular boy in the class. (He is the leader of the fort in the playground.) The boys who really do the most work in the class, Richard and Peter, and the girls too, Pam and Shirley, are not the most popular. Richard is well liked by everyone, but he is very much a loner. Larry, who does almost no work, is also among the most popular ones.

Thus the anti-intellectual student culture described by Coleman for high schools[4] is already present in the second and third grades, at least in this school. But the main point is that peer group subcultures are more important in open classrooms than in traditional ones. In traditional classrooms, work is individual; peer groups carry on their activities during recess, athletic periods, and other interstices of the school day. In the open classroom, children are permitted for most of the day to work with self-chosen groups. This means that the peer groups invade and influence the central dynamics of the classroom and affect the children's work in fundamental ways. That will be even more apparent in the next class we discuss.

A Fifth-Sixth-Grade Open Classroom Team

Nancy Stuart's fifth-grade class and Manny Levine's sixth-grade class were teamed. They occupied rooms located at right angles to each other in a corner of the second floor corridor. There was no connecting door between the rooms, and since the fifth and sixth graders were not separated for most of their work, there was a constant flow of children through the corridor from one room to the other. Nancy specialized in teaching language arts and Manny taught math. Social studies was handled by one of the two student teachers, and science was not taught at all during the period of our observation.

By contrast with Carol Stone's room, or the K–1–2 open classroom at Coolidge, Nancy's room showed a great dearth of materials. There was a two-tiered loft where children could sit, play, and read. It had been built by a shop teacher with the help of some pupils. There was a pyramid-shaped castle, the walls of which displayed children's writing. There were some art materials and a class library. There were cages for the hamsters and gerbils, but the cages were not well-made, and the animals kept escaping and dying in closets and other hiding places. Some placards on the walls suggested topics for stories children could write. There were two TV sets, a phonograph, and some tables and chairs. The space was not organized in any discernible pattern, so that activities would be clearly located in certain places, and traffic flow through the room would be facilitated.

The only new materials Nancy brought into the room during two and a half weeks of observation was some colored tissue paper. She showed the children a collage of fir trees in various shades of green and yellow that she had made by cutting out the tissue paper and mounting it on a white board. She said she was going to prepare some tissue paper and board and show anyone who wanted to learn how to do it.

Manny's room was a bit smaller than Nancy's. In the center, running from front to back, were three tables with chairs around them. A carpeted space on one side of the room was surrounded on three sides by mathematics games on shelves. Another little space had Manny's desk. There was a third space, a kind of alleyway made by a wall between the classroom and the clothing closets, in which children often sat on the floor and worked. The room had a display of mathematics books and math problems and puzzles on cards. There was a calculator as well.

Toward the back of the room was a box of miscellaneous materials—tools, fabrics, paper, foam rubber, styrofoam, nuts, bolts, buckles, and electric plugs—from which the children made diaramas in shoe boxes.

Manny's room was often overcrowded because the fifty children on the team spent more time there than in Nancy's room. This may have been due to the fact that the tables and carpeted spaces were well-suited to working in groups. The room was also tidier than Nancy's, which had a lot of trash on the floor, closets left open, and materials left around in disarray.

The team organized its work around a contract system. Each week each child made a contract with one of the teachers to do certain things. The children wrote the contracts themselves and had them approved by a teacher or student teacher. A typical week's contract had five tasks on it: "1. Write a story. 2. Draw a picture of anything. 3. Play chess. 4. Read a mini-library math book. 5. Do a math problems card." Another contract read: "1. Read two books and do a project in connection with one of them. [That usually meant doing an illustration for the book.] 2. Math project. [Unspecified.] 3. Work in recycle center. [This was the center with all the materials.] 4. 'Yellow.' [This meant playing a certain math game with another student.] 5. Write a story. 6. Work with Arthur. [This was a learning disability specialist who came to the school regularly.] 7. Fix room. 8. Work with arithmetic." A third contract read: "1. Chips [a math game] and this was marked 'Finished. I played with John.' 2. Read a book and do project. 3. Play Quinto. [Another math game.] 4. Make a maze for the hamsters." This was marked "Looks OK to me" and initialed by a student teacher.

We calculated that these contracts took up a little less than half the children's school time during the week. They went to gym classes, music classes, and art classes and had an afternoon

of optional activities. Once or twice a week they received whole-
class lessons in mathematics, and they also worked as a class on
"Man, A Course of Study," the well-known elementary school
social-studies curriculum.* Any remaining time the children
had, and they had quite a lot of it, they were free to do what
they chose. The classrooms didn't offer many possibilities for
constructive independent work. There were several flourishing
business enterprises going on among the children, which the
teachers knew about and didn't interfere with. Some children
drew pictures to order and sold them for a fee. Others bought
and sold baseball cards. One boy constructed an ingenious spin-
ning pointer on a dial which his clients spun for a fee; where it
rested there was printed a "fortune" for the client. Some
fortunes were catastrophic and some were wonderful, but all of
them were funny.

Children did not write their contracts individually. Rather,
the members of a clique all wrote their contracts together.
Sometimes there was cheating. For instance, a girl trying to
curry favor with a popular child said to her, "I wrote a report on
the kidney. You want to read it? You could put a report on the
kidney in your contract and copy mine." It might seem surprising that the children could get away with this, but they could
and did, because their teachers did not check carefully each
week to see that the work in the contract was done. Rather, they
"took the kids' word for it" that they had completed their
contracts. Manny told us that the children were truthful and
trustworthy about this, but observation revealed that many of
them were not. Many were not mature enough for the responsibility the loosely supervised contracts put on their shoulders.
And others were not inventive enough to keep themselves occupied. One of the student teachers observed:

> I see a number of kids who are just sort of swimming around aim-
> lessly all the time. Certainly not a majority of them, but enough
> of a minority so that I think this is a question of great concern.
> Maybe it's something inherent in the open classroom itself which
> requires a larger teacher-to-student ratio.

This contention, that open classrooms require a high adult-
to-child ratio, was reiterated many times to us by open
classroom teachers. Without at least one adult for every twelve

*Created by the Educational Development Center, Newton, Mass.

children, American open classrooms[5] do not seem to work. At least those we observed which had a lower ratio than that—like Abe Winner's class at Southside—were often disorganized.

A form of neglect that Nancy and Manny's pupils suffered was that their teachers hardly corrected their spelling, punctuation, or grammar. The children's writing was filled with errors to a degree quite surprising for their age, intelligence, and background in reading. The more formal fifth- and sixth-grade classroom teachers did correct such errors systematically, and it was our impression that their pupils' writing was more correct than that of the open classroom team. We do not believe it was so much a scruple about not stifling creativity, as sheer laziness, which kept Nancy and Manny from correcting the children's written work. Here are some examples of their writing from an exercise which was a blank page headed; "I felt, I was, I am, I did, I learned, I improved, I experienced, I wish, I can, I tried, I overcame, I started, I finished, I know, I . . . .":

> this year I think I did pritty good. it was fun this year and I learned a lot of things in math and soashal studies. I did finish a lot of [s]peed math tests and I go[t] [a] fare number of them right. My contract work it satisfis me but I wish I had more freinds in schoo[l]. tried to do some things that other kids did to see if I could make some more feinds but it didn't work. I feel like every time I walk in to the room every body walks out and never want to do any thing with me. and that is all I can say for this year.

> This year I learned new kinds of math. But I did not improve in multipucation then I did in the Beginning of the year. I'm allrite in social stuids the Part I liked most was the Babons. I like the new class myths its rely fun. Im rely lousy in spelling as you can see. And same with my pucuation. contracs are fun most of the time I get them in late But I dont think Ive gotin any 8 ball notes. I love optionals on wed. They class I like the most is FolkDancing and this is my second time Before that I taoke weaving and folkdancing in writing I get good idears for storys But I never write them down good one story I wrote was about a candy maker who Bad a candy rocket that was one of the Best story I ever did in this class this year

> This year was pretty good. I learned about the salmon and the Herring, gulles and the Eskamoes in social studies and the classes were pretty good but Gabriel [the student teacher] kept on taking a fit and we never got anywere. I also like talking about myths and how they were maid up. Miss Marks teaches myths and she's

really nice Gabriel teaches math and so does Mr. L. but Gabriel teaches most of the time.

I think that this year is my best and I really like Mrs. S. and Mr. L. We have contracts and my contracts I think are pretty good. but some times I can't finish them in time and I get really frustrated. I am not so good In math or reading. in fact Im terrible. Some times my contracts don't get finished by Wednesday and I get scared I'm going to have to com back. I have never come back and I never got a 8ball note.*

This year I have met a lot of new Friends and this is the best class because all the teachers arn't like teachers There like Friends and that why I like this class. We have optionals and they are really great but the optional that I like best is the one I'm in now Entering Adolesens and it's great when we talk about having babies. I have done some book projects that I think are pretty good. And have had a wonderful year! ! ! !

I wish I could start the year over
I ttried to do better and projects
I was scar ed tha last weeks because of the play
I know that 6th grade is fun
I started I think with better projects
I did great thingstoo like. .the puppet show my ABC book,
Dictonairy vocabulairy I am happer I felt sad at the begging of the year
I can do a fractions I overcame being scared
I experienced being yelled at a lot
I finished my cross number puzzle book
Mrs. Stuart said I improved behaveyor
I learnd how to make a teacher mad

Both Nancy and Manny said in their interviews that affective goals for pupils were as important to them as cognitive ones. An example was an agreement they had with the mother of one girl that they would try to help her overcome her excessive dependence:

Julie came up to Mrs. Stuart and pointed out that a piece of furniture had half collapsed. Mrs. Stuart said, "Julie, I think you had better do something about that." Julie went and fixed it; it was quite easy to do. The next day Julie asked Manny for some rubber bands and he said, "You know where they are. That helplessness of yours is what your mother and I talked about."

*Apparently an 8-ball note was given by one of the teachers to a pupil whose contract was not finished on time. The pupil then had to stay after school to finish it. We never saw this happen.

A floating substitute teacher in the school described to us how Mrs. Stuart once had a fifteen minute discussion with the class about the feelings of a boy from whom something was stolen. Nancy felt the child was upset and that others had had similar experiences; it was important to get these feelings out in the open and talk about them. Mrs. Stuart was particularly skilled at leading such discussions. On another occasion, after we had delineated for her the sociometric structure of the team,* she decided to talk about cliques with the children. She began by asking them what was nice about having "special friends." The children talked a good bit about this, and then, spontaneously, they moved over to the question of what was "not nice" about their cliques. They mentioned the pain of exclusion. They mentioned their own unkindness to outsiders. They mentioned the fact that they often hid their own true opinions in order to conform to the majority view in the group. Mrs. Stuart did not draw any moral. There was no need to. The children themselves concluded that they had been grossly unkind to some new transfer students, who were excluded from the cliques simply because they *were* new.

The cliques also reported some of their norms of behavior. One girls' clique prescribed dungarees and body shirts as the sole acceptable costume for its members. A boys' group required each member to insult all the others once every day, and the insulted party was supposed to come up with a fast and witty retort. Games of ritual insult like this occur in many cultures. What this boys' clique at Coolidge did, resembled in many respects the way the black children at Johnson played "the dozens." In both cases the "winner" is the person judged by the audience to have been coolest, fastest, and wittiest. However, youngsters at Johnson frequently "lost their cool" and got into a physical fight in the classroom, corridors, or playground. Boys at

---

*Sociometric structure is a term sociologists use to describe the pattern of cliques, of isolates, and of popularity in a classroom, depending on the answers to questions such as "Whom do you like best in the class?" "Whom do you like least?" "Whom would you most like to have as a partner on an art project?" etc. We did not ask sociometric questions until after we had observed for a while, and then we did it as an interview with each child, rather than a paper-and-pencil questionnaire. Today there are some computer programs for deriving the sociometric structure of a class from data like those we collected in this team. We, however, used the answers to the questions only to check whether the groupings we observed day after day reflected fairly accurately the pupils' verbalized feelings of mutual attraction and dislike. They did.

Coolidge were more likely to maintain their aggression at a verbal level, though not always. Sometimes, a boy who went too far was "creamed" on the way home from school.

Nancy and Manny worked more closely together than many of the other two-person teams in the school. In the nonopen fifth-grade team and the nonopen sixth-grade team, the teachers simply divided up the subject matter and each taught the two classes his or her own way, without consulting the other party, except for occasional chats about individual pupils. However, the very closeness of their collaboration created certain difficulties for Nancy, or so she said. She complained that Manny, who was in his mid-20's, was very immature:

> He's a baby. And I find that very difficult. Up until this year he used the children for his own ego gratification. He was very dependent on their love of him. One day a girl who was in love with one of the boys told him a dream she'd had and he told it to the other kids and he had her sobbing. He played into emotions that he should not have played into with preadolescent children. He used to do that kind of thing all the time.

In contrast to the K–1–2 teachers and the 2–3 open classroom teacher, who spent evenings and weekends planning for their rooms and their pupils' work, neither Nancy nor Manny did much preparation. Nancy said she did some planning on Tuesday and Thursday afternoons when the children had gym or art or music. But she never brought work home, except for the writing of anecdotal reports to the parents, because she had her own two children who needed her attention. Manny said that he taught "off the top of my head."

Peer Group Functioning in the Fifth-Sixth-Grade Team

As one reads philosophical accounts of the open classroom, one gains the impression that children choose their activities individually, that those who have made the same choice form a temporary task group which dissolves when the activity is over, and that new groups re-form easily around new individual choices.

This suggests great social fluidity in the open classroom. The sociometric literature tells us that young children are more fluid in their social groupings than older children. However, one of the K–1–2 teachers at Coolidge told us about very strong peer groups in her room:

> In last year's first-grade class there was a group of boys who were the closest thing to a teenage gang at the age of six I've ever seen. It was unreal. They were totally exclusive. Unfortunately, they were all very strong leader types whom other children like to emulate. We had enormous problems with children being very unhappy who were not included, and the group was being very nasty, very cruel to other children. This year we broke them up. We separated them. Now I have another situation this year which is a group of second- and first-grade boys who are just super kids. Everyone wants to be their friend. There are some children who are very unhappy that they are not really good friends with them. But they are not unpleasant; they are not nasty. Their support of and help to each other is just phenomenal to watch. We just try to use what happens constructively.
>
> Question: "In what way?"
>
> Answer: "We can use some children's desire to be friends to structure the situation so that they are at least communicating."
>
> Question: "Do these peer groups present a different problem in open and traditional classrooms?"
>
> Answer: "Absolutely. In a traditional classroom they are there, but nothing happens within the classroom. It's mostly kept on the outside. In the informal classroom they are there in the middle of the classroom all the time."

Each clique on the 5–6 team had a customary gathering place. This territory, which was usually a certain table or corner of the room, performed the same function for the children as the street corners they frequent perform for young adult gangs; they made it easy for the members to find each other.

The members of a clique collaborated on their weekly contracts. Children in each clique took care to sign up for roughly the same amount and kinds of work. The norm for a "fair week's work" was indicated by such comments as, "If you put that in, it will be too much." It was indicated too by the comparisons among children of the number of pages of original writing they turned out each week and by the gentle or not so gentle razzing of members who had done "too much." We validated the existence of "output norms" by examining the contracts themselves which, rather than being individual, were strikingly alike for members of the same clique.

The fact that self-chosen peers did most of their work together on the 5–6 team had several consequences. First, the members helped each other. This was a desired outcome, except when it degenerated into feeding each other "right" answers. Second, tasks which were meant to be individual became a group product—like writing a poem by having each member contribute a few lines. Third, and most important, there were large chunks of time when there was no clear-cut division between being "on-task" or "off-task."[6] The work was carried on simultaneously with purely social conversation. For instance, a group of girls sat around "their" table. One was writing a book report; one was reading a book; one was drawing a picture; and one was doing a cross-number puzzle. As they worked, they discussed a slumber party they were planning for the following week. In the background there was rock and roll music on the class phonograph. The attention of each member of the group fluctuated continually between the work and the conversation, with the background music also claiming some attention. The children seemed able to fulfill contracts in a way acceptable to the teachers, while working in this manner. There is some question in our minds as to whether children who have worked this way for several years can easily learn to work any other way; viz., with their attention fully concentrated on the task. They seemed to be acquiring a trained incapacity to concentrate their attention. On the other hand, they were learning to work with others.

The larger and more enduring the peer group, the more likely it was to have a differentiated internal structure, with a leader and a hierarchy of influence and prestige. The main criterion of leadership was interpersonal skill. Popular children were described as being "nice," "never mean," and "never letting you down." When very popular leaders were observed for a while, it became clear that they were helpful to and supportive of their followers. In order to be helpful, they had to be good at activities valued by the clique. One leader of a girls' clique was good at drawing and gymnastics. She was "pretty" and "into" boy-girl relationships. Above all, she had the requisite interpersonal skill. These criteria are like those Coleman described in

The Adolescent Society.[7] However, in the open classroom this girl's leadership extended to academic work. She was asked for her judgment of their work by clique members who were academically her superiors. On one occasion a girl in the clique complained to Manny that more work was expected of her than of the leader. Manny explained that that was due to the fact that she had greater skills. But the girl persisted in regarding the teacher's demands as "unjust."

Boys mentioned athletic skill and "being a good kid" as the criteria of popularity. The importance of interpersonal skill among them was demonstrated one day in art class when each clique was working on a large painting. In one of these groups the outstanding artist at first took the lead in deciding what they would paint and how. But because he could not organize the activities of the others successfully, he quickly lost his place to the usual leader of the clique.

As in the 2–3 classroom, academic ability was not a criterion of popularity for either boys or girls. Best-liked youngsters tended to do little academic work, and youngsters who did a lot of academic work were not liked. Output norms were set by peer groups, and they were low.

This last point was an aggravated issue at Coolidge in the fifth and sixth grades. Teachers and students in the nonopen fifth- and sixth-grade rooms both claimed they did much more work than the 5–6 open classroom team. Teachers and students on the team insisted this was not so. It seemed to us that it was so, but the explanation was uncertain. Since Nancy and Manny did not work very hard themselves, that might have been a sufficient explanation of why their students didn't work much either. It is possible too, that at the 5–6-grade level—which is very cliquish in any case—the centrality of peer groups in the open classroom, and the intense preoccupation of the preadolescent cliques with the requisites for social success, make it likely that pupils will do little academic work if the teachers let them get away with it.

While the fixed rows of seats in the traditional classroom encourage individual—if not individualized—work, the open classroom makes it somewhat difficult for a child to work alone. The degree of difficulty varies with the ratio of space to number of pupils. Open classroom teachers recognize the need for places in the room where a child may have some solitude and privacy, but it is not always possible to provide them in overcrowded rooms. Even when they are provided, the child working alone must be capable of doing so surrounded by intensive social interaction.

Not all children in an open classroom are members of a peer group. Among those who are not, it is necessary to distinguish between loners and isolates. Loners are children who prefer to work alone most of the time, but who are attractive to their classmates. We encountered several such loners at Southside. Usually they were highly able youngsters who did not wish to be pulled toward the peer groups' mediocre norms of achievement. They were liked because they emerged from their invisible shells periodically, and made themselves available to help others with work. Loners seemed to be left alone when they wanted to be, partly because what they were doing was too difficult for many others to share and partly because they gave off signals which indicated when they were ready to be approached, and when they were not. When they wanted company, they did not hesitate to take the initiative in seeking it. They knew they would not be rejected.

Isolates are children who are rejected by others. The isolate is the victim of verbal and sometimes physical aggression. He can often be seen on the spatial periphery of a group watching, listening, and attempting to participate.

To be an isolate in an open classroom is more painful than it is in a traditional classroom, where the life of the peer group does not color the whole school day and nearly all of the work. One newcomer-isolate on the 5–6 team clung to the teacher for the support which was not forthcoming from his classmates. He was a good student who, out of ignorance of peer group output norms, did "too much" work. He read 500 pages one week. The teacher publicly praised him for this, thereby worsening his situation with his peers.

While this particular isolate overproduced, it was more common for isolates to "underproduce." At first they were preoccupied with their social problems. Later they became depressed about those problems and the depression made working difficult. Maurice Gibbons and Katherine Cobb, who conducted an open classroom in English at a junior high school and wrote about it as participant-observers, suggest that the need for companionship in the open classroom is so basic that compatible persons should be imported into the room if necessary for such children.[8]

All of the open classrooms at Coolidge were strongly affected by the children's peer groups. In the 2–3 classroom and the 5–6 team, we observed this for ourselves. In the case of the K–1–2 team, we had the teacher's testimony that it was so. Yet the range of problems which peer groups can create are not discussed in the literature of open education. Open classroom teachers vary in their awareness of peer groups and their effects. Some know quite well what the membership of the groups in their rooms is, and others, like Nancy Stuart and Manny Levine, do not. Some, like the K–1–2 teacher at Coolidge, are aware of both destructive and constructive effects that peer groups can have, and they try to manipulate these as best they can. However, they are also aware that there are limits to what a teacher can do in influencing peer groups. "You cannot legislate a friendship," as the K–1–2 teacher said.

Our hypothesis, deriving from these observations, is that children's peer groups take on added importance in the open classroom over and above the importance they have always had in school. In particular, to the extent that they are also the task groups, social considerations tend to interfere with and override considerations of academic effectiveness. Time after time, we saw children whose skills for a task made them the natural leader of the group for that task, displaced because the group would follow only its established leader. It happened to the best artist of the 5–6 team, when the task was to paint a mural. It happened when academic leadership was ceded to the most popular girl in the main girls' clique on the 5–6 team, although she was inferior as a student to many members of her group. In addition, in a classroom where much of the work is done in small groups, rather than individually or by the class as a whole, the child who is a social isolate not only lacks *social* companions, he has no one to *work* with and sometimes, thereby, is rendered unable to work at all.*

---

*The reader will recall that this happened to a pupil at Johnson, who was isolated from her table for a while, as a punishment.

If our hypothesis is correct, open education has consequences not intended by its practitioners. By allowing children
to group themselves spontaneously for work as well as play, they
have admitted into the classroom—in the form of strongly organized and stable cliques—powerful social forces which are
neither understood nor controlled.

Chapter 13

The Conflict over Open Classrooms

Tension over Teaching Styles

On our very first visit to Coolidge, we were interviewed by Dr. Williams, who asked us to describe to him in detail what we wanted to do. We said we wanted to look at some "open" and "nonopen" classrooms at the upper elementary grades. Dr. Williams immediately told us that we were not, under any circumstances, to present our project as a comparison of "open" and other classrooms. In fact, he didn't want us to use the term "open classroom" at all in discussing our project with the staff. As he said this he turned to the school psychologist and remarked jokingly, "They think we're paranoid and we are."

On our second day in the school, Williams had arranged for us to meet with some fifth- and sixth-grade teachers to discuss the possibility of observing in their classrooms. We took care to comply with his instructions. However, the first teacher we talked to told us we would never understand the school if we stayed in the fifth and sixth grades, because "the split in the staff over open education runs through the school from top to bottom." A sixth-grade teacher whose room we visited for an hour asked us what kinds of things we wanted to observe. We mentioned peer groups. We remarked that it was interesting, for instance, that when she gave her pupils a chance to change their seats at tables all the shifts were in the direction of segregating girls and boys more completely. Miss Callas snapped, "The same thing would happen in an open classroom."

So the fact that there was tension in the school over open education made itself apparent from the first moment we were there. Later we learned that there was tension over the issue among parents as well. Dr. Williams' insistence that we avoid the term was part of his effort to minimize conflict by defining

193

each classroom as unique rather than as an exemplar of one of two types, "open" and "not open."

In this chapter we shall examine the cleavage concerning open education within the school and among parents.

Cleavage in the School

In the light of our discussion of Coolidge policies—such as the shift to an anecdotal report card, the dropping of grammar as a subject, and the abolition of ability grouping—it should be clear that when we talk of cleavage we do not mean cleavage between open and "traditional" classrooms. There were no traditional classrooms at Coolidge. All the classes were at least mildly progressive. The whole school practiced a relaxed discipline. Projects were commonly used as a medium for teaching. And most pupils had a certain amount of choice in their work.

Just as the open classrooms were variable, so were the others. However, despite the principal's efforts to delabel them, there were some teachers who called their classrooms "open" and others who did not, and within the school these labels were widely accepted. We followed these common understandings in our interviews.

The teachers of nonopen classrooms usually commented negatively about open education:

> I can't see when children really learn skills in an open class. I don't believe this stuff about how the children can teach themselves. They are trying to tell me that another kid could teach division as well as I can. I've been in teaching for thirty years. A child has 106 hours during a week, twenty-five of which are devoted here, not to play, not to fooling around, but to learning. If we are not here doing our jobs in front of a class teaching children skills, we have no business here.

> It seems to me that the kids in the open classroom are playing all the time. They never seem to be working. I'm right next door, but I don't know for sure what's going on.

On one occasion a teacher conducting a discussion during a Wednesday afternoon "optional" encouraged a student to criticize the fifth-sixth-grade open classroom team:

> A boy said there was a great difference between the classes downstairs, the nonopen sixth grade, and Nancy and Manny's

team upstairs. Miss Callas said, "Oh, what? I really want to hear this." He said, "Well, when I walk upstairs, it is like a party; the music is blasting and there are kids just sitting around together." Miss Callas asked, "Is it just during recess?" He said, "No. It is going on all the time. They just sit around and have a good time."

All the open classroom teachers we interviewed expressed their awareness of the critical views surrounding them:

> She said she believes the kids in our classroom are allowed to do nothing if they choose to do nothing. We were talking about Charles Stevens, whom they were having trouble with, and she said she would never recommend that he be put in a room like ours. If a kid wanted to sit and look at a gerbil all week, that's all he would have to do. There are no expectations of the children in our classroom. It's just a free-wheeling circus. That's simply not the case. But she believes it is.

> I think that the problem is that when you have alternatives like this, which noboby planned but just sort of happened, there isn't acceptance. It's like a Mexican stand-off at this point. Which way is it going to go? It frightens people. Maybe these people are worried that it's somewhat of a trend in education today and they are going to be out. Maybe they think we're more on the inside track. Maybe they think we're having more fun or something, like Rebecca saying to Harry that my class was nothing but a zoo.

> There are a lot of people who still have total misconceptions about some of the things we do in here, whose idea is that the children all day long do exactly what they please, which is very far from the fact.

In the upper grades at least, the tension among the teachers carried over to the pupils. The children were very much aware of the differences between classrooms and had a variety of feelings about it. One girl expressed a preference for the more structured kind of room:

> Louise said she was in the open class last year and hated the freedom. She said she likes to be told what to do.

Another pupil, a boy, was ambivalent. He liked the greater choice of the open classroom, but he claimed it was sometimes hard to work while surrounded by such intense social activity:

> I have a problem. I think this class is better because there's more to do. You can do a math card; you can do different kinds of math.

> If you're in Mr. Seligman's class, you have a sheet in front of you and that's all you have to do. Sometimes it's easier to do something in Mr. Seligman's class, because if you're trying to do it, you don't have somebody next to you who's talking to you all the time you're trying to do it. And that makes it easier to do. Sometimes here I end up in the coatroom just to get a little bit of privacy.

The children in the more structured classrooms accused the open classroom pupils of doing less work than they did:

> Tania came up from downstairs to visit her friends. She was having a conversation with them and also with Mrs. Stuart, and she said, "Well, I know you do some work here, but you don't do nearly as much work as we do." The kids in the class defended themselves and said, "That's not true. We work very hard. We do just as much work as you do, maybe more." and Mrs. Stuart said, "We do. It may not look that way, but we really do a lot of work here."

A teacher with a fairly formal classroom commented:

> I've had kids in Elizabeth's [nonopen sixth grade] room say things to me about Nancy Stuart that you just would not believe: She's a horrible teacher. She doesn't teach. The kids are not learning anything up there. They spread this around. They say it freely. And I just wonder to myself, "What's the problem?"

There were differences between open and other classrooms in behavioral norms for pupils which, trivial though they might seem, created a potential for conflict. For example, children in the open classrooms were permitted to snack all day long, whereas in most other classrooms they were forbidden to eat except at lunchtime. In the open classrooms the children handled the gerbils and hamsters and were even allowed to carry them to special classes, like art class, whereas in other classrooms they were not allowed to touch the animals. In the open classrooms the children had background music on the phonograph constantly, even while they were working, whereas teachers in other classrooms allowed the phonograph to be played only at special times. In the open classrooms, children worked with self-chosen partners, so that cliques were always together, whereas in the other classrooms teachers broke up the cliques during work periods, because they saw their socializing as an interference with the task. A student teacher in a nonopen room pointed out how these differences became a problem for the teachers:

> The freedom which some teachers allow their children, which perhaps a more traditional teacher won't allow, is felt by the kids very strongly. They say, "Mrs. So-and-So lets her kids play with gerbils. Why can't we? Mrs. So-and-So and her hamsters in the creative writing class. Why can't we?" The teachers feel this. I mean these issues are "So-and-So's class plays music all day, and I won't let my kids have music on while they're doing arithmetic." These are conflicts.

An example of the tension generated by such different standards came up at a faculty meeting which tried to reach agreement about rules for pupil behavior in the corridors:

> Someone said something about not letting kids play ball in the corridor. Someone else suggested a rule against running or shouting. Alice said she objected to playing in the corridor for two reasons. First, because parents came through the corridor and saw the children playing there and then went out and generalized about how the children at Coolidge spend their time playing. Second, it disturbs other classes. Beverly said she objected to Alice's first reason. But she accepted the second one. She said, "If I stop this kind of activity, I have to explain it in some way to the children and justify it to them. It really is kind of weak to say that it looks bad to the parents, but you are on solid ground when you tell them it disturbs other classes."
>
> Lillian said that on occasion she stopped Bill's kids from playing ball in the hallway. She sent them in to tell Bill why, but they didn't tell him. Manny said, "Children's attitudes come from home. The school can't change them. I will tell kids to stop running in the hall, but they will continue to do it." Lillian said, "Not if you have a teacher in every corridor to stop them," and Manny retorted, "Then we would become policemen."
>
> After a while they seemed to be nearing a consensus that there should be a rule against running or playing ball in the corridors. But the fifth-grade open teacher said there were some people not present who used the corridors for just that purpose, and they shouldn't pass such a rule in their absence. Some people protested, saying, "What is the point in talking for hours if we can't reach a binding decision?" It was left unclear as to whether they had agreed on this rule or not.

At this meeting the majority of teachers wanted a rule against running or playing ball in the corridors, but some open classroom teachers opposed the rule. It proved impossible to reach a consensus, and the two groups left the meeting feeling quite irritated with each other.

It was the cumulation of such small irritations which built up bad feeling in the school. The open and nonopen classes had mutually inconsistent expectations for pupil behavior. On the whole, it was the nonopen teachers who seemed to feel that their discipline and their work demands were in danger of being undermined by the freer discipline, and what they supposed were the lower work demands, of the open classrooms.

Cleavage among Parents

We have already recounted how one open classroom teacher whose methods angered many of his pupils' parents was fired the year before we came to Coolidge. Other open classroom teachers also felt a good deal of pressure from parents and were put on the defensive:

> It was very unpleasant last year when we went through a big hassle. There are still a lot of people who don't believe their children learn to read in this kind of room—that sort of thing. And we've done some pretty serious looking at some of the allegations. I think the allegations are unprovable, which is one of the things that makes all of us feel uncomfortable. "My child did not learn to read in the open first grade and he's learning to read in a much more structured second grade." That's true. I don't question that for a minute. But I do say that we aren't looking at everything if we simply say, "You guys didn't teach him to read and whoever is teaching him in the second grade is teaching him to read." I contend that particular children wouldn't have learned to read in the first grade anyway, that it took age maturity. It took the kind of attention our reading consultant gives to second grade, not to first grade. So there are a lot of extenuating circumstances.

In our interviews with parents we found both criticism of open classrooms and support for them. One of the chief complaints of the critics was that open classrooms give pupils more choice than they are mature enough to handle. Mothers felt that children would choose easy things to do or would too often choose to do nothing:

> I don't think at all that I approve of the open classroom where

children are just trotting around making choices all day long. I think the children are barraged with too many choices. I've found, in observing my own children, that they need some limits put on and some help in their different choices, and I think that we make a mistake if we think that children at ten or eleven can make sensible choices all day long. It's no service to them.

The child does not have the maturity to determine what is optimal for their eventual growth. Give her her choice and she'll major in basketweaving or cooking. I would too, at that level. The point at this level is to get yourself disciplined so that later on when you are faced with a choice of schedule, you can schedule intelligently, first filling in your basics. They're giving the kids the whipped cream without giving them the meat and potatoes first.

I think he's in a classroom where he does what he pleases, and he happens to be the kind of child who needs to be told what to do and not to be, you know, just given choices and allowed to do nothing if he feels like doing nothing.

One mother said that having to make choices was anxiety-provoking for her child:

She likes structure. She prefers structure. I think she feels very pressured, even a little frightened, by having to figure out what to do by herself and decide for herself whether it's the right thing to do.

Another common kind of complaint about open classrooms was that their academic standards were too low; the teachers didn't teach; and the children weren't learning basic skills:

My philosophy of education is that the public schools are there to teach youngsters how to read, write, and compute. And in open classrooms they are not learning that. That's it. Period.

He is not learning how to do the basic fundamentals. He is not confident of his skills. If he is asked to do some paper work, he is not confident of his ability.

I don't think very much of the class. Unfortunately, the permissiveness is a bit much. True, I realize that children today don't sit in school and fold your hands and have this dictator shouting at you. It's a different way of living today. But I feel that a great deal of their work is done out of workbooks. My son, in particular, has expressed a desire to be taught. In other words, he would like someone to stand there and say, "Now today we're go-

ing to do such-and-so," instead of having to make out a contract
himself for what he's going to do during the week.

I have a feeling that there's a sense of accomplishment lacking.
Perhaps it's the fact that what they do accomplish they are given
too much credit for. I mean their standards aren't high enough.
You know, "You can do a whole lot better, Sara, if you just try a
little harder and finish the job." That's the sort of thing I would
be inclined to say to her. I'm rather hard, I think, in my estima-
tion of what they should do and what they actually accomplish.
I'm not too happy about it.

One mother with a son in Nancy and Manny's fifth-sixth-grade
team had the same complaint as a student we quoted above.
There was so much social interaction going on that it was difficult to work uninterruptedly:

He would prefer a quiet room. He doesn't like fights going on in
the classroom. He doesn't like kids bothering him all the time
when he is trying to work. He's very unhappy with what's going
on in schools today.

The parents who supported open classrooms were as enthusiastic as the others were negative. One particularly satisfied
mother said the room allowed her son to explore all his interests:

I think Carl's class is fantastic and I'm really thrilled and delighted with the way things have been going. He has an in-
credibly wide range of interests, and I think he's really being
allowed to explore all of that. And he's passionately in love with
all the drama things which seem to carry over not only in the
Drama Club, but he's constantly making up plays. I guess the
teacher allows them to write, produce, direct, cast, star in
them—and it's just been fantastic for him.

Quite a number of mothers felt the open classroom relieved
their children of academic pressure which was harmful to them:

I think it is good for Richard. I think he gets restless in a
classroom that's too structured. Last year he had Mrs. Sanders,
who allowed them a lot of independent work and so on, but I
think was more demanding as far as results, as far as actually producing things. I think he was under quite a bit of pressure last
year. He's an awful worry wart. He has worried this year, too.
But I think this open type of thing may be a little easier for him.

He's for the first time learning something about math and beginning to understand it. I don't know if I would say that he's enjoy-
ing it. But he's had terrible fears about it. And he seems to be
overcoming that, which I'm delighted about. I think that's great.

He's very verbal and he's not very good in written work, and
therefore he had a much tougher time of it in the traditional,
structured room with a great deal of emphasis on paper work and
neatness and penmanship, because that's where he really doesn't
do well. When he does do well is when he's allowed to take off on
projects and do a lot of oral work instead of written work. He has
a tremendous zest and enthusiasm for life that finds its way into
an open classroom. For him it's been ideal.

Some parents liked open classrooms because they seemed
to meet their children's emotional needs:

I like the open classroom, if I can use that overused phrase. It's
especially good for him because of his history. He had a very hard
time at the time of our divorce. In the fourth grade, he was in an
extremely structured room with a teacher who was much more of
an authoritarian figure and very cold and impersonal with the
children. It was not a good year for him. And then he came into
this room and it was like a whole new world for him because the
teacher was very aware of him as a person.

The parents did not disagree much about the characteristics of open classrooms. They disagreed about what they
wanted. Those who wanted structured classes were interested in
having the teacher make the decisions as to what should be
studied. They wanted academic demands to be high. And they
wanted a quiet, businesslike atmosphere, at least when
academic work was in progress. The advocates of open classrooms were more concerned that their children be free to
develop their interests. They wanted a lightening of academic
pressure. And they wanted teachers to be responsive to
children's affective needs.

Who Shall Control Pupil Placement?

The first year that Dr. Williams was principal of Coolidge the
staff decided which classrooms the children would be promoted

to. That meant that quite a number of children were placed in open classrooms without the parents having played any part in the decision. The parental reaction was very strong. At the primary level, the parents' hostility seemed to be focused on the multiage grading:

> They said he [the principal] was combining grades without consulting parents and that he was not able to document his reasons for doing it. There wasn't any reason why kindergarteners shouldn't be with kindergarteners, first graders with first graders, and so on. And evidently they must have pushed him in a corner at one meeting, and he said he would document his reasons and then he didn't deliver any pieces of paper to them, and they told him he was a fraud and a liar for saying he would give them some documentation and he didn't.

There were many parental requests for transfers out of the multiage primary classrooms, and there were also many requests for transfers out of the two fourth-grade single-age, open classrooms after students started the semester. Dr. Williams could not have honored the requests even if he had wanted to, since to do so would have left some teachers with very small classes and other rooms overcrowded. However, the pressure on him was unremitting, and he felt quite threatened by it. At a PTA meeting, he promised the parents that the next year they would have a chance to say where their children were going to be placed. That created some logistical problems for the school, but the parents were quite satisfied:

> He got himself a little bit in a corner by saying that. Obviously you could end up with some classes double size and other classes no kids at all or all girls or all boys or something like that. But it seems to have been worked out. There have been very few complaints or requests for change this year. There were lots last year.

Although the parents were well pleased with their new option, officials in the district and Dr. Williams' fellow principals were not. One district official thought that giving the parents a choice between open and "traditional" classrooms was dangerous:

> So far as Dr. Williams is concerned, I have had a lot of conversations with him. You know last year he gave the parents an option between open and traditional at every grade level. I think that's

very bad. It's dangerous to polarize a community and staff that way. We talked about it quite a lot.

Dr. Williams himself reported to a faculty meeting that his fellow principals were worried that the unusual option given to parents at Coolidge might lead to similar demands by parents on them:

> I was just at a principals' meeting and principals were saying to me, "We hear that Coolidge parents are saying that they are choosing their kids' teachers for next year." I'm not at all advocating that we shouldn't listen to what parents say. But I don't want them to say "I chose her," meaning they chose the teacher.

Toward the end of Williams' second year, the question of placements for the following fall came up again. Dr. Williams wanted to take back some of the power over placements that he had relinquished to parents. The faculty differed among themselves. Since parent-teacher conferences were due to be held, and parents were likely to raise the question of placements at these conferences, the faculty had several long meetings to thrash out how placements should be handled. At the first of these meetings, Williams expressed his dilemma. He wanted to regain control over placements for the school. But realistically, he knew he could not do that in one stroke. It would have to be a gradual process:

> We should try to work toward the situation where the school makes the placements. For a number of reasons, the parents have a feeling of control over these placements. That's very unfortunate. We should listen to them, but we should take the responsibility for making the placements. Our judgments are more informed. However, that's all in the future, and we have to think about the present when the parents still feel they have the power, and do, in fact, have the power.

A minority of teachers felt it was right for the parents to choose their children's classrooms:

> I think the parents are entitled to a choice. If they have a strong preference, they should get it. In the conference I write down what they say right under their noses so they can see I'm writing it down.

More teachers felt the opposite way. They felt the school should make the placements. Some who held this view thought the school should place each child on the basis of a careful assessment of what kind of classroom environment was best for that child:

> We as professionals, have the right to decide. The kid has had one kind of experience this year. The sending teacher may feel he needs a similar or different kind of experience next year. We ought to be able to talk to the receiving teachers and say, "Is that what your classroom is like?"

Other teachers thought the school should decide, but not in this way. They felt judgments about classroom environments involved invidious comparisons of teachers which were divisive. Instead, they wanted all the receiving classrooms to be considered alike and the placements to be made on some purely objective criteria:

> You can minimize the divisiveness. I was in a school where the teachers made the choices, but we had some criteria. All the fourth-grade teachers got together and made choices about where the kids should go. And we had three criteria. We spread the leaders around. We had heterogeneous ability grouping. And we spread the problem children around. And on those three criteria, we did it.

Particularly difficult for the teachers was the fact that parents tended to ask them in conferences to recommend a classroom for the child for the following year. Dr. Williams said they should avoid such discussions in conferences, but the teachers said that was not possible:

> I don't see how you can keep it out of the conferences. It was already coming up in February, and parents were much more demanding about it than they were even last year.

> Some parents want my opinion. Others have made up their minds. You can't keep it out of conferences.

A few teachers said that recommending either specific teachers or types of classrooms to parents simply intensified the divisiveness produced by trying to fit children to appropriate environments.

> If we say, "Your child would do well in a free situation," that im-

plies that the other situation is a jail. We have to stop doing that sort of thing.

I don't think we should discuss the kinds of classrooms kids should go into with the parents. I don't think we should discuss specific teachers. I respect the notion that some children would profit by being in a particular classroom style. But I also think we may be wrong about the environment in which the child will learn. I think there are very few children at this age who have a definite enough learning style to be either hurt or benefitted by those placements. I don't want to begin again this great search for categorization of styles and categorization of personalities.

Teacher recommendations to parents, as to what classes their children should go into, were a major cause of tension and suspicion among the staff. It is not hard to see why. Some teachers, like Nancy Stuart in the fifth grade, complained that her fourth-grade colleagues, excepting those with open classrooms, gave her a bad press with the parents. But Mrs. Stuart, in turn, was very hostile to the nonopen sixth grades and in subtle ways gave them a bad press in conferences with her parents. So factionalism among the faculty was intensified in these attempts to influence parental choice.

At the time we left Coolidge, matters rested there. The parents believed they had the right to choose their children's classrooms. The principal was attempting to modify their control over placement into something more like input into the decision. The teachers had to handle the matter as it came up in conferences with parents. In theory, they were supposed to avoid recommending any placement to the parent. Instead, they were supposed to tell the parents that they could write a note to the principal expressing their preferences, and that their comments would be taken into account at the placement conference. In fact, the teachers did not altogether trust each other to express no judgments of other classrooms. Some open classroom teachers thought their nonopen colleagues gave them a bad press, and vice versa, and they were right.

Other principals in the district were putting pressure on Dr. Williams, because they feared the notion of parent control of placement might spread to their schools. However, retrieving the power yielded to Coolidge parents was not likely to prove easy. Parents felt strongly pro and con open education. They thought that the differences among classrooms were important. And they did not want to return to the situation of two years previously, where their children were placed in open classrooms without their consent.

Dr. Williams' strategy of delabeling the classrooms and defining the school as having a rich diversity of teaching styles had not yet worked, although it had considerable foundation in fact. Within the school, the structured teachers had much more respect for the primary level open classrooms than for those in the upper grades. Parents, too, to a limited extent, thought in terms of the reputations of particular teachers. But the open-versus-structured-classroom dichotomy still dominated their thinking.

The open classroom teachers cultivated their support in the community and the structured classroom teachers cultivated theirs. So long as parents controlled placement, it was inevitable that teachers would seek to build a constituency in the school district, in order to guarantee that they would receive a respectable number of choices every year. At the end of the year we were in Coolidge, the absence of an open fourth-grade classroom led to a serious underchoosing of Nancy Stuart's fifth grade—which was an embarrassment to her and a difficult logistical problem for the school. Such an event cannot occur when the school controls placement, as it usually does. The implication of this occurrence is that the parents—by underchoosing open classrooms—can greatly curtail this innovation which the teachers originated. If the parents maintain their control over placements, and if open classroom choices dwindle significantly, the innovation could conceivably be wiped out. Thus the parents would have exercised veto power over a policy made by the professionals.

Conclusion

At the second school we considered, Southside, we saw that the absence of any choice between open and structured classrooms in grades one through three led to a situation where some teachers participated in the innovation somewhat unwillingly and many parents participated unknowingly.

At Coolidge we see that alternative types of classroom

within the same school led to divisiveness among the staff, and some tension for pupils old enough to be aware of the differences. And an option for parents was beginning to turn placement decisions into a popularity contest which threatened the teachers' professionalism.

Many people, including open classroom advocates like Professor Wylie in Walton, believe that parents are entitled to choose whether or not their children are in open classrooms. But the provision of such a choice within a single school leads to polarization of the staff, because the norms of behavior which govern open classrooms contrast sharply with the more usual elementary school norms. It is very difficult for a single organization to maintain two such different sets of expectations for its pupils. As we saw in this chapter, the more structured teachers tend to fear that their less permissive demands will be undermined by the visibility of a more permissive regime down the hall. Perhaps the only solution to this problem is to provide parents with an option between schools. This policy is already followed in a few towns where an "alternative school" is provided for parents who want their children to have an open education. Alternative schools, rather than alternative classrooms within a school, make it somewhat more difficult for parents and pupils to change their minds about the teaching style they prefer, but the advantages of a consistent teaching style within a school are probably worth the price.

The importance of pupil peer groups in the open classrooms at Coolidge led us to the view that peer group dynamics are more central to open classrooms than to other types of classes. In open classrooms, peer groups often become taskgroups. When this happens, social skills take precedence over individual ability and curiosity. Success with one's peers becomes the "hidden curriculum." This is not what the theorists of open education have in mind when they describe their ideal, but they have made the error of envisioning the child, freed to make choices as an individual, acting on his own preferences and judgments. In reality, the child nearly always seeks to become a member of a peer group. The peer group has a structure, customs, and norms whose authority in an open classroom replaces, in part, the withdrawn authority of the teacher. Peer group consensus relieves the anxiety of the child, who is often too immature to shoulder the responsibilities of choice which the open classroom places on him.

Finally, Coolidge is an example of a school where an unusually well-qualified staff, supported by district headquarters, had to struggle to maintain its professional prerogatives against parents who were articulate, powerful, and intensely involved in their children's education. In spite of the parents' intrusiveness, the staff made many pedagogical decisions. It was they who decided to drop the formal teaching of grammar, to abolish the traditional report card, to substitute heterogeneous for homogeneous ability grouping, and to introduce open classrooms into the school.

On the other hand, the parents succeeded in squelching a sex-education program they had voted for themselves, because they did not trust the staff members who were to run it. They succeeded in getting an open classroom teacher who was too "far out" fired, and a principal whose style they didn't like transferred. But most important, the indignation of the parents at having their children placed in multiaged open classrooms without their consent had frightened the principal into giving them the right to choose their child's classroom placement. Since this is traditionally the right of the school, other principals and district officials were dismayed. They feared that demands for a similar right would spread to other schools. Dr. Williams was eager to recapture the power he had given away to parents, but felt that it would have to be a gradual process. In the meanwhile, as we pointed out, the parents could, by underchoosing open classrooms, wipe out the innovation in the school.

The contrast between the way open education was introduced into Coolidge and Southside is striking. At Southside, Professor Wylie saw to it that the parents most involved in the school supported the introduction of open education. No equivalent process of consultation with parents occurred at Coolidge, although the proportion of families who took an interest in the school was higher. Instead, the introduction of open classrooms was left to the initiative of individual teachers. The parents' reaction to this was to attack the school for introducing multigrade classrooms without consulting them. Since the principal was intimidated by the parents, he conceded them the right to choose their children's teachers. At the time we left

Coolidge, parents were well satisfied with this situation and counted on its continuation. On the other hand, the principal, as well as his colleagues and the district officials, felt it was necessary to recapture this prerogative for the school.

The teachers were split about the virtues of open education and distressed about their own involvement in helping parents to make a choice. Some felt they could make such recommendations on professional grounds and that this was quite legitimate; others believed that the recommendations would be based on personal likes and dislikes, and so should be avoided.

Coolidge was caught in an organizational dilemma. It had brought the parents into very close relationship with the school, and then had introduced a radical innovation without either consulting them or offering them a choice. When the parents vigorously protested, the principal made too large a concession. Instead of a choice between open and nonopen classrooms, he allowed them to choose the particular class their child would be promoted to. This decision is traditionally in the domain of the school, and to let parents have it has several consequences which create difficulty for the school. First, it causes logistical problems, since some rooms may be over- and others under-chosen. Second, it forces each teacher to cultivate a following in the community in order to ensure that her classes will be adequately filled. Third, it causes the formation of alliances and enmities among teachers, who make a point of recommending or not recommending certain classes to inquiring parents.

As a result, Coolidge School was in trouble, both internally and externally. Open education caused a cleavage among teachers and among parents. The question was how to pacify its supporters as well as its enemies. The strategy the principal chose—of defining each classroom as unique and avoiding the open versus nonopen dichotomy—was not working. It seemed more sensible to face up to the dichotomy and find a way of dealing with it. We have suggested a choice for parents between alternative open and nonopen schools as a solution. But that was not on the horizon in Sundale when we left.

PART IV

Conclusion

Chapter 14

Implementing Organizational Innovations

Until now we have been dealing with processes of innovation unique to each of our schools. In this chapter, we discuss innovation in elementary schools on a more general level, using our three cases as illustrations. Many of the points we make are similar to those which have emerged from other case studies. Our data offer further support to several of these earlier generalizations and help to extend some of them.

How Prevalent Is Innovation?

There has long been a feeling among both laymen and experts that schools are resistant to innovation. Schools are "domesticated organizations"; that is, organizations with a guaranteed clientele for whom they need not compete. Therefore they have little motivation to try to improve their effectiveness. However, there is some contrary evidence from Havelock and his associates who found, by means of a mailed questionnaire, that there was a high rate of innovation in U.S. schools.[1] Of course, this rate is probably somewhat exaggerated, since schools are inclined to claim they have innovations which exist in name only.

We, of course, selected for study schools which had already adopted innovations, and thus, if the "domesticated organization" hypothesis is correct, our schools are atypical. However, when we observed them, each of our schools proved to have innovations over and above the one we had come to see. More significantly, the innovations we saw were not a matter of the moment. All three of the schools had been continually innovative for a considerable period of time, or were embedded in a continually innovative school district. Nor were these constantly innovating schools of a single type. One was a black ghetto school; one was an urban integrated school, serving pupils of high and low income; and the third was a white school in an affluent suburb.

The fact that we found innovation to be the norm rather than the exception in three such different schools leads us to believe that the hypothesis of the noninnovating "domesticated organization" needs amendment, and that Havelock's finding of widespread innovativeness in schools is more valid for the sixties and early seventies. Our observations suggest that widespread criticism is threatening to school personnel, and that they often cope with criticism through attempts to change. We can pinpoint a threat and an innovating response in two of our three cases. Johnson's era of innovativeness began as a reaction to the announcement of a boycott by black parents, made against a background of national civil-rights agitation. The Board of Education in Centerville was clearly influenced by these events when it appointed Dr. Phillips as principal of Johnson with a broad mandate to experiment, free of district control.

The superintendent of District 7 in Walton, where Southside was located, explicitly presented the district's Individualized Reading Program as a response to demands from parents for accountability. He warned the principals that unless they implemented this innovation, and others like it, public education might be overwhelmed by public disapproval, and disappear.

In the Sundale school district, where Coolidge was located, we uncovered no specific threat which had triggered the district's long-standing openness to change. However, this district was the one most vulnerable to criticism from a sophisticated, affluent clientele which had demonstrated its power to have school personnel removed. Part of this clientele was politically and culturally liberal, receptive to the radical critiques of the public schools which were written in the 1960's and to the movement for open education.

Thus, we conclude that the "guaranteed clientele" of the

schools by no means makes them invulnerable to the climate of opinion in their environment. Strongly critical outside opinion may trigger innovation.

Once innovation is initiated, what makes it persist as a pattern of action for some schools and districts? In the case of Johnson, constant innovativeness was an attempt to maintain legitimacy for the school's special status of autonomy within the district. At the time we studied Johnson, district officials were talking of withdrawing this status and the principal was determined that it should continue. In District 7 of Walton, the continuing innovativeness was a response to intense demands for community control, which rose out of articulate and organized discontent with the schools on the part of parents. Another factor in District 7's ferment of innovative activity was the availability of federal and foundation funds for innovation. Both Title III money and foundation money were financing many undertakings in the district.

In Sundale, innovativeness went back at least to the post-Sputnik curriculum reforms of the 1950's. The innovativeness of this district was a function of the power of the parents and their determination that their children should have the "best" in education. Sundale was kept at the forefront of educational change by its knowledgeable and involved parents and by its superior school personnel. The administrators and teachers played their roles in a more professional manner than most schoolmen, and this included keeping abreast of new developments and maintaining mechanisms for recurrent professional training, which facilitated the adoption of new educational ideas.

Thus we have concluded that, while resistance to innovation may be the stance of some school districts, continuing innovativeness is the stance of others. Resistance to innovation has been generally evaluated as "bad." It does not follow, however, that constant innovativeness is constructive. In the case of Johnson, we saw that innovations which followed each other in rapid succession over a period of six years were often extremely superficial. To be more precise, Johnson adopted many innovations, but failed, partially or wholly, to implement them. This brings us to a useful set of distinctions.

Educational innovation can be broken down into stages. We choose to differentiate three: the stage of *adoption* of the innovation, the stage of *implementation,* and the stage of *routinization.* When we say that schools are quite likely to meet criticism by innovating, we mean that they are likely to *adopt* innovations. Adoption is a declaration of policy that the innovation will become part of the school's regular organization. *Implementing* innovations which have been adopted is another matter. Most of the literature on educational innovation has dealt with the determinants of adoption. However, some recent works have made it a point to emphasize that the adoption of an innovation does not guarantee that it will be implemented.[2] Implementation is the process of making changes and readjustments in the school's performance of its functions so that the innovation can be incorporated as a regular part of those functions. *Routinization* means that the change process has been completed and that the innovation has become a stable, permanent part of the school's procedures. When innovations are only partially or superficially implemented, routinization does not occur and the innovation tends to disappear rather quickly.[3]

In this book, our main focus has been on the implementation stage of innovation. Implementation is especially important since we have chosen to deal with organizational innovations of considerable scope, and these are the most difficult to put into effect. It is relatively easy to implement the use of a new curriculum, a new facility, or a new bit of technology; but extensive organizational change has many ramifications which are difficult to foresee and to control. Therefore they are especially vulnerable to failure at the stage of implementation.

Implications of Pattern of Adoption for Implementation

Some aspects of the manner in which an innovation is adopted have consequences for its chances of implementation. An innovation may be adopted as a response to a need felt by the school, or it may be adopted opportunistically—for example, because some outside agency has offered to fund it.[4] The latter type of adoption occurred often under the provisions of Title III of ESEA. Implementation efforts will obviously be more serious if the innovation answers to a need felt by the school. The adoption of open classrooms by teachers in the Coolidge School and by those teachers drawn into the OCT program in its first year at Southside conformed to this pattern. In both of these situations, implementation was partially successful. The main exception was the fifth-sixth-grade team at Coolidge, which isolated itself from the expert help available.

On the other hand, the Individualized Reading Program at Southside was adopted because of district coercion, and the Individualized Learning Program was adopted by Johnson because the principal wanted to put the district in his debt, and because Title III funding was expected. Neither of these innovations responded to a need felt by the school, and both largely failed at the implementation stage. Opportunistic innovativeness was a Johnson pattern. Innovations were adopted for political or public relations reasons, implemented very superficially or not at all, and dropped when the next innovation came along. So our findings confirm those of Berman et al., that innovations arising out of a locally experienced need are more likely to be implemented than those adopted opportunistically.[5]

Another dimension of adoption which is related to implementation is the level of the organization from which the proposal is initiated. David Livingstone says that many innovative proposals originate at the diverse lower levels of complex organizations, but that few of these are adopted. Few proposals originate at high levels, but those which do, have a good chance of adoption.[6] However, if the adopting unit and the implementing unit of the organization are different, and if the tasks required of the implementing unit are complex, the implementing unit can ignore, resist, or sabotage a decision to innovate. Since the teachers' innovative tasks are complex, they will not infrequently fail to implement the decision of their superiors to innovate—often for good reasons. An example is the total failure of District 7 in Walton to implement the District Superintendent's decision to adopt the Individualized Reading Program.

Another well-known student of educational innovation, Matthew Miles, finds the following:

> . . . we collected data showing that up to 75 percent of teachers had thought of innovations that might improve education in their districts outside of their own classrooms, but only half of the 75 percent had in fact talked with *anyone* else about the innovations,

and that only 5 percent reported that any action had ensued. Anti-collaborative norms can be inferred. [7]

We have some evidence on innovations which originate at a low level in the school system, namely with the teachers. At Johnson, these were the DISTAR reading and math program and the use of Kephart perceptual-motor tests to diagnose learning disabilities. These innovations were adopted by those teachers who proposed them, and DISTAR spread to some of the initiators' fellow teachers at Johnson. However, these new patterns seemed unlikely to diffuse any further for lack of support from the principal and the district. In Sundale, on the other hand, about half the primary classrooms were open at the time we studied the Coolidge School; so the open classroom innovation which had originated with the teachers diffused widely through the district.

Johnson probably represents a more usual situation than the Sundale school district. Generally, teachers have only a limited audience for their professional ideas, an audience confined to colleagues within their own school. They have no way of contacting colleagues beyond the school's boundary unless the district provides it. Johnson was quite isolated within its district in any case, since its autonomy was a sore point with other district schools. While there were no anticollaborative norms at Johnson—the teachers there were accustomed to collaborating in teams—the teachers did not conceive of themselves as agents of innovation. It did not occur to them to document their claims for DISTAR and to present this documentation to other teachers in the district. There was no ready channel of communication through which they could have done so.

The difference between Johnson and Coolidge lay not so much in the teachers' behavior as in the district's. In both schools, the teachers implemented innovations in their own classrooms. But the Sundale school district made a point of attending to the teachers' professional behavior. When open education became a matter of interest to a sufficient number of teachers in several schools, the district provided it with a support system. Another difference was that the innovations of the Johnson teachers were not at the time widely fashionable, whereas open classrooms were becoming fashionable when Sundale's teachers began to adopt this mode of teaching. Teachers in many Sundale schools adopted the open classroom more or less simultaneously, not because of influence flowing from each other, but because of influences coming from the national educational media.

On the whole, then, it seems correct to say that innovations originating with teachers have little chance of widespread adoption and implementation in a school system. That is so because no mechanisms exist for providing teachers with a means of reaching a large audience of colleagues beyond their own schools, and because the teacher-as-innovator is not part of the usual definition of the teacher's role.

If we look now at innovations adopted at the top of the school district, like ILP in Centerville and District 7's IRP in Walton, we see that high-level adoption of an innovation does not guarantee its implementation. The Centerville district, unlike Walton, at least took pains to get the consent of the Johnson principal for ILP. The principal, in turn, had the teachers vote on whether or not to adopt it, and they voted for it. The principal's consent, however, was opportunistic rather than backed by conviction, and the teachers' vote was largely conditioned by their expectation of Title III funds, which were subsequently denied them. Nevertheless, the consent of principal and teachers would seem to be a necessary, if not sufficient, condition for implementation.[8] District 7 tried to impose its reading program on Southside and the other schools in the district by a combination of threats and offers of assistance, neither of which was forthcoming.

These observations suggest that principals and teachers, if they wish, can sabotage the implementation of innovations which a higher level of the school system has forced them to adopt. The district is helpless against passive resistance at the levels where the real implementation must take place.

Another illustration that teachers are crucial to implementation is the Afro-American studies program which originated with the principal of Johnson. He made compromises to secure the support of the Soul team. They adopted the proposal, but proved unable to implement it. They couldn't implement it because it was badly thought out and the necessary resources were not provided.[9] Nonimplementation did not prevent the principal from proceeding to broaden the adoption of the innovation in its second year, but it is clear that, regardless of adoption, implementation would not take place unless better resources were provided.

What emerges from these observations is that the key people in *adopting* an innovation and the key people in *implementing* it are not the same. Teachers in a single school may adopt and implement an innovation in their own classrooms, but it cannot be widely adopted without the support of district administrators. Formal authority is necessary for wide adoption, and that is concentrated at the top of the school district.

The situation with respect to implementation is different. Implementation of intricate organizational innovations requires action of a highly complex kind on the part of teachers. The action can neither be specified nor supervised in detail; it must be left in considerable degree up to the teachers' initiative. Therefore, teachers must be at least willing, and at best highly motivated, to undertake the innovation. Second, the action required of them must be realistically possible in the sense that the required resources are available. If either the motivation or the resources are lacking, the teachers will not or cannot innovate. Implementation of organizational innovations in schools stands or falls on the teachers' willingness and capacity to pattern their interaction with each other and with pupils in new ways.

Sufficiency of Resources for Implementation

A great deal has been written about the pervasive insufficiency of resources for carrying out educational innovations. Our data underline what has been said by other observers.

There are two separate aspects of resource needs. First, any innovation, no matter how inexpensive it may become once it has been routinized, requires some extra resources during the period of implementation. At a minimum, time is needed for planning how to implement the innovation and for modifying it so that it fits into local procedures. Second, many of the organizational innovations which schools experimented with in the 1960's and early 1970's were more expensive than traditional, whole-class teaching. The lack of recognition, and sometimes even the denial, that individualized instruction and open classrooms cost more than whole-class teaching has been an important cause of failure to implement and routinize these innovations.

The required resources can all be translated into money, of course. But to see how resources affect the implementation process, it is more useful to think of them as expertise, personnel, time, and materials.

Expertise

In their book *Implementing Organizational Innovations*, Gross, Giaquinta, and Bernstein showed how the failure to provide willing teachers with needed expert help, caused a total failure of Cambire School to implement open classrooms.[10] In none of our three cases was there a complete absence of expertise, but there were variations in the adequacy of the expert help provided.

ILP at Johnson was backed up by the least expertise. There was a summer workshop for the teachers, a kit of printed and visual materials for team leaders, which went unused for lack of time, and a part-time change agent who visited the classrooms infrequently. As a consequence, teachers had only a hazy idea of what ILP purported to be. They translated it into teaming— which was a part of the ILP format—and into reorganization of pupils into more homogeneous ability groups—which was directly opposed to ILP doctrine. The central goal of ILP, custom-tailoring a school program for each child, was approached in only one out of four teams intensively observed, and that team succeeded due to a fortuitous combination of circumstances not easy to replicate.

Southside and Coolidge were comparatively well provided with expertise in open education. There was an extensive literature which explained open education doctrine and described its practices. Some of the Coolidge teachers were given preservice training in it. The teachers of both schools had workshops available to them, which they claimed to find very useful. Southside had, in addition, two change agents who visited the school twice weekly, working with the teachers in their classrooms and at meetings. One would imagine that this was the most effective service of all, but its usefulness was undermined because the teachers did not regard the change agents as experts. In addition, they were hostile to the change agents because the agents held power over them. Despite explicit claims by the head of Open Classroom Teaming in Walton that teachers, change agents, paraprofessionals, and parents were all treated as equals in the program, the change agents at Southside threatened to expel from the program one teacher whose commitment they questioned, and they chastised all the teachers for failing to form a team. Thus, though they claimed to act as status equals with the teachers, they actually acted as status superiors. Their power was not viewed as legitimate by the teachers, who doubted that the change agents really possessed the superior expertise which would have, in part, legitimated it.

It is axiomatic that an innovation which imposes a new layer of authority over teachers will arouse hostility for that reason alone; teachers will question the legitimacy of any authority which is not customarily found in a school system. And consultants who cannot convince their clients that they are expert will give advice in vain.

Personnel

Most classrooms in the United States have a teacher-to-pupil ratio somewhere between one-to-twenty-five and one-to-thirty. We have repeatedly noted that the adult-to-pupil ratio in the classrooms we observed ranged between one-to-ten and one-to-fifteen. Not all the adults were teachers. Some were student teachers, Teacher Corps members, paraprofessionals, and parent volunteers. Still, it is striking that we rarely saw a classroom, where individualization or open education was being attempted, without at least two adults in the classroom. Furthermore, the teachers who were engaged in these experiments consistently told us that they could not succeed unless there were more adults in the classroom than there are in traditional schools. In the exceptional case where a teacher was alone in an open classroom with twenty-five children—for instance, Abe Winner's room at Southside—the class teetered on the brink of disorganization.

There are a number of reasons why the organizational innovations we have studied require more personnel than traditional, whole-class teaching. One is that the teacher's role comes to include a tremendous amount of planning which takes place *outside* of the classroom. Instead of making one lesson plan to be taught to the whole class simultaneously, the teacher now plans for each individual child or small group. If she plays her new role as it is ideally prescribed, she will do less direct teaching but more of many other things. She must diagnose each child's learning status. She must select from available curriculum materials those which are appropriate for each child, or else must create appropriate curriculum herself. She must keep detailed records of each child's academic and social-emotional development. She must introduce new and stimulating materials into the classroom environment, materials which she has either bought or made. If she is a member of a team, she must devote considerable time to planning with her teammates. What is demanded of teachers by these innovations has been called a "role overload."[11] To accomplish even part of what is prescribed, teachers must either work prodigiously on their own time, or they must be freed from the classroom for considerable periods while they do this enormous amount of out-of-class preparation. If the latter course is taken, other personnel must cover their classes during teachers' preparation periods, and these other people must be competent to carry on in the spirit of the innovation. We saw that at Southside, when open classroom teachers had "prep" periods, their classes were covered by inept traditional teachers, whose every word and act was incongruous with open education.

Inside the classroom as well, open education and individualized instruction require more adults than whole-class teaching. Most of the instruction in such classes takes place in the form of the teacher working with small groups and individuals as she circulates around the room. While she works with one group, other pupils must either be able to work constructively on their own, or they must have some supervision. Only certain types of young children have the self-control and independence to work for extended periods with no adult supervision. Many cannot do it at all, and many can do it only to a limited extent. For the most part, at least one, and sometimes two or three adults in addition to the teacher, are present to give assistance and to meet the children's varied needs. If they are not present, some classes deteriorate into chaos.

Time

Time is a resource all too often in short supply when innovations are implemented. This is true in two senses. The length of the period required to implement an innovation is usually underestimated by adopters and funding agencies. If a school tries to implement a complex organizational innovation all at once, rather than doing it gradually, it will be overwhelmed by unanticipated consequences.[12] Yet the Centerville Board of Education ordered the administration of achievement tests in Johnson and Merrill Schools at the end of the first year of ILP to see whether the very partially implemented innovation had raised the pupils' test scores. It hadn't. Even if ILP had been implemented more effectively than was actually the case, one year was far too soon to expect that kind of outcome. The Board of Education's time perspective for implementation was overly optimistic.

The other sense in which time is scarce is indicated in our above account of the new components in the teacher's role. Most of these new role components must be enacted outside the classroom. The teacher needs a great deal of time for them. Even when "prep" periods and team planning meetings are institutionalized, there is not enough time during the school day for the teacher's out-of-classroom duties. Teachers customarily take some work home, but the innovative role demands far more homework than is customary. In fact, the demands of the innovative teacher's role are unrealistic. Only teachers working from morning until night every day could fulfill them. The teachers at Johnson did this for a few years under the spell of Dr. Phillips' charismatic leadership. But such extraordinary dedication cannot be routinized.* The obvious substitute for additional time is additional personnel. So the teachers' role overload may be viewed as another reason why more personnel are needed for innovative than for traditional teaching.

---

*It is a "Hawthorne effect," in sociological language. The term refers to an effect which comes about, not because of an experimenter's change in the "treatment" given to his experimental subjects, but because of their feeling flattered and important at being the subjects of a study. Phillips made the teachers feel that what they were doing, with his leadership, was of great significance.

Materials

One of the fundamental ideas of open education is that young children do much of their learning through the exploration and manipulation of concrete materials. A learning environment which is rich in such materials, and which constantly has new materials fed into it, is an indispensable condition for this innovation. At Southside, in the early years of OCT, materials were abundantly provided through foundation funds. After the funds were stopped, teachers were left in the position of having to make their own materials—as Natalie Roseman made games for her classes and spend their own money—as Abe Winner spent his for materials for his class to build a boat. The change agents helped the teachers scrounge for materials; for instance, the waste of some industrial plants which could be turned to classroom use. Like the excessive time commitment of teachers under Dr. Phillips, these, too, are extraordinary measures which cannot be expected to persist as routine practices. Open-classroom materials are costly and budgets must be planned accordingly.

Individualization is also expensive in materials. It means that one reader and one arithmetic text for the whole class will no longer do. There must be books on different levels of difficulty, and books with varying approaches to the same topic, if the needs of different individuals are to be met. We saw, in our discussion of the Soul team at Johnson, how destructive it was for the teacher not to have available books on the appropriate level of difficulty for her slower pupils. Having neither the books nor the time to write reading exercises of the kind they needed, she assigned the students books which were too advanced for them. As a result, they suffered a punishing frustration.

Since the literature is unanimous that innovations founder often on the rock of inadequate resources, the real question is why the costs are so regularly underestimated. Schoolmen do not ordinarily think in economic terms. Most innovations are not carefully cost-analyzed. Innovators sometimes insist that their "product" costs no more than traditional school practices—apparently to encourage their adoption. However, it is also true that costing-out an educational innovation is difficult. Costs vary with the quality of the teaching personnel and the characteristics of the pupils, so that the same innovation entails different costs in different schools. Still, a certain amount of obvious unrealism could be abandoned with benefit. Innovations like the open classroom and individualized instruction cost more than traditional teaching, not only during the implementation phase. They cost more after routinization as well. The needs for more adults in the classroom, more planning time for teachers, and more materials for the classroom are inescapable. If an attempt is made (as at Southside) to take the extra costs out of the hides of the teachers by getting them to commit their "own" time to the innovation, the commitment breaks down as soon as the novelty of the innovation has worn off, or the teachers become exhausted.* Making impossibly heavy demands on teachers is not the way to solve the cost problem or to insure adequate implementation of a new program.

Underdeveloped Innovations

Another way of looking at the problem of teacher "role overload" in innovative teaching is to think of the innovation itself as underdeveloped. ILP, for instance, asks teachers to diagnose children's "learning styles" with no specification as to what is meant by that vague term. In contrast, the Individualized Reading Program in District 7 of Walton included diagnostic tests of specific reading skills. The firm which sold the program scored the tests and returned the scores to the teachers. Unfortunately, they did not return the specific skill profiles which the teachers needed.

Other producers of individualization "packages" evidently have learned through experience that their programs must do more for teachers than ILP does if they are to be implemented. Some now provide diagnostic tests and show teachers how to score and interpret them. They also provide curriculum appropriate for each diagnosis, or they direct the teacher to appropriate curriculum in any of a large number of commercially available texts. [13] This groundwork relieves the teacher of heavy burdens, but it carries price. It programs the teacher to analyze

*Unfortunately I cannot recall where I saw the term, but some clever social scientist, taking the title of Graham Greene's novel, has generalized such exhaustion among participants in innovation and calls such a person "a burnt-out case." The concept is very useful.

skills in a preordained way, and it determines, by the way it selects curriculum, how reading and arithmetic will be taught. While some teachers are grateful to be relieved of the tasks of diagnosing every child and prescribing curriculum for each, others feel that such programs interfere with their creativity and their excercise of professional judgment.

The Public Relations Facade

Most observational case studies of educational innovation report failure. Yet when Havelock and his associates tried, through a mailed questionnaire, to find examples of innovative failure they could turn up no schools which would admit to it:

> There was an apparent reluctance on the part of our respondents to own up to negative consequences and innovations that ran awry. We tried to get reports specifically on "unsuccessful" or "problematic" innovations in our pilot work but drew a blank.[14]

This says a great deal about the atmosphere in which educational innovation takes place. It is not a climate of detached experimentation, but rather a climate of advocacy.[15] If the knowledge base for educational innovation were strong, the element of advocacy would be unnecessary. But most educational innovations have a weak knowledge base. In the absence of a demonstrated superiority to existing practice, there must be, behind many educational innovations, an element of charisma, of "true belief."[16] This faith provides the necessary motivational strength to undertake the innovation in the absence of objective knowledge of effectiveness. However, it also gives rise to a facade of success which is maintained regardless of actual outcomes.

The Johnson School is our clearest example of such a facade. Johnson kept up a pretense, under two principals, of good and rising achievement scores when, in fact, the achievement scores of neighborhood children had not risen, despite years of various kinds of innovation. The principals felt they had to maintain an aura of success in order to justify the continued autonomy and extra resources of the school. Yet the pretense of rising achievement prevented Johnson from facing its real problem—the persistence of very low achievement. Not only was nothing done about the low achievement, but children were made to feel a sense of failure because they were given work which was far too difficult for them.

The lack of a firm knowledge base for educational innovation in the United States is a consequence of the lack of educational research which is generalizable and cumulative.[17] However, the charismatic element in educational innovation is also due to the fact that education consists of socialization as well as instruction. While instruction is a matter of effective techniques which can be dealt with in scientific terms, socialization is a matter of values. Changes in values come about through social movements rather than through scientific experimentation, and this explains why educational innovations, like progressive education and open education, have often resembled social movements. We deal further with this valuational aspect of the innovations in our three schools in the next chapter.

"Too Much" Innovation and Goal Conflict

When innovations are introduced into a school in rapid succession, with little thought as to how they fit together, there may be goal conflicts. For instance, the Soul team at Johnson was asked to undertake the development of an Afro-American curriculum before it was well into its second semester of implementing ILP. As the principal pointed out to us, the emphasis in ILP was on the individual child. He disapproved of this. His goal for the Afro-American curriculum was to develop a collective solidarity among the children around their African heritage and their experience of being black. The conflicting goals of the two innovations did not seem to disturb the principal. He regarded ILP as a political favor to the district headquarters which he traded off for permission to go ahead with his Afro-American curriculum. His official position was that the two innovations would continue simultaneously. This stance would have placed the teachers in an impossible situation, except for the fact that neither innovation was really implemented. The Soul team did not individualize instruction and neither did it develop an Afro-American curriculum.

Events at Southside illustrate even more clearly what can happen if innovations are introduced on top of one another with no thought as to how they fit together. The Individualized Reading Program of the district interfered with the reading programs of the open classrooms. The individualized program asked teachers to fill out every two months a diagnostic instrument on reading, with behaviorally formulated skills, for each of their pupils. Since open classroom teachers do not instruct pupils in skills in a behavioral fashion, the task was meaningless and obnoxious for them. But it was some time before the head of the Open Classroom Advisory was able to negotiate with the district to substitute an instrument more acceptable from an open-education viewpoint. Even this compromise did not eliminate the conflict between the district's holding teachers "accountable" for certain levels of mastery by their pupils and the open-education philosophy that children should be permitted to progress at their own individual pace. Open education, following Piaget, teaches that children's learning progresses through an unvarying sequence of stages, but at different rates. If a child does not learn to read, it is because he is not "ready" to do so; the teacher cannot be held responsible.

Another goal conflict which loomed for Southside was the contradiction implicit in providing a choice of open or traditional classrooms at each grade level, and the standing policy that every classroom be ethnically integrated. There was a very real possibility that, given a choice, a majority of Hispanic and black parents would opt for traditional rooms, while the white upper middle-class mothers would opt for open classrooms. If this happened, either some parents would not be granted their choices, or classes would become *de facto* ethnically segregated, in contravention of district policy.

Teaming: Potential Conflict in Teachers' and Pupils' Roles

Team teaching was a frequent accompaniment of the educational innovations of the 1960's. It existed at Johnson and Coolidge, and it was a goal not yet achieved at Southside.

That team teaching often accompanies individualization and open classrooms is not an accident. It comes about partly because these innovations consume resources so heavily. The division of labor on a team is supposed to increase the teachers' "output." Whether it does so or not isn't clear, but it is clear that teaming is a major organizational change in elementary schools. It deprives teachers and pupils of some of the gratifications of self-enclosed classroom. It provides a new set of gratifications and a new set of problems. During the period of implementation, when teachers and pupils are in transition from the self-enclosed classroom to the team, the new role requirements may come into conflict with the old.

There are several types of teaching teams. At Coolidge many two-teacher teams split up the subjects they had to teach. The team handled two classes by exchanging them from period to period, each teacher remaining in her self-enclosed classroom, with a minimum of communication between them. Such teaming has little transforming effect on the role of the teacher. At Johnson some teams divided their pupils into ability groups for each subject, and each group was taught by a single teacher in a self-enclosed classroom. These teams, however, had regular meetings to plan certain activities which they undertook as a team. Teachers in this situation are part of the way down the path from the self-enclosed classroom to teaming. However, when teaming involves first, collaboration in carrying on instruction, and second, mutual visibility of teachers as they go about their daily tasks, it radically transforms the teacher's role. Examples of such teams were the Butterflies at Johnson and the Soul team during the period when it worked in an open-space building at the university. At Coolidge examples were the fifth-sixth-grade team and the K–1–2 team. With the exception of Soul, these teams did not function in areas designed to be "open spaces," but they treated their traditional classroom *as though* they were open spaces, with several small groups and teachers working in full view of each other in the same room and with fluid movement of pupils between rooms.

As a result of this kind of teaming, the individual teacher no longer "owns" her pupils and her space, as the self-enclosed traditional teacher does. Instead, she shares both with other teachers. As we noted in our chapter on Johnson, this gives rise to a need for normative consistency among the teachers on a team. They must negotiate with each other concerning the rules for pupil behavior. The team teacher also surrenders other aspects of a traditional teacher's autonomy. She can no longer treat her space as she pleases. This can lead to conflicts of personal style. On the Soul team, a compulsively neat teacher and an habitually sloppy teacher, who had no trouble while each had her own classroom at Johnson, came into head-on conflict in the open space building at the university.

Team teachers cannot take sole credit for the gains of pupils. This is the traditional teacher's main source of satisfaction.[18] On a team, it must be shared.

Two important norms of behavior among traditional teachers are equality of status and avoidance of mutual criticism. The equal status norm is violated when there is a team leader. This was well illustrated in Johnson, where we saw the principal urging team leaders to exert authority over teachers on their teams, and the difficulty team leaders felt in assuming authority. Unless the position carries some kind of tenure, team leaders are unlikely to use their presumed authority.

The mutual visibility of teachers on a team means that the members know a great deal about each others' professional strengths and weaknesses. Mutual evaluation of professional competence follows inevitably. The fear of this kind of exposure to colleagues is alleviated if the team has good interpersonal relations and evolves into a mutually protective primary group. If such an evolution does not occur, we would predict that collaboration must in some way break down, though we have no example of such a case.

Teaming offers teachers new gratifications. First, they enjoy collegial contact—sharing their professional problems. Second, team teachers feel more influential in matters of school policy than traditional, self-enclosed teachers do.[19] This is a realistic feeling. If a team achieves consensus on an issue—as the Soul team did on the issue of the Afro–American studies curriculum—the principal is far more constrained to make concessions to their position than he would be to the position of an individual teacher.

Third, the teaching team supplies the teacher with a small group of colleagues as a regular audience. Members of the team often adopt each other's practices. This also contributes to the feeling of being influential.

At the same time, it is possible that team leaders may interpose a new layer of authority and a new channel of communication between the teachers and the principal. This did not happen at Johnson, since every teacher felt able to approach the principal directly. However, it is easy to see how it could occur in a large school with a less informal principal.

Teaming affects pupils as well as teachers. The main effect for elementary school pupils is that they no longer have a single teacher as a surrogate parent with whom to identify closely. Instead, they may have two to six teachers. For young children, the need to shift from one teacher to others may arouse considerable anxiety. We saw this at Johnson when pupils rebelled at going to rooms other than that of their homeroom teacher and when they refused to accept the authority of other teachers. The problem seemed to arise when pupils were given enough time in self-enclosed classrooms to form a strong tie to a homeroom teacher and *then* were expected to shift to a team situation. The Butterflies, who were teamed with several teachers from the beginning of the school year, experienced no difficulty in adapting to this organizational pattern, although they were the youngest pupils in the school.

Teaming, however, may also carry emotional benefits for pupils. As we saw, if one teacher did not establish rapport with a child, another teacher on the team frequently could and did. So children were less dependent on their capacity to relate to a particular adult for a whole school year.

Finally, Gilles Ferry has pointed out that teaming helps where the role of the teacher has become problematic because change is in progress.[20] It allows some coordination in the way the role is played and avoids complete incoherence. It also alleviates teachers' insecurities. We saw this at Southside, where there were meetings of open classroom teachers with change agents, even though there was no fully developed teaming. At these meetings, teachers raised the issue of how much pupil autonomy was mandated by open classroom doctrine and how much teacher authority was permissible. Teachers who felt the need to "give orders" sometimes, were reassured about the appropriateness of such behavior.

Yet Southside also illustrates the potential difficulty of teaming. It was hard to see how Natalie Roseman, a structured open classroom teacher, and Abe Winner, an unstructured one—each expressing strong doctrinal objections to the other's style—could be brought together in the same team.

Organizational Problems of Individualization

All three of the schools we studied were presumably individualizing instruction. The guidelines of the Individualized Learning Program (ILP) at Johnson proposed a fairly formal kind of individualization. Open classroom doctrine specifies a kind of individualization which the teacher carries out informally. However, in each of the schools, individualization was actually quite limited. We suggest that this was so because individualization has consequences which make it inherently difficult for a school to carry out.

A major structural characteristic of schooling is that it is sequential. One cannot enter grade four without completing grade three, or college without completing high school. Sequentiality is a coordinating mechanism; it enables pupils to transfer from any part of the national school system to any other part and be correctly placed. But more important, it guarantees that pupils move along a curricular pathway of increasing difficulty. Once they have mastered certain fundamentals of a subject, they move on to higher levels for which these are prerequisite.[21] They do not get caught in a tangle of backtracking, repetition, or nonprogress.

Sequentiality may be endangered by individualization. Grade level organization may be abandoned, together with the keying-to-grade-level of most commercial curriculum materials. Where this happens, the work of the children must be sequenced by the teachers. The teachers must know the curriculum sequence. At Johnson, where there were multiaged primary and intermediate teams, many teachers did not know how curriculum should be sequenced. The two curriculum facilitators found it necessary to work out an ordered progression of curriculum goals in each subject, for the use of inexperienced and poorly trained teachers.

Another problem of individualization is that it increases the need for detailed communication among the child's successive teachers as to his level of achievement and the specific work he has done. The traditional third-grade teacher assumes that a child entering her class has been exposed to traditional second-grade work. No such organizational principle applies in an individualized or open school. The function of communicating between teachers is supposed to be performed by careful record keeping, but as we saw in Johnson, the records are often neglected. Each successive teacher may diagnose the child herself. But in the case of a slow child—for instance, one who at fourth grade has still not learned to read—the child may find himself repeating the identical work in the same books that he has used in previous years. This is profoundly demoralizing to pupils. It happened not infrequently at Johnson, where communication within teams was good, but communication between teams was almost nonexistent.

Another consequence of individualization is that it increases the dispersion of achievement in any group of children. Whole-class teaching presents the same material to all at the same pace and thereby keeps the dispersion within limits. But if children are literally allowed to progress at their own pace, the variance in achievement among them is very quickly broadened. So are the problems of the teacher. The more heterogeneous the class, the more work the teacher must do to make the curriculum appropriate for each child. The usual response of teachers to such a situation is to stream within the group.[22] That is what the teams at Johnson did. At Southside and Coolidge, streaming was against the policy of the school and against the philosophy of open education as well. Yet three of the five classes we observed at Southside streamed children within the class for reading. The streaming, however, was not the rigid traditional kind. There were as many as six reading groups in a class of twenty-five, an indicator that the grouping was responsive to the actual heterogeneity of the class rather than a preordained structure into which the children were fit.

This pattern of teaching many small groups, rather than either a whole class of twenty-five to thirty, or individual pupils, is what one usually finds in programs labeled "nongraded" or "individualized." The classifying, "batch-processing" nature of the traditional school's structure is modified. Rather than a few classifications, like grade level and stream, there are many, making the organization more flexible and the match between individual pupils' needs and school offerings potentially better. Complete individualization is seldom encountered. Its resource requirements are too immense. The school is always impelled to reduce the demands on its resources by grouping pupils in some way and "treating" them collectively. Since flexible pacing of work lowers the correlation between age and achievement, age is used less as a principle for grouping and achievement is used more. Thus we find multiaged teams and classes in Johnson and Coolidge. At the same time, the ability grouping which has been abolished *between* teams and classes is reintroduced *within* teams and classes in a modified, more flexible form.

We may summarize the major problems of implementation found in our schools as follows:

1. The people who can adopt innovations on a broad scale are the heads of school districts, but the people who must implement them are the teachers. Teachers cannot effect widespread adoption unless they persuade the officials at the top. The district officials cannot implement the innovations they adopt unless they have the willing cooperation of the teachers, and have supplied them with the necessary resourses.

2. Extra resources are needed for any innovation during the period of implementation.

3. Individualized instruction and open classrooms are more expensive than whole-class teaching. This fact is too seldom acknowledged.

4. Educational innovation in the United States has a weak knowledge base. It is carried on in a climate of cultism rather than an atmosphere of scientific experimentation. This prevents the separation of successes from failures and the cumulation of knowledge as to what makes for success.

5. Some schools and districts indulge in excessive amounts of innovation, in a somewhat haphazard way, leading to goal conflicts.

6. Team teaching removes the traditional teacher's main source of gratification, which resides in control of "her" pupils and space and the increase in achievement perceived as an outcome of "her" teaching. It substitutes gratifications arising out of collegiality, but it seems to require excellent interpersonal relations in order to work.

7. Individualization calls into question some of the basic organizational principles of the traditional school. It requires new mechanisms for insuring sequentiality in the pupil's curriculum. It widens the dispersion of achievement and leads to a reintroduction of ability grouping as a mechanism for keeping this dispersion within reasonable bounds.

Chapter 15

The Social Organization of Innovative versus Traditional Classrooms

The liberal school reform movement of the 1960's and early 1970's was not a mere collection of unrelated programs.[1] There was an underlying unity among seemingly diverse innovations. The movement attacked the traditional school and proposed a radically different social organization for elementary education, which we shall simply label *innovative*. In sociological terms, we can say that the traditional school was authoritarian, universalistic, and competitive, while the innovative school is egalitarian, particularistic, and cooperative.[2] But these terms need specification.

In this chapter we shall show that the above structural features of the innovative school were present in all three schools we studied, regardless of the particular innovation being implemented at the time of our observation. Some of these structural characteristics of the innovative schools had been incorporated before we arrived on the scene. Since the schools were very different in social composition and had different histories, their convergence on the major aspects of the innovative pattern of organization testifies to the coherence of the liberal reform movement. In order to show how the innovative school's organization departs from that of the traditional school, we start with Talcott Parsons' classic description of the traditional elementary classroom. We shall find that the classrooms in our schools differ from it in nearly every particular:

> the main process of differentiation (which from another point of view is selection) that occurs during elementary school takes place on a single main axis of *achievement*. . . . That the differentiation should occur on a single main axis is insured by four primary features of the situation. The first is initial equalization of the "contestants'" status by age and by "family background," the neighborhood being typically much more

homogeneous than is the whole society. The second circumstance is the imposition of a common set of tasks which is, compared to most other task areas, strikingly undifferentiated. The school situation is far more like a race in this respect than most role-performance situations. Third, there is the sharp polarization between the pupils in their initial equality and the *single* teacher who is an adult and "represents" the adult world. And fourth, there is a relatively systematic evaluation of the pupils' performances. From the point of view of a pupil, this evaluation, particularly (though not exclusively) in the form of report card marks, constitutes reward and/or punishment for past performance; from the viewpoint of the school system acting as an allocating agency, it is a basis for *selection* for future status in society.[3]

According to this account, pupils in the traditional school are engaged above all in a contest. Marks are distributed on a normal curve. High marks are scarce by definition and pupils compete for them. Some must be winners and others losers, in a race which is run according to rules which apply to all alike. The initial status of the contestants is equalized by age and by home background which tend to be fairly homogeneous in a neighborhood elementary school.[4]

In contrast, none of the three schools we studied held a competition for grades. All three had abolished the practice of marking. Johnson sent home a report card which listed skills and indicated which the child had mastered and which he had yet to attain. Southside and Coolidge sent parents a narrative report on their child's progress. Each child was measured against his own past performance; pupils were not compared to each other. Since there was no contest, it was not necessary to "equalize initial status," and pupils at Johnson and Coolidge were often in multiage groups.

Nor are our innovative schools so concerned as the traditional schools with achievement—in the sense of mastery of a specific body of knowledge. They are more concerned with what they call "learning how to learn"—or with processes which lead to understanding and creativity. This is the express philosophy of open education.

The imposition of a common set of tasks, which Parsons mentions as a condition of the competition in traditional schools, is the antithesis of individualized instruction. While individualization was only imperfectly achieved in the classrooms we studied, the difference in underlying premises is nonetheless important. The school as a race where all must go through the same curriculum under the same rules applies when a major aim is to perform the selection function "fairly." According to Parsons' account, marks in school are the initial basis "for selection for future status in society."[5] It has long been recognized that the selection function of school interferes with the optimal conditions for learning. Once selection is abandoned, as it is in innovative classes, the school can try to optimize conditions for learning. Individualized instruction is an attempt to do this by adapting the work to each child's needs rather than assigning uniform tasks to the class.

The sharp *polarization* between the pupil and the *single* teacher, which Parsons says characterizes the traditional elementary school, is also modified in the innovative school. For one thing, there is less likely to be a single teacher. Even the youngest children may have several teachers—a situation which breaks sharply from the structure of the home and does not permit the child to identify in school with one adult. Second, the polarization between teachers and pupils is not so great in innovative schools. The innovative school can reduce the social distance between pupils and teachers, because the teachers need no longer sit in judgment on the relative quality of the children's work. Whereas the traditional teacher must above all be "fair" in her evaluations, the innovative teacher, who makes no invidious comparisons, is freer to be warm and nurturant.

These contrasts between the innovative and traditional school imply change in the roles of pupils, parents, and teachers which we now take up in more detail.

Changes in the Role of the Pupil

The spatial organization of the innovative classroom is the clue to change in pupils' roles. In the traditional classroom, each pupil sits at "his" desk, an isolated individual, surrounded by competitors with whom communication—especially about work—is severely limited. In the classrooms we have described, pupils sit around tables with self-chosen peers. They interact freely, and they move freely about the room from activity to activity. The changed spatial relationships are a necessary condition for the changed work relationships. The children do most of their work in small groups. In open classrooms, cooperation on tasks is explicitly encouraged. On the ILP teams in Johnson, too, children at the same table worked together, and this was permitted and sometimes promoted. In traditional classrooms, collaboration on their work by children is defined as "cheating." But where pupils are not in competition, the help which they can give each other is valued.

We have also shown that in some open classrooms, the authority of the peer group fills the vacuum left by withdrawal of the teacher's authority. Choices, instead of being made individually, are made by the peer group. If the contract system is used—as at Coolidge School—contracts are kept carefully within "output norms"* set by the peer group. And pupils plan their contracts collaboratively to insure that they will be able to work together. Pupil peer groups, rather than competing individuals, are central to the dynamics of such a classroom. Getting along with peers at work and at play is the "hidden curriculum."

By eliminating competition and whole-class teaching, the innovative school reduces pupil anxiety over performance and fear of public humiliation over a poor performance. Children are not marked on performance, nor are they forced to "recite" with the entire class as an audience. It is part of the ethos of the innovative school to promote each child's self-esteem. We have seen that ideally this is done by tailoring the work to the child in such a way that he experiences growing mastery. Although Johnson did this very poorly, its proclaimed goal nonetheless was self–esteem for all its pupils. A favorable self-concept is also a stated goal of the open classroom.

Still another consequence of the breakdown of competition in the innovative school is the breakdown of universalism in the teacher-pupil relationship. In the innovative classroom, the teacher-pupil relationship is particularistic. Not only do innovative teachers individualize instruction, they also adapt the socialization process to the emotional needs of each child.

Pupils in innovative classrooms have higher status vis-à-vis the teacher than those in traditional rooms. They are permitted some choice as to what work they will do. Learning how to make

---

*This term is used by sociologists to describe what happens within informal work groups, e.g. in a factory. The group collectively keeps output within certain limits.

good choices and carry them through—in short, learning to be autonomous rather than obedient—is a major aspect of socialization in open and individualized schools. It is exemplified in the 5–6 team at Coolidge, except that here it was poorly carried out. Pupils were permitted to make undemanding contracts and there was little effort to insure that contracts were fulfilled.

Also, pupils in innovative schools are treated in more egalitarian fashion by their teachers than is customary in the traditional school. Johnson had its students' bill of rights. The reader will recall that at a class meeting in Mrs. Waters' homeroom, pupils were highly critical of a substitute teacher. Mrs. Waters accepted their criticism as legitimate and said the substitute would have to "change his behavior since it is not satisfactory to you." At a meeting of teachers with change agents at Southside, a teacher asked whether it was all right to "give orders" to pupils on some occasions. For a traditional teacher to raise such a question is inconceivable.

To summarize, the major differences for pupils between the innovative and traditional school are that first, the innovative school abolishes competition and with it much anxiety; second, children do much of their work cooperatively in small groups and the authority of peers comes to substitute in part for the authority of the teacher; third, it establishes more particularistic and egalitarian relationships between pupils and teachers; and fourth, work is less oriented to learning facts and more to the development of problem-solving ability.

Change in the Role of Parents

In a traditional school, the teacher must maintain a universalistic attitude toward her students, treating them all alike under the code of rules, so that none will be given an unfair competitive advantage. By contrast, the proper role for the parent vis-à-vis the child is always particularistic. She must take account of his special needs and put his welfare before any other considerations. Thus there is a built-in conflict between parent and teacher, since the parent may request special consideration for her child which the teacher cannot conscientiously accord.[6] This conflict makes it necessary for the traditional school to keep parents at a certain distance.[7] The principal mediates between parents and teachers. It is a norm among traditional teachers that the principal must always defend their actions in front of parents no matter how severely he may reprimand them privately. If this solid front is not maintained by the principal, the teachers deny him their cooperation.

The particularism of the innovative school eases the parent-teacher conflict, making it possible for the two to collaborate in the child's interests. In addition, the innovative school puts less emphasis on academic achievement and more on social-emotional development than does the traditional school. Thus it shares the parents' concern for the affective side of the child. As a result, innovative schools usually try to involve parents deeply in school affairs. This happened at Johnson and Southside. Johnson's teachers made mandatory visits to their pupils' homes to learn more about their backgrounds and to form a liaison with their parents. The principal did his best to involve parents in the governance of the school. There were many parents inside the school in the role of paraprofessional teacher aides.

At Southside there was a core of very active parents who did volunteer work in the classroom and who cooperated with change agents and administrators to promote Open Classroom Teaming (OCT). The administrators had plans to broaden community participation to include minority parents, who were badly under-represented.

At Coolidge the parents were *too* deeply involved in school affairs from the standpoint of the staff. They had seized the prerogative of choosing their children's classroom placement, a decision which the principal and teachers wanted to regain for themselves. They were extraordinarily active, both collectively, through the PTA, and individually, looking out for their children's interests. What the Coolidge staff needed was to free the school of parental control, to some extent, rather than to involve parents further.[8]

Change in the Role of the Teacher

The innovative teacher is frequently a member of a team. Teaming was practiced at Johnson and Coolidge, and it was a goal of the change agents at Southside. The team teacher is no longer isolated in her self-enclosed classroom, but becomes part of a group of peers who cooperate on instructional tasks. In this situation, getting along with peers becomes as important for teachers as it is for pupils in innovative classrooms.

When teachers are teamed, their collective influence rises and their role relationships become more egalitarian. They have greater leverage vis-à-vis the principal than any single teacher would have, and they are less authoritarian vis-à-vis their pupils.

A major concern of the traditional teacher is gaining control of the class and maintaining order. The underlying premise is that pupils are in school against their will and must be coerced into letting themselves be instructed.[9] To this end, the traditional school imposes regimental routines on pupils—lining up in straight lines, "sitting up tall" in seats, maintaining silence while the teacher talks, looking at the teacher, raising hands to be called on when one wants to speak, and so on. The teacher keeps the whole class under detailed surveillance to see that the numerous rules are not violated. Her desk is at front and center so that all the children are in view. When violations occur, the offenders are punished. All this is believed necessary if the teacher is to give lessons to an attentive class without distraction.[10]

In the innovative classroom, the teacher's desk is usually in an inconspicuous place. It is not necessary for the teacher to be able to see the whole class, since pupils, ideally, are not under continual adult supervision. The teacher moves through the room from group to group, working with one or a few children at a time, while others work on their own. The teacher spends much of her time preparing materials *outside* of the classroom for the pupils to work with in class. Materials which teach—without the teacher—are essential to the innovative school. The regimentation of the traditional classroom disappears. The order is more loose, more flexible, and allows for much more pupil spontaneity. These freer conditions are necessary if pupils are to work autonomously. They are left to create a self-directed order. They order their own time to complete tasks by deadlines agreed on with the teacher. They order their own actions to achieve agreed on goals. They must exercise self-control to preserve discipline, rather than relying on the external control of the teacher.

If pupils are not capable of self-control or of working independently, the innovative classroom is in danger of breaking down. There is a breakdown in the learning process if the pupils cannot work on their own with the materials they are given. This situation was pervasive at Johnson. As we saw, the work assigned was too difficult for the students, so they went through an elaborate charade of copying rather than actually working. If a breakdown of self-control occurs, discipline dissolves into chaos. This happened occasionally at all three schools. But on the whole, Johnson, Southside, and Coolidge maintained good discipline in the flexible, innovative style.

The change in the teacher-pupil relationship is best captured by saying that in traditional schools teachers are active—they talk a lot—and pupils are passive—they listen a lot. In the innovative classroom, pupils are active. They engage in many different activities designed to further mastery of skills and understanding of subject matter. Teachers are active, too, but in a different way from the traditional teacher. They prepare the environment so that the children's activities can go on. They observe and diagnose pupils at work. They give help and advice to sustain or further the pupil's activities. They keep records of what has been mastered so they will know what kinds of tasks should be undertaken next. The innovative teacher's role is more varied and demanding than that of the traditional teacher. The variety, along with the collegiality of teaming, would seem to make it more interesting as well. However, as we saw, the innovative teacher typically suffers from "role overload." The increased cost of innovation is all too often hidden in the excessive demands made on teachers. If this fault were corrected, teachers probably would find the innovative role more gratifying than the traditional one. But to correct it would probably cost more than our society is willing to pay.

Perhaps the most serious question one can raise concerning the social organization of the innovative classroom is: Is it possible to extend this pattern to higher grade levels? It is well known that at present most innovative classes are found at grade levels K through three. Fewer are found in the upper elementary grades. And while experiments with innovative high schools and colleges were not infrequent in the United States in the sixties, they nowhere nearly matched the frequency of early childhood innovation, and they had a high rate of failure.

What was the reason for this? Our answer is that the key to the innovative classroom is its abandonment of the function of *selection* which, according to Parsons, is the central task of traditional classrooms. Virtually all the structural characteristics of the innovative classroom flow from this one crucial fact. No need for selection means no need for competition, for marks, for universalistic rules, for distance between the teacher and pupils, for distance between the teacher and parents, for a ban on academic cooperation among pupils, and so on. The innovative classroom can be cooperative, egalitarian, and particularistic *only* because it need not select.

The early elementary grades can afford to eliminate the selection function because virtually all young people today stay in school to junior high school and beyond. So selection and streaming can be postponed beyond elementary school. But that does not mean that selection has disappeared from the school system. It has simply moved up to higher levels. And if this argument is sound, the innovative pattern of school organization cannot be implemented at those higher levels because selection and the innovative pattern of organization are functionally incompatible. Only if the schools as an institutional complex abandoned selection entirely could innovative education become the predominant style. And that is unlikely. The occupational system depends heavily on the school system for a preliminary sorting of people according to educational attainment.

The school system continues to do that sorting, though at a later age and grade level than when schooling was less widespread than it is today. The innovative pattern of social organization tends to be confined to those grade levels where competitive performance doesn't yet "matter," and our prediction is that, to the extent that it survives, it will remain confined to those levels.

The Backlash against the Innovative Classroom

Not only is innovative schooling not moving to the upper grades, however; today—in the mid-1970's—there is a heavy backlash against it at the lower grades as well. Obituaries of innovative education are appearing with increasing frequency. Five years ago, Roland Barth, author of *Open Education and the American School*, began writing articles which suggested that we forget about open education.[11] In the autumn of 1974, Fred Hechinger, education editor of the *New York Times*, wrote that the newest suburban fashion in education was a return to the traditional teaching of the three R's.[12] A few weeks later, *Newsweek* carried a report to the same effect.[13] And the October, 1974, issue of *The Journal of Educational Research and Development* contained an article called "Why Open Education Died."[14]

Partly, this backlash is due to external circumstances. The seemingly guaranteed affluence of the 1960's, which made parents feel they could "afford to turn to such values as cooperation, egalitarianism, social skill, and freedom of choice, have given way to the straitened circumstances of the 1970's, where parents feel that even upper middle-class children must be trained for a stern competition for scarce rewards. While objectively, the sorting of pupils into different academic streams could be postponed at least until junior high school, from a subjective standpoint, parents and teachers feel that pupils must learn to be competitive early, if they are to learn it at all. And so the teaching of the "cultural nightmare," as Jules Henry called the competitive attitudes, and fear of "failure," which early selection fosters,[15] is returning to the primary grades.

In good part, however, the backlash is due to factors which we have noted throughout this book. For the low-income, minority children at Johnson, a decade of fashionable innovations—including open education and individualized instruction—has failed to bring about any change in their achievement levels, which is their crucial need.

Until recently, the bulk of research on open education seemed to indicate that it had no effect on achievement levels, neither raising nor lowering them. Moreover, there was very little firm evidence that it improved creativity or self-esteem, its own proclaimed goals. Parents, however, do not read research; they make their judgments on the basis of their children's experience. And on this basis many parents, like some of those of the fifth-sixth-grade team pupils at Coolidge, felt that open education was failing to provide their children with basic skills. We saw that the children on this team, who had well above average IQ's, were nevertheless very poor at spelling and punctuation. The parents complained that they were also behind in computational skills, while the teacher pointed out that they were advanced in their conceptual understanding of mathematics. Both these statements were true, but the parents—right or wrong—believed computational skill was more important.

In the city of Walton, we heard many parental complaints about open classrooms which were "completely out of control," and we observed one—Abe Winner's class—which on occasion was very nearly so.

Other parents—along with many "traditional" teachers—faulted the open classroom for allowing many children to get away with doing very little work in school. Again we observed this situation among some children on the 5–6 team and in the 2–3 class in Coolidge. It was also true for most children in Abe Winner's class at Southside. But it definitely was not true for Natalie Roseman's class in the same school.

Many parents have become aware of the strength of peer-group norms among very young children in open classrooms and have felt that they would prefer their children to identify at that age with an adult.

Parents have also become aware that, as Roland Barth points out,[16] open education has no curriculum. The curriculum emerges as an interaction between the materials the teacher happens to bring into the room and what the children choose to do with them. It is not thought necessary to teach the three R's directly. Rather, they should be learned as they become necessary for carrying out the child's own projects. They benefit thereby from his intrinsic motivation to learn them in order to complete the projects.

Critics of open education feel that this, and many other premises of this school of thought, are simply wrong for many, if not the great majority, of children. Skills *do* need to be taught directly. Extrinsic motivation must be used in the classroom or children will fail to learn essential material. Now a large British study has been published showing that children in "progressive" classrooms achieve less in academic subjects and also show less creativity than children in traditional classrooms. If results like these stand the test of criticism and become widely disseminated in this country, open education will have received the final blow.[17]

What are the chief lessons which can be drawn from our case studies? One is that organizational innovations in schools are very difficult to implement. Most of the innovating which occurs is a very imperfect realization of what the innovators intended. That may be due to their lack of realism, or to some lack in the innovating schools, or both. In any case, it is clear that educational innovation in the United States needs a stronger knowledge base than it now has. Innovations should be tried out on a limited experimental basis and assessed with care and sophistication before governments and foundations undertake to fund their broad dissemination to schools.

A second implication of our case studies, brought out in this chapter, is that the innovations of the 1960's and early 1970's were largely the expression of a set of values—a pale reflection of the counterculture—which flourished in the upper middle-class while the economy was growing rapidly—and died when the economic growth ran into trouble.

The humane values of the innovative classroom can only be sustained in an environment of abundance, where the need of the individual to compete for scarce material rewards, and of the society to use the schools as a preliminary mechanism for allocating people to different levels of the occupational and social structure, have eased. Just as soon as material abundance for virtually all the offspring of the upper middle-class is no longer assured, the schools reflect the change in the economy by returning to "traditional" schooling with its harsher value system, geared to the harsher realities of the economic situation. That is what is happening today.

The future of our economy and society are contingent on such a complex combination of factors that our best social critics are groping their way haltingly through analyses to forecasts. No one can forecast the future of education in such circumstances, except that, as always, education will reflect the needs of dominant social groups. Educational styles depend on such needs. Education does not change society; it reinforces major social trends.

APPENDIX, NOTES, AND INDEX

Appendix: Research Methods

The first thing that needs to be said here is that I was misled, by the experience of many of my colleagues in the sociology of education, into believing that I would have to send out many requests to schools for permission to study them, in order to receive a small number of invitations to do the study. I began sending out requests in the spring of 1972. The study was to begin the following autumn. I received three turndowns, thirty-two letters which said their schools didn't qualify under *my* guidelines,* and sixty-one invitations to study the school—before I began sending out form letters, in late August, saying that I regretted having to turn down the invitations, but the schools to be studied were already chosen. Unfortunately, I do not have a completely reliable figure for the total number of letters I sent out; so I don't know the number of non-responses, but I do recall that it was small. The proportions of different types of responses I received and have kept on file suggests no difficulty in gaining entry; quite the contrary. And the number of favorable responses is an underestimate, because it excludes the ones which eventually received the form with our regrets. It was the end of August; I had my schools; and I stopped keeping the letters—certainly a methodological error, as was my failure to record the number of non-responses.

The contrast between this experience and that of other re-

*I specified that the school had to be at least K through six, that the innovation should extend to the upper elementary as well as primary grades and that it should have been in progress for at least a year. As the reader knows, I lowered the specifications along the way (i.e., during the late spring, before the study began). I did that because many schools were writing that they would like to be in the study, but didn't meet all three specifications. If I had started with the lower specifications, the figure for favorable responses would be higher.

searchers is puzzling. The only clue I have is that many replies emphasized the impression made by the proposal,* written for the Spencer Foundation and other foundations to which I applied for funds, and which I enclosed with each request sent out. Just what it was about that proposal which had this effect, I don't know. There were a few schools which almost begged me to come. They seemed to think I could and would help them solve their problems. Also relevant is the fact that I was not proposing to conduct a study in a highly tense, controversial atmosphere such as surrounds the busing issue. There was some tension and controversy present, though, as the reader will recall, especially in District 7 of the city of Walton.

The methods Schorr and I used to collect data were participant-observation, interviewing, and the gathering of relevant documents and records.

Much of the interviewing consisted of long conversations which sprang naturally out of our interaction with the people we were observing. Our formal interviews were also with people we had been observing for some time. Although we asked a few standard questions in all of these interviews, for the most part each was unique. They were designed to clarify for us the meaning of some actions of interviewees which we had not fully understood, and to elicit their views on matters which seemed to us to be critical.

Laura Schorr and I went into the field clearly identified as researchers. We had little choice in this matter, since our schools were selected after a country-wide search† for elementary schools which had organizational innovations in progress and which were willing to be studied. We had little choice in another sense, as well, since neither of us was qualified as an elementary school teacher—nor did we wish to spend the whole year in one school. We could not, as Gerald Levy so ably did, teach in a school for a year, while acting as an observer, unbeknownst to any save one other person.[1]

The role we played in the schools we studied was mainly that of teacher aide. During our sojourn in a classroom, we volunteered to help the teacher in any way she wished, with the

---

*The proposal is quoted in the Introduction. Almost all of it is included there.

†I decided on the regional limitation, mentioned in the Introduction, *after* I was flooded with invitations from all over the country to study schools.

sole proviso that we not be sent out of the room to do chores which removed us from the scene of the action. As it turned out, by virtue of differences in age and academic status, I established better rapport than Schorr with the staffs of the schools, and Schorr, due to a natural gift for relating to children, established better rapport with the pupils. For at least two days, well separated in time, in each school, I accompanied the principal on his or her rounds, observing a principal's everyday tasks. The principals were helpful in elucidating the meaning of events, when necessary. They were interviewed formally as well, sometime after the observations had taken place.

In our own minds, as we began the study, we took the classic position of participant-observers that we would disturb the setting as little as possible.[2] But there were a few occasions when we did intervene in a situation. For instance, I told the principal of Johnson about the perceptual-motor tests being carried out by one of his primary teams and suggested that he make the procedure a standard one for all incoming pupils. The principal refused, on the ground that the problem was massive and sufficient funds for remediation unobtainable. He was probably right on both scores. Nevertheless, his own solution for the pupils' academic problems—to politicize them—was not working either politically or educationally.

On another occasion I discussed the peer group structure of her class with one of the fifth-grade open classroom teachers at Coolidge and discovered that she did not know about it. I described it for her, at her insistence. Shortly after, she had a discussion with the students about it, making them more aware of it than they had been. I also asked the district official in charge of reading at Centerville why he did not investigate the teachers' claims for DISTAR. The reader may have spotted additional interventions. Lending a sympathetic ear is itself an intervention. That struck home to me when two teachers told me that they never would have gotten through the year without me to listen to their gripes.

Our observational procedures included taking notes on the scene when practicable, which was often the case amidst the bustle of an open classroom. When we could not do that—for instance, during a tense meeting—we noted down some key words immediately afterward to help us recall the content and sequence of the discussion. We dictated our observations at the end of each school day into a tape recorder, for later transcription by a typist. This is an expensive procedure, but I recommend it to participant-observers who can afford it. Typing is tiring. It tempts one to condense and to leave out things which seem unimportant at the moment, but might turn out to be very important later on. Talking into a tape recorder is much easier and leads to fuller notes. At least that is my experience.

We ended the study with nearly 2,000 pages of field notes, in four copies: one for each of us to work with, one for cutting out excerpts to insert into the text as illustrations, and one to be kept in a different place, as a hedge against destruction of the notebooks.

To reduce the materials to manageable form, we made up a code; i.e., a list of categories and subcategories we wanted to write about. Each of us then read through a set of the field notes. Every time material relevant to a category appeared, we noted the page numbers under that category. Then we combined our two code books.

This proved a very convenient device. Whenever we needed material on some specific category, the code book told us where it was. On the occasions when we wanted to write about a remembered incident not included in the code book, we had to try to recall the approximate date and make a search through the field notes to find it. That can be a frustrating procedure if one's memory isn't good. It is also one of the reasons why it is important for participant-observation studies to be written up as soon as possible after the field work is completed.

In my case, the constraints of teaching obligations ruled out the highly desirable procedure of leaving the field, writing for a while, and then returning to the scene of the observations to check whether they hold up.

A major problem of the method of participant-observation is that of reliability. Would another observer have seen what I saw? The fact that Schorr was in the same schools at the same time, though in different classrooms, helped. We discussed the schools constantly, agreed, disagreed, went back to look again, and, I believe, held in check each other's biases.

Participant-observation is valuable because it gives a "whole" picture of a social setting in terms of the functions and dysfunctions of particular social patterns. One of the problems of sociological research is that, despite what the methodology texts say, field studies usually do *not* produce hypotheses easily translatable into the language of variables, which can be tested by quantitative methods. Or if they do produce such hypotheses, the survey researchers and experimentalists don't test them. But participant-observation does help us to understand how a social setting functions and malfunctions, whereas explanatory survey research (and experimental designs) usually deal with analytical variables, useful for testing hypotheses but not for this kind of wholistic analysis. Learning how to make the language of field work (and functional analysis) and the language of variables and surveys mutually translatable, and the respective styles of research mutually supportive, is a task still undone.

Notes

Introduction

1. The study was made as the basis of a background paper for an OECD international conference on teaching. The five schools included three which were elementary, one middle school, and one high school. In addition, it drew on two case studies in unpublished dissertations. These were Roland S. Barth, "Open Education," Harvard Graduate School of Education (HGSE), 1970, and Maurice Gibbons, "The Search for a Scheme of Individualized Schooling," HGSE, 1969. My paper is available as Leila Sussmann, "*The Role of the Teacher in Selected Innovative Schools in the United States,*" in *The Teacher and Educational Change: A New Role*, Part 2, Experts' Papers (Paris: OECD, 1974), pp. 37–144. Both Barth and Gibbons later turned their dissertations into books: Roland Barth, *Open Education and the American School* (New York: Agathon Press, 1972); Maurice Gibbons, *Individualized Instruction: A Descriptive Analysis* (New York: Teacher's College Press, 1972).
2. Barth, *Open Education*, pp. 108–174.
3. Charles Silberman, *Crisis in the Classroom* (New York: Random House, 1970), e.g. pp. 224–225, 229–231, 233–235.
4. "The powerful social forces that gripped our class took me completely by surprise" (Gibbons, "Search for a Scheme," p. 195).
5. Neville Bennett et al., *Teaching Styles and Pupil Progress* (Cambridge, Mass.: Harvard University Press, 1976), pp. 24–25. Bennett found that anxious children do less well in open classrooms than in "formal" ones.
6. Gibbons, "Search for a Scheme," p. 195. The author claims that in his classroom members of the same peer group tended to be alike in academic ability and in "level of energy."
7. For a quasi-experimental study which compared the self-esteem of pupils in open classrooms with those in more traditional ones, see David D. Franks et al., "The *Effects of Open Schools on Children: An Evaluation,*" Project #3-1347, National Institute of Education, Grant #NE-C-00-30209, U.S. Department of Health Education and Welfare, Washington, D.C., 1977.
8. "The teachers in the non-graded Old Bethpage had some problems with parents. . . . Parents were given detailed information about their child's progress through levels and anecdotal reports concerning his effort—but no information comparing his performance with that of other children. . . . However, parents reinterpreted every bit of information they received in terms of competitive comparison with other children" (Leila Sussmann, *Innovation in Education—the United States* [Paris: OECD, 1971], p. 25). The information comes from Lillian Golgan and Murray Fessel, *The Non-Graded Primary School: A Case Study* (West Nyack, N.Y.: Parker, 1967).
9. Patrick Suppes found that " . . . when students are given the opportunity to progress at will, the rate at which the brightest children advance may be five to ten times faster than that of the slowest children." Although he began with a group of students very homogeneous in initial measures of ability—I.Q.'s ranged from 122 to 167—after a year and a half, the achievement spread was "almost two years." Quoted in Sussmann, *Innovation in Education*, p. 45. In another case study it was reported that the spread became so wide that the teachers found it unmanageable

253

and they began slowing down the fastest students, for instance by refusing to give them any homework. See Richard O. Carlson, *Adoption of Educational Innovations* (Eugene, Ore.: The Center for the Advanced Study of Educational Administration, 1965).

10. The phrase "middle range" theory was invented by Robert K. Merton in pleading for less grand theorizing and less trivial research in sociology Robert K. Merton, *Social Theory and Social Structure* (2d ed.; Glencoe, Ill.: Free Press, 1957), pp. 9, 280, 328.

11. Talcott Parsons, "The School Class as a Social System: Some of Its Functions in American Society," *Harvard Educational Review* 29 (Fall 1959): 297–318. The article was reprinted in Jean Floud, A. H. Halsey, and Arnold Anderson, eds., *Education, Economy, and Society* (Glencoe, Ill.: Free Press, 1961), pp. 434–435. All page numbers cited in these notes refer to the latter publication.

Chapter 1

1. Samuel Bowles, "Getting Nowhere," *Society* 9 (June 1972): 1–8.

Chapter 2

1. The argument that open education works with middle-class children who have been socialized to independence, but not with working- or lower-class children who have not been so socialized, has been made often; for instance, in Roland Barth, *Open Education and the American School* (New York: Agathon Press, 1972). The argument seems plausible, but there is as yet little systematic research on the topic. One research project in Canada reported that inner-city schools with open programs showed consistently lower achievement scores than those with less open programs, while in the suburbs, there was no consistent relationship (Ross E. Traub and Joel Weiss, "Studying Openness in Education: An Ontario Example, " *Journal of Research and Development in Education* 8 (Fall 1974): 54–55.

2. Eugene Litwak and Henry J. Meyer, *School, Family and Neighborhood* (New York: Columbia University Press, 1974), p. 44.

3. James S. Coleman et al., *Equality of Educational Opportunity* (Washington, D.C.: U.S. Office of Education, 1966).

4. Christopher Jencks et al., *Inequality* (New York: Basic Books, 1972).

5. Barth, *Open Education*, chap. 3.

6. Morris Rosenberg and Roberta Simmons, *Black and White Self-Esteem: The Urban School Child* (Washington, D.C.: The Arnold and Caroline Rose Monograph Series in Sociology, 1971).

Chapter 3

1. E. G. W. W. Charters, Jr., et al., *The Process of Planned Change in the School's Instructional Organization* (Monograph 25; Eugene, Ore.: Center for the Advanced Study of Educational Administration, University of Oregon, 1973).

2. Matthew Miles, "A Matter of Linkage: How Can Innovation Research and Practice Influence Each Other?" in S. V. Tempkin and M. V. Brown, eds., *What Does Re-*

search Say about Getting Innovation into the Schools: A Symposium (Philadelphia: Research for Better Schools, 1974).

3. The Bereiter-Engelmann program in an earlier form was referred to by Jensen in his *Harvard Educational Review* (Winter 1969) article entitled, "How Much Can We Raise IQ and Scholastic Achievement?" The early Bereiter-Engelmann program to which Jensen referred was a preschool program. Jensen said, "The pre/post gains (not measured against a control group) on the Stanford-Binet IQ are about eight to ten points. Larger gains are shown in tests that have clearly identifiable content which can reflect the areas receiving specific instruction, such as the Illinois Test of Psycho-Linquistic Abilities and test of reading and arithmetic. Bereiter and Engelmann, correctly, I believe, put less stock in IQ gains than in the gains in scholastic performance. . . . [The] scholastic performance was commensurate with that of children 10 or 20 points higher in IQ. . . . An important point of the Bereiter-Engelmann program is that it shows that scholastic performance the acquisition of basic skills—can be boosted much more, at least in the early years, than can the IQ, and that highly concentrated direct instruction is more effective than more diffuse cultural enrichment" (p. 106).

4. J. S. Fuerst, "Report from Chicago: A Program That Works," *The Public Interest* 43 (Spring 1976): 59–60. Fuerst says in a footnote: "Reading tests are given to second-graders in the eighth month of the ten month school year. Thus the expected standard score is 2.8."

5. "10 Years of Health Care Called a Success," *New York Times*, June 8, 1975: ". . . young children of the lower socioeconomic level had a much higher frequency of severe problems including . . . neurological diseases and nutritional deficiencies. . . . Further improvements are expected through a new . . . program of early childhood health screening which will provide even more complete examinations for Head Start children and their siblings."

6. The Moynihan Report, as it is popularly known, was a government policy paper called *The Negro Family: The Case for National Action*, published in March 1965 by the Office of Policy Planning and Research, United States Department of Labor, and authored by Daniel Patrick Moynihan for a White House conference on children. Because it was highly controversial, its contents reached a wider audience. Moynihan blamed many of the problems of Negroes (the term then current) on forces which had undermined the position of the man as head and main supporter of the family, leaving a large number of Negro families headed by women. He implied that this situation was "pathological" and was the source of many other problems. For a reprint of the original report, see Lee Rainwater and William L. Landy, *The Moynihan Report and the Politics of Controversy* (Cambridge, Mass.: M.I.T. Press, 1967), pp. 39–124.

7. Paul Berman and Milbrey Wallin McLauglin, *Federal Programs Supporting Educational Change*, vol. 4 (Washington, D.C.: U.S. Office of Education, Department of Health, Education, and Welfare, April 1975), p. viii. Berman and McLauglin make the point that innovations arising out of a need felt in the school are much more successfully implemented than those adopted opportunistically.

Chapter 4

1. Gertrude Noar, *Individualized Instruction: Every Child a Winner* (New York: John Wiley and Sons, 1972).

2. The staff of a traditional school with self-enclosed classrooms, on the other hand, could have both low cohesion and low conflict. For the effects of teaming in open

space on teachers, see John Meyer and Elizabeth Cohen et al., *The Impact of the Open-Space School upon Teacher Influence and Autonomy (Technical Report No. 21; Stanford, Calif.: Stanford Center for Research and Development in Teaching, Stanford University, Oct. 1971).*

Chapter 5

1. Dan C. Lortie, *Schoolteacher* (Chicago: University of Chicago Press, 1975), p. 104, points out that teachers cite their successes with individual pupils as a major source of gratification.

Chapter 6

1. Given this attitude on the part of the Director of the OCT Advisory, the reader may wonder how we managed to study open classrooms in Southside. The answer is that the director didn't learn we were in the school until we ourselves sought him out for an interview. By that time, our work was nearly finished, and it was too late for him to deny us access to Southside.
2. Title I of the Elementary and Secondary Education Act (ESEA) awards federal assistance to school districts based on the proportion of pupils in a school who come from families below the poverty line.
3. In the Coleman study, "high fate control" meant disagreement with the statements that "Good luck is more important than hard work for success"; "Every time I try to get ahead something or someone stops me"; and "People like me don't have much of a chance to be successful in life" (James S. Coleman et al., *Equality of Educational Opportunity* [Washington, D.C.: U.S. Office of Education, 1966], p. 320).

Chapter 7

1. E.g. Neal Gross, Joseph Giaquinta, and Marilyn Bernstein, *Implementing Organizational Innovations* (New York: Basic Books, 1971), state that participation of subordinates in initiating innovation has been held to be very important in most of the literature, but they deny that there is conclusive evidence that it is indispensable.

Chapter 8

1. Open education was borrowed by U.S. educators from Britain, where it originated. However, it underwent some change in crossing the Atlantic. This was natural, since British and American societies, not to speak of their school systems, are different. British teachers are more professional than American, and British children are more deferential to adult authority. Those two facts alone are enough to account for considerable variation in the way open education is implemented in the two countries.
2. Roland Barth, *Open Education and the American School* (New York: Agathon Press, 1972), chaps. 1 and 2. Where direct quotes are used, page numbers are given in the text.

3. Most American studies find that open classroom pupils score neither better nor worse than traditional pupils on achievement tests. See Diane Levin and Leila Sussmann, "A Review of Research in Open Education," Medford, Mass.: Tufts University, Nov. 1974 (mimeo.). One study conducted by the Ontario Institute for Research in Education suggested that "inner city children," in this case French-Canadians, achieved less well in open classrooms than in traditional ones. See Ross E. Traub and Joel Weiss, "Studying Openness in Education: An Ontario Example," *Journal of Research and Development in Education* 8 (Fall 1974): 54–55: "The results for Inner City schools stood in marked contrast to those for suburban institutions. The achievement results consistently favored Inner City schools with less open programs over Inner City schools with more open programs." A large British study, published in 1976, showed that children in "progressive" (this includes open) classrooms scored distinctly less well in achievement than children who were "formally" taught (Neville Bennett et al., *Teaching Styles and Pupil Progress* [London: Blackwells, 1976])

4. This is, of course, the classic problem of communicating accurate information upward in a hierarchical situation. This was not a very elaborate hierarchy, yet the advisers were surely motivated not to report their failures to the director, if they were aware of them, and the director might have been motivated not to hear of such failures. To quote Harold Wilensky, "Matching the motive and opportunity of the subordinate to remain silent are the superior's motive and opportunity to close his ears" (*Organizational Intelligence* [New York: Basic Books, 1967], p. 44).

Chapter 9

1. The reader will recall that DISTAR is the highly programmed reading and mathematics curriculum devised by Bereiter and Englemann and used by some of the teachers in the Johnson School, who found it extraordinarily effective. As we reported, it has since been found highly effective with inner-city children in a large experiment in Chicago (J. S. Fuerst, "Report from Chicago: A Program That Works," *The Public Interest* 43 [Spring 1976]: 59–60).

2. Herbert Walberg and Susan Thomas, "Open Education: An Operational Definition and Validation in Great Britain and the United States," *American Education Research Journal* 9 (1972): 197–202.

3. As we said above, many of the minority children in this school came from families which were upwardly mobile. It was the principal who first pointed this out to us.

4. Science Research Associates.

5. Charles II. Rathbone, "Open Education and the Teacher" (Ph. D. diss., Harvard Graduate School of Education, Harvard University, 1970), pp. 58–59.

6. Willard Waller, *The Sociology of Teaching* (New York: John Wiley and Sons, Inc., 1965). This book was first published in 1932.

7. Roland Barth, *Open Education and the American School* (New York: Agathon Press, 1972), pp. 143–144.

Chapter 11

1. Eugene Litwak and Henry J. Meyer, *School, Family and Neighborhood* (New York: Columbia University Press, 1974).

2. Ibid., p. 24.

Chapter 12

1. One of the student teachers was in the room during the entire period of observation. The other joined the class in the middle of the observation period.
2. There is a considerable literature on the powerful effects of others' expectations on behavior. A book which deals with the problem specifically in relation to the effects of teachers' expectations on children's school performance is Robert Rosenthal and Lenore Jacobson, *Pygmalion in the Classroom* (New York: Holt, Rinehart and Winston, 1968).
3. Roland Barth, *Open Education and the American School* (New York: Agathon Press, 1972), p. 144.
4. James Coleman, *The Adolescent Society* (Glencoe, Ill.: Free Press, 1963).
5. In Britain there is often only one teacher with thirty children. When people speculate as to why this does not lead to disorder, as it would here, they usually say that British children are more deferential to authority and British teachers less hesitant to exercise authority, even in the open classrooms, than their counterparts in the United States.
6. Joseph Grannis, Walter Freeman, and Sally Kamensky, "Leaders' and Pupils' Roles in Variously Structured Classroom Settings and Subsettings" (paper presented at American Education Research Associates Meetings, Chicago, Apr. 1972).
7. Coleman, *Adolescent Society*, chap. 2.
8. Maurice Gibbons, "The Search for a Scheme of Individualized Schooling" (Ph. D. diss., Harvard Graduate School of Education, Harvard University, 1969).

Chapter 14

1. R. G. Havelock and Mary C. Havelock, with assistance of Elizabeth Markowitz, *Educational Innovation in the United States*, vol. 1: *The National Survey: The Substance and the Process*, project report for the National Institute of Education (originally U.S. Office of Education) (Ann Arbor: Center for Research on Utilization of Scientific Knowledge, Institute for Social Research, University of Michigan, June 1973), pp. 11, 19, and 111.
2. Neal Gross, Joseph Giaquinta, and Marilyn Bernstein, *Implementing Organizational Innovations* (New York: Basic Books, 1971).
3. An example would be the Individualized Reading Program at Southside.
4. This point is made in Paul Berman and Milbrey Wallin McLaughlin, *Federal Programs Supporting Educational Change*, vol. 4 (Rand Corp., Santa Monica, Calif., 1974, prepared for U.S. Office of Education, Department of Health, Education and Welfare), p. viii. Seymour Sarason made a similar distinction between changes arising from a felt need and those imposed from outside. He pointed out that teachers who are subjected to conditions like those in Johnson develop a "Here we go again" response to innovation, which leads to non-implementation (*The Culture of the School and the Problem of Change* (Boston: Allyn and Bacon, 1971), pp. 36–37.
5. Ibid., p. 24.
6. David Livingstone, "Organizational Innovativeness," The Ontario Institute for Studies in Education, Ontario, Feb. 1970 (unpub. paper), pp. 31–33.
7. Matthew Miles, "A Matter of Linkage: How Can Innovation Research and Practice Influence Each Other?" in S. V. Tempkin and M. V. Brown, eds., *What Does Re-*

search Say about Getting Innovation into the Schools: A Symposium (Philadelphia: Research for Better Schools, 1974), p.205.

8. The point was first made to me about ten years ago by a Boston School Department official who was overseeing the adoption of a program of individualization in several Boston schools. She indicated that the Department never tried to introduce the program unless the principal wanted it, because if he didn't want it, the chances of implementation were nil.

9. This situation, rather than negative attitudes, often prevents implementation. We discuss it in more detail below.

10. Gross et al., *Implementing Organizational Innovations*.

11. Ibid., pp. 180–181.

12. This is the chief message contained in Louis Smith and Pat Keith, *The Anatomy of Educational Innovation: An Organizational Analysis of an Elementary School* (New York: John Wiley and Sons, 1971), see especially pp. 84–88.

13. See Ronald K. Hamilton, "Testing and Decision-Making Procedures for Selected Individualized Programs," *Review of Educational Research* 44 (Fall 1974): 371–400.

14. Havelock, *Educational Innovations*, p. 94.

15. "One simple shift in political posture which would reduce the problem is the shift from the advocacy of a specific reform to the advocacy of the seriousness of the problem, and hence to the advocacy of persistence in alternative reform efforts should the first one fail" (Donald Campbell, "Reforms as Experiments," in *Evaluating Action Programs*, ed. Carol Weiss [Boston: Allyn and Bacon, 1972], p. 189).

16. Smith and Keith, *Anatomy of Educational Innovation*, use the term "true believers" to apply to the teachers who implement an innovation out of a deep faith in it.

17. "While a large body of literature has recently evolved which describes open education practices (Bartel, 1972), little has been published describing the overall effect that these programs have on children. Friendlander (1965) proposes that caution must be used with educational innovations lest they become universally accepted as a new orthodoxy without detailed and firm evidence that they can fulfill the expectations for improvement held for them. Walberg and Thomas (1972) noted in reference to the growing move toward open schools, 'There has been very little research and validation on Open Education, aside from the testimonials by exponents and reporters' " (Robert J. Wright, "The Affective and Cognitive Consequences of an Open Education Elementary School," *American Educational Research Journal* [Fall 1975], p. 450).

18. Dan C. Lortie, *Schoolteacher* (Chicago: University of Chicago Press, 1975), pp. 102–106.

19. John Meyer and Elizabeth Cohen et al., *The Impact of the Open-Space School upon Teacher Influence and Autonomy* (Technical Report No. 21; Stanford, Calif.: Stanford Center for Research and Development in Teaching, Stanford University, Oct. 1971), pp. 126–134.

20. Gilles Ferry, "The Role of the Teacher in Selected Innovative Schools in France," in *The Teacher and Educational Change* (Paris: Organization for Economic Cooperation and Development, 1974), pp. 119–174.

21. In part, the sequentiality of schooling is based on the presumably sequential structure of the subjects studied. But subject-matter sequentiality is limited and the school system carries the principle further organizationally than subjects demand. Another basis for organizational sequence is the increased socialization which advanced subjects demand. For instance, one does not, in social studies, introduce serious critiques of the pupil's own society until fundamental loyalty has presumably been internalized.

The importance of the sequential character of the educational system was first brought home to me by Professor Thomas F. Green's several unpublished working papers, "Toward a General Theory of Educational Systems" (Education Policy Research Center, Syracuse University Research Corporation, Syracuse, N.Y., 1972–1973).

22. Robert O. Carlson, *Adoption of Education Innovations* (Eugene, Ore.: Center for the Advanced Study of Educational Administration, 1965), points out that some teachers responded to the situation by deliberately slowing down the fast learners—they gave them no homework—and jacking up the slow learners with extra help.

Chapter 15

1. There was also, simultaneously, a conservative reform movement which has been mentioned only in passing in these pages. It was behavioristic in outlook and used such key terms as "teacher accountability," "performance-based" instruction, and "competency-based" teacher training. An excellent article bearing on both the conservative and liberal reform movements is Christopher J. Hurn, "Theory and Ideology in Two Traditions of Thought about Schools," *Social Forces* 54, no. 4 (Summer 1976): 848–865. The author kindly sent me a copy of this paper prior to its publication. This chapter owes a good deal to the thoughts it stimulated.

2. "Universalistic" is a sociological term which means that all persons playing a given social role, e.g. that of "pupil," are treated and evaluated according to the same set of performance standards, insofar as that role is concerned, "Particularistic" means—in this chapter—that players of the same role may be treated and evaluated differently, in a way which takes into account the individual's special circumstances. This is not precisely the meaning given to "particularistic" by Talcott Parsons, who invented both concepts; "universalistic" and "particularistic," and used the former to describe the appropriate stance of the teacher toward her pupils and the latter (by implication) to describe the appropriate stance of a parent toward his or her child. For the parent, the child is unique and should be treated as such; but for the teacher in the traditional school, "particularism" is a deviation from the proper role (Talcott Parsons, "The School Class as a Social System: Some of Its Functions in American Society," first printed in the *Harvard Educational Review*, vol. 29 [Fall 1959], and reprinted in Jean Floud, A. H. Halsey, and Arnold Anderson, ed., *Education, Economy, and Society* [Glencoe: Free Press, 1961]). The page number cited here refers to the reprinted article. Page 439 speaks of "how far teachers can and do treat pupils particularistically in violation of the universalistic expectations of the school." This chapter owes a great debt to this classic article, as will become clear later.

3. Ibid., pp. 436, 437–438.

4. Vide ibid., p. 438.

5. Ibid.

6. To give an example, the parent of a child who writes very slowly cannot legitimately request of the traditional teacher that her child be given extra time to write class assignments and especially tests. But there would be no difficulty in accommodating to this characteristic of the child (which probably signifies poor small muscle control) in an open or individualized classroom.

7. This is true, for instance, of the Boston school system, known for its traditionalism. A story in the *Boston Globe*, Feb. 4, 1976, p. 12, quoted a member of one of the

Parent Advisory Councils set up by the federal court under its desegregation order as follows: "It's snobbery on the part of school administrators to say that most parents 'don't care'. Up until this past year, most parents had only a token involvement in the schools. . . . It is the result of years of conditioning, years of peripheral contact with a system that didn't want parents looking over teachers' and principals' shoulders. Parents were made to feel stupid and treated like intruders. It will take work to undo that kind of conditioning."

8.   Eugene Litwak and Henry J. Meyer, *School, Family and Neighborhood* (New York: Columbia University Press, 1974), discuss this problem, p. 146.

9.   Willard Waller, *The Sociology of Teaching* (New York: John Wiley and Sons, 1965), e.g. chap. 20, "Focal Points of Student-Teacher Antagonism," pp. 339–353.

10.   This "regimentation" is described as an object of the radical critique of the schools by Christopher Hurn, "Theory and Ideology," cited above, note 1.

11.   Roland Barth, "Should We Forget about Open Education?" *Saturday Review,* Nov. 6, 1973, pp. 58–59.

12.   Fred M. Hechinger, " 'New' Education and the Old Three R's," *New York Times,* Sept. 15, 1974, IV, 15:1.

13.   "Back to Basics in the Schools," *Newsweek,* Oct. 21, 1974, pp. 87–97.

14.   "Why Open Education Died," Donald A. Myers, *Journal of Research and Development in Education* 8, no. 1 (Fall 1974): 60–67.

15.   Jules Henry, *Culture Against Man,* (New York: Random House, 1963), p. 305.

16.   Roland Barth, *Open Education and the American School* (New York: Agathon Press, 1972), p. 50.

17.   The British study is Neville Bennett et al., *Teaching Styles and Pupil Progress* (Cambridge, Mass.: Harvard University Press, 1976). Several recent reviews have faulted it on statistical grounds.

Appendix

1.   Gerald Levy, *Ghetto School: Class Warfare in an Elementary School* (New York: Pegasus, 1970), pp. xiv–xv.

2.   For a different view of participant-observation—one which suggests that the observer should "be himself," intervene when he feels impelled to do so, and observe how the setting changes with his interventions—see Michaele Bodemann, "A Problem of Sociological Praxis, the Case for Interventive Observation in Field Work," unpub. paper, Department of Sociology, University of Toronto, Aug. 1974. Parts of the paper were originally presented at the meetings of the American Sociological Association, Montreal, Aug. 1974.

Index

Accountability, teacher, 20–21
Achievement, academic. *See* Pupils' skills
Adult/child ratios in classroom. *See* Teacher-pupil ratios
Administrators, school. *See* Principal, role of, *and* School officials, district and city
Advisers. *See* Change agents
Assessment of achievement levels. *See* Pupils' skills
Assistant principals. *See* Principal and assistant principal, role of
Administrators. *See* Innovators, district officials as, *and* School officials, district and city

Barth, Roland, xii, 22–23, 115–117, 152, 179
Black English, 30–31
Busing, school, 18, 28, 29, 46, 91, 93, 99, 104
Boundary spanners, 19
Brown, H. Rap, 44

Change agents, 57, 61, 62, 80, 96, 109, 110, 112, 114, 119, 219–220, 223, 239; Open Classroom Teaming Advisory (OCT Advisory), 96, 97, 113, 117, 121, 123–126, 127, 130–131, 136, 138, 140, 141, 155, 156, 227
Change in moral climate of school, 9–10, 116, 117, 170, 226
Children. *See* Pupils
Classroom materials, 7, 13, 25, 53, 64, 68, 69, 70, 72, 75–76, 83, 88, 92, 116, 117, 122, 133–135, 137, 142–143, 147, 148, 149, 171–172, 174, 180, 181, 221, 223–224, 244
Classrooms, social organization of, xvi, 28, 234–245
Cleaver, Eldridge, 44
Cliques. *See* Pupils' peer groups
Cobb, Katherine, 190
Coleman, James C., 179, 188–189
Coleman report, 20
Community control of schools, 18, 103, 104

Community relationships with school. *See* Parents, role of
Consultants. *See* Change agents
Competition among pupils, 9, 235, 237, 238, 243
Cooperation among pupils, 237, 238, 243
Corporal punishment, code concerning, 15–16
Curriculum, xi, 5, 6–7, 14, 17, 46, 48, 50, 52, 55, 56, 60, 63, 76, 80, 81, 83, 100, 112, 114, 116, 154, 161, 173, 182, 207, 221, 231, 232, 244; continuity and sequentiality in, 7, 59, 60, 233. *See also* Innovations, specific, Afro-American curriculum

Dewey, John, xvi, 115, 116
DISTAR (Direct Instructional System for Training for Arithmetic and Reading). *See* Innovations, specific, DISTAR
Discipline patterns in school. *See* Socialization patterns in school
District, school. *See* School officials, district and city
Dozens, playing the, 27

Egalitarianism in schools, 116, 130–131, 163, 220, 229, 236–238, 240
Ethnicity. *See* Race and ethnicity in the schools

Falsification of test scores, 90–91

Gibbons, Maurice, 190
Grades (marks), xiv, 3, 4, 8, 9, 116, 235, 236
Green, Thomas F., xxix
Grouping. *See* Instructional groups

Head Start, 40

Innovation, xi, xiv, 9, 12, 34, 92, 95, 96, 104, 109, 110, 111, 113, 245; prevalence of, in U.S. elementary schools, 211–214
Innovation, continual, 4–7, 213
Innovation, process of, xii, 1–7, 34, 35, 37–48, 92, 93, 114, 118–139, 154–157,

Innovation, process of(*cont.*)
170–173, 209, 212–221, 223, 225–226, 245

Innovations, mutually contradictory, xv–xvi

Innovations, specific: Afro-American curriculum, 18, 41–53, 56, 79, 92, 226; bilingual classes, 100, 104; DISTAR, 35–39, 128; district-wide option in choice of school by parents, 105; Flanders Rating Scale, 105; individualized instruction, xi, xiii, xiv, xv, 53, 54, 60, 62, 63, 65, 68, 69, 70, 71, 74, 78, 79, 82, 85, 113, 141, 144, 146, 175, 177, 218, 220, 221, 223, 224–225, 229–233, 235–236, 243; Individualized Learning Program (ILP), 53–61, 62, 78, 81, 82, 84, 85, 92, 93, 113, 215, 217, 219, 222, 224, 226, 231, 237; Individualized Reading Program (IRP), 104, 108, 109–115, 154, 215, 217, 224; integrated day, 116–117, 123, 140, 150; Johnson-on-campus, 2–3, 40, 46, 52; open classrooms, xi, xiii, xiv, *see also* Open classrooms; Open Classroom Teaming (OCT), 96, 115–131, 132, 223, 239, *see also* Open classrooms *and* Open education; open space, 40, 47–51, 82, 83, 228; Pelham-on-campus, 2, 46; perceptual-motor remediation, 35, 39–40; political training of parents, 18; political training of pupils, 6, 12, 51; Superior Educational Achievement Program (SEAP), 2, 3

Innovators, 34; district officials as, 34, 53–61, 217, 222, 233; principals as, 34, 40–64, 217–218; teachers as, 34–40, 52, 215–217, 233

Instructional groups, 35, 58, 60, 62, 70–71, 76–77, 79, 83, 84, 85, 105, 113, 140–141, 142; homogeneous-heterogeneous ability groups, 64–65, 68, 71, 91, 105, 120–121, 136, 138, 162, 194, 219, 232–233; small group instruction, 62, 64, 65, 68, 74, 177, 232; teams as, 62, 77

Integration, racial. *See* Race and ethnicity in the schools, segregation and integration

Isolates, 190–191

Jencks, Christopher, 20 and n

Johnson-on-campus. *See* Innovations, specific, Johnson-on-campus

Kephart Perceptual-Motor Tests, 39

Kids. *See* Pupils

King, Martin Luther, Jr., 23, 44

Learning style. *See* Pupils' learning styles

Levin, Diane, 132, 174

Levy, Gerald, 248

Litwak, Eugene, 19, 168, 169

Loners, 190

Marks. *See* Grades

Marshall, Thurgood, 44

Master teachers. *See* Change agents

Materials. *See* Classroom materials

Meyer, Henry J., 19, 168, 169

Moynihan report, 45

NAACP (National Association for the Advancement of Colored People), 23, 44, 102

Neighborhood. *See* Parents, role of, relationship to teachers

OECD, Organization for Economic Cooperation and Development, xi, xii

Open classrooms, 64, 84, 97, 107, 115, 117, 119–121, 127, 129, 132–153, 159, 160, 163, 173, 174–192, 193–201, 208, 218–220, 223, 224, 227, 230, 231, 237, 244. *See also* Innovations, specific, Open Classroom Teaming (OCT), *and* Open education

Open education, 5, 13, 23, 95, 96, 115, 116, 117, 126, 129, 130, 131, 132, 139, 140, 150, 151, 152, 153, 156, 170, 171, 172–173, 174, 176–177, 193, 194, 209, 219, 220, 221, 223, 227, 235, 243, 244. *See also* Innovations, specific, Open Classroom Teaming (OCT), *and* Open classrooms

Open space. *See* Innovations, specific, open space

Paraprofessionals, 19, 31, 53, 54–56, 63, 75, 78, 101, 102, 106, 129, 142, 220

Parents, role of, 2, 4, 16, 17–18, 19, 95, 96, 98, 99, 100, 102, 103, 104, 106, 107, 117, 118–120, 130, 142, 155, 160, 165–169, 207; relationship to principal, 16, 17, 98, 107, 128, 186, 201–206, 208–209; relationship to teachers, 4, 9, 18, 79, 97, 107, 126, 128, 129, 130, 155, 156, 162, 172, 201–206, 208–209, 238,

239; relationship to their children as pupils, 15–16, 67, 69, 98, 138, 164, 201–206, 208–209, 243–244

Parsons, Talcott, xvi, 234, 235

Participant-observation, xiii, 191, 248, 249–251, 262 n

Peer groups. *See* Pupils' peer groups

Perceptual problems, 31–33, 39–40

Piaget, Jean, 115, 227

Principal and assistant principal, role of, xiv, 3, 11–14, 17, 22, 37, 39–40, 41, 43, 51–52, 53, 55–57, 62, 90, 96, 97, 98, 99, 100, 101, 102, 107, 113, 114, 118, 129, 155, 158–160, 163, 167, 201–206, 239; relationship to higher administrators, 18–19, 92, 109–110, 112, 202; relationship to pupils, 15; relationship to teachers, 13–15, 17, 20, 25, 37, 40, 43, 48, 81, 82, 110, 111–112, 114, 126, 172, 240. *See also* Innovators, principals as

Principal as charismatic leader, 3–4, 222

Public relations of schools, 7–9, 37, 51, 90, 91, 92, 225–226

Pupils, 21, 62–63, 68, 74, 77, 83–84, 86–87, 88, 89, 91, 146–147, 163–165, 175, 179, 182, 207, 232, 240–241. *See also* Parents, role of, relationship to their children as pupils; Principal and assistant principal, role of, relationship to pupils; *and* Teachers, role of, relationship to pupils

Pupils, competition and cooperation among, 138, 141, 148, 177. *See also* Parents, role of, relationship to their children as pupils; Principal and assistant principal, role of, relationship to pupils; *and* Teachers, role of, relationship to pupils

Pupils' fighting, 26–28, 148, 149, 151, 164, 178–179, 190, 200

Pupils' learning styles, 54, 60–61, 116

Pupils' peer groups, xiii, xiv, xv, 27, 28, 30, 33, 148, 173, 178–179, 180, 182, 185–192, 193, 196, 207–208, 221, 232, 238, 244

Pupils' self-concept, xiv, xv, 4–5, 29–30, 32, 45, 48, 50, 51, 54, 70, 79, 116, 232, 243

Pupils' skills, 8, 10, 23, 34, 37, 40, 54, 58–59, 60, 62–63, 64, 70–71, 72–73, 74, 77–78, 81, 83, 84, 86, 88, 89, 91–92, 93, 116, 117, 133, 138, 142, 146–147, 161–162, 175–176, 183–184, 235, 239, 243–

244; dispersion of, xv, 22, 70–71, 79, 83, 88, 176, 232

Pupils' verbal aggression, 27, 164, 178, 190

Race and ethnicity in the schools, xii, 2–3, 4, 5, 9, 10, 12, 13, 15, 16, 17–19, 22–23, 28–29, 30, 41, 42, 44–45, 63, 69–70, 72–73, 79, 91–92, 99, 100, 101, 102, 103–104, 105, 106, 120, 133, 138, 141, 147, 148, 151, 157, 165; black separatism, 11–12; segregation and integration, 2, 5, 11, 16, 17, 18–19, 28, 29, 69, 92, 99, 104, 105, 106, 120, 227

Regrouping. *See* Instructional groups

Researchers' role, 248–249

Role conflict, 57

School district, xxx, 8, 9, 13, 15, 18, 33, 37, 38, 43, 53, 63, 93, 95, 96, 97, 98, 104, 107, 111, 114, 161, 170, 171, 172. *See also* School officials, district and city

School officials, district and city, 2, 3, 6, 8, 16, 17, 18, 19, 34, 35, 37–38, 40, 41, 42, 51, 52, 53, 57–58, 64, 90, 92, 93, 96, 97, 98, 99, 100, 101–102, 103, 104, 108, 109, 111, 114, 155, 160, 163, 165, 167, 170–171, 202

Schorr, Laura, ix, 63, 174

Seale, Bobby, 44

Selection, competitive, as a function of the schools, xiv, xv, xvi

Self-concept. *See* Pupils' self-concept

Sex, pupils' self-segregation by, 28, 138, 148, 178–179

Sex education, 165–166, 168, 208

Silberman, Charles, xii

Social class in schooling, xi, xii, 9 n, 12–13, 15, 22, 25, 27, 28, 40, 92, 105, 106, 107, 139, 141, 147, 151, 157, 174; class subcultures, 26–27, 33, 92, 93

Social mobility, 31, 106

Socialization patterns in school, 6, 10, 12, 47–48, 226, 238

Space, structuring of, in classroom, 10, 28, 47, 49, 58, 66, 82, 133–136, 142–143, 150, 171, 174, 180, 181, 236

Spatial perception. *See* Perceptual problems

Teacher Corps, 41, 42, 63, 65, 67, 69, 70, 71, 220

Teacher-pupil ratios, 63, 69, 78, 133, 139,

Teacher-pupil ratios *(cont.)*
    151, 158, 182–183, 220
Teachers, role of, xi, xiii, xiv, 4, 8, 15, 17,
    19–25, 38, 41, 50, 53, 59, 78, 80–81, 96,
    97, 98, 102, 106, 109, 110–111, 112,
    114, 116, 118, 122, 123, 129, 137, 143–
    144, 147, 149, 152, 160, 161, 162–163,
    167–168, 170–171, 172, 208–209, 220–
    221, 222, 224, 228–233; relationship to
    district officials, 37–38, 40; relationship
    to other teachers, xiv, 34, 49–50, 66–
    67, 70, 78, 81, 83, 142, 204–205, 207,
    209, 229; relationship to parents/com-
    munity, *see* Parents, role of, relation-
    ship to teachers; relationship to prin-
    cipal, *see* Principal and assistant prin-
    cipal, role of, relationship to teachers;
    relationship to pupils, 15, 19–24, 49,
    62–63, 70, 73–74, 76–77, 79, 88, 89, 90,
    91, 113, 129, 136, 138, 145, 146, 148,
    168, 179, 183, 184, 185, 186, 230, 237,
    240, 241; relationship to staff specialists,
    44–49, 50, 79, 137; relationship to team
    leaders, 55–59, *see also* Team leaders
Teachers, student-, 13, 20, 75, 78, 107,
    136, 163, 220

Teachers, unrealistic demands on, 7, 52,
    60, 92–93, 113, 114, 222, 224
Teachers' union, 102, 104, 107, 108, 110,
    128, 130, 155
Team leaders, 14, 20, 22, 25, 41, 42, 45,
    46, 53, 54–57, 60, 63, 67, 68, 69, 75, 76,
    77, 78, 79, 80, 81, 91
Team teaching, xiv, 6, 20, 48, 50, 53, 54,
    62, 66, 67, 68, 74, 75, 76, 78, 82–83, 84,
    104, 118, 126, 127, 180–186, 219, 221,
    227, 228–229, 239–240, 241; interper-
    sonal problems, 49, 186, 229–230, 233
Teaming. *See* Team teaching
Time, structuring of, 24–25, 135–136,
    143–144, 150, 174–175, 181–182, 222,
    240

Urban League, 44
Urban Teaching Interns, 63, 67, 75, 78

Walberg (Herbert)–Thomas (Susan) scale,
    132
Waller, Willard, 152
Wilkins, Roy, 44

Young, Whitney, 44